MANAGING GLOBAL PROBLEMS

Books by C. Maxwell Stanley

WAGING PEACE (1956)
THE CONSULTING ENGINEER (1962)

C. MAXWELL STANLEY

A Guide to
Survival MANAGING
GLOBAL PROBLEMS

THE STANLEY FOUNDATION

MUSCATINE, IOWA 1979

Library of Congress Cataloging in Publication Data

Stanley, Claude Maxwell, 1904–
    Managing global problems.

    Includes bibliographical references and index.
    1. International relations. 2. Security, Inter-
national. 3. International cooperation. I. Title.
JX1395.S7   327   79–17797
ISBN 0–96031–121–1
ISBN 0–96031–122–X pbk.

The Stanley Foundation, Muscatine, Iowa 52761
© 1979 by C. Maxwell Stanley. All rights reserved
Printed in the United States of America

Distributed by the University of Iowa, Iowa City, Iowa 52242

*To my grandchildren
May the world of their children be
managed in the interests of justice and peace.*

CONTENTS

PREFACE

This book is an effort to clarify thinking on how the world community can best cope with global problems of mounting complexity and seriousness. Such an examination seems timely in view of the meager progress toward this end since World War II. No way has been found to assure international peace and security, the dominant issue of early postwar years. Meanwhile, grave problems of an economic, social, and humanitarian nature continue to exist.

The world community's management of serious global problems is so inadequate that survival of millions of people, if not of civilization, is uncertain. Even if nuclear holocaust, ecological disaster, and agricultural deficiencies are avoided, aspirations for greater human dignity and a suitable quality of life are thwarted by poor management.

I am motivated by a strong personal conviction that the world community can and must do a better management job, even within the existing nation-state international political system. I believe, too, that more effective management within today's framework is the only way to progress toward the political and economic orders necessary to assure peace and security, enhance justice and human rights, and improve quality of life. We need to foster a management climate more conducive to the creation of political and economic institutions endowed with essential extranational and supranational authority.

These convictions arise from more than thirty years of concern about foreign affairs, particularly international cooperation and world organization. During these years, I have been active in several organizations focusing attention upon these subjects. For more than twenty years, I have been personally involved in the problems of developing countries through the activities of Stanley Consultants. I have observed the functioning of the United Nations and the manner in which nations use and abuse it.

Twenty years ago, having a basic confidence in the decency and brotherhood of mankind, Mrs. Stanley and I established The Stanley Foundation, a private operating foundation, as a vehicle to contribute to the search for secure peace with freedom. Our interest in world organization developed from a mounting conviction that the United Nations was insufficient to the task. Our then college-age son was a further persuading influence.

As president of The Stanley Foundation, I have organized and chaired some 50 international conferences and seminars, seeking ways to strengthen US foreign policy, improve the United Nations, and manage global problems. These gatherings have been supplemented by discussions and correspondence with diplomats, statesmen, political leaders, scholars, academicians, and businessmen from many nations. As a consequence, I believe that nation-states can, if they will, vastly increase the effectiveness of their cooperation and better manage critical world issues.

As an engineer and executive, I have great respect for the importance and effectiveness of sound management procedures. The world community needs to make greater use of basic management principles, suitably adapted to the politics of national and international decision-making.

My nongovernmental perspective centers upon the lack of innovative leadership by the United States. Our overall posture falls short of near-term and longer range needs; we have not faced the realities of a changing and more interdependent world.

The proposals presented in this book are focused upon approaches, procedures, and mechanisms to manage global problems more effectively. They emphasize the interrelationships of the critical issues and the importance of dealing comprehensively with them. They are more procedural than substantive; they are not simple solutions. My comments are directed to generalists concerned with overall approaches, people who are opinion-shapers and decision-makers.

My appreciation and thanks are extended to those who have helped in the preparation and review of this book. I especially mention my two sons, David and Richard, together with Jack M. Smith, John R. Redick, and Roger L. Lande, who reviewed an early draft of the manuscript and Willard Boyd who reviewed the chapter on human rights. Joni Axel and Claudine Harris have given great assistance in drafting and editing. Joan Walling and Margaret Fuller typed the many pages several times. My wife Betty has contributed ideas, suggested modifications, and tolerated the many hours I have spent in writing the book. I am grateful for the encouragement of the faculty in world order studies at The University of Iowa.

C. Maxwell Stanley
Muscatine, Iowa
August 15, 1979

I TODAY'S PREDICAMENTS

1 CHANGE

Like the legendary horseman, the world community seems at once to ride off in all directions.

Is it possible for a world community of over four billion people represented by more than 150 sovereign nations varying in size, power, population, wealth, ideology, culture, and interest to manage critical world problems? How can we get together? How can we rise above narrow, short-term concerns to deal with far-reaching global issues? These are the paramount questions world scholars must study and national leaders and global statesmen must face. Awareness of global problems and of the need to deal with them is widespread, although opinions regarding their relative seriousness vary. No consensus exists, however, on how a hoard of bickering, suspicious, and selfish nations can overcome real and perceived differences in order to cooperate.

Problems and chaos are chronicled daily and analyzed continually by commentators and columnists. News presents war, suffering, injustice, stalemate, and frustration—not peace, comfort, justice, progress, or confidence. Occasional hopeful international events or agreements are too often preludes to setbacks and controversies. Despite some exaggeration, the media accounts do mirror correctly the dissonance and confusion, and the lack of consensus among nation-states, not only on world community priorities but also on actions to advance them.

Indeed we have failed to comprehend and manage the staggering pace and scope of global change in recent decades. Remarkable technological development, immense industrial expansion, and unprecedented political change have created wholly new and unexpected world conditions. The capacity of traditional political and economic systems to resolve today's complex and controversial problems has been outpaced. Governments are floundering in efforts to respond.

The world is suspended between a battered, centuries-old political system, which nations prefer to use, and a fledgling new world order more responsive to the demands of peace, justice, and human dignity. The international political system that has served nations for centuries is unable to deal with the problems of the post–World War II era.

The same state of flux applies to the world economy. Archaic, overloaded systems are unable to meet the demands of a more interdependent world whose crowded inhabitants seek a higher quality of life. While the slow transition to new political and economic orders is apparent to most scholars, many statesmen, and some politicians, the parameters are indistinct and the pace of emergence is uncertain.

Nation-state centered political and economic systems do not fully describe today's structure. Nation-states are still the leading actors on the world stage, but the cast of characters and the setting are becoming more transnational. Many regional, multinational, and international organizations—private as well as governmental—have been established. Nevertheless, world discord and disorder are aptly symbolized by the United Nations as it attempts to manage political and economic problems.

The Issues   In United Nations circles, global problems are often divided into two categories: political (meaning peace and security issues) and economic (embracing most other issues). This classification is overly simplistic and illogical—all international problems are fundamentally political; resolution depends upon actions of national governments using political processes. One school of thought suggests four value-oriented categories: (1) minimization of large-scale collective violence; (2) maximization of social and economic well-being; (3) realization of fundamental human rights and conditions of political justice; and (4) maintenance and rehabilitation of ecological quality.[1] Other groupings have been suggested by other writers, scholars, and observers.

Any grouping is somewhat arbitrary, but for this discussion, six critical issues have been selected.

All are urgent priorities on the world community's agenda. They are complicated and interrelated; none can be individually resolved.

PEACE AND SECURITY Developing adequate systems to assure peaceful settlement of international differences and to protect the

1. Richard Falk, *A Study of Future Worlds* (New York: Free Press, 1975), pp. 11–30.

security of nations against overt or covert intervention, thus removing the need for threat and use of armed force

ECONOMIC ORDER Improving the various systems and mechanisms comprising the world economic order to better handle expanding trade, commerce, and development

DEVELOPMENT Achieving an acceptable pattern and a tolerable pace of economic and social development for the less developed two-thirds of the world's population

RESOURCE/POPULATION BALANCE Managing the finite resources of the earth and stabilizing population growth to achieve and sustain a quality of life compatible with human dignity

BIOSPHERE Protecting and managing the biosphere to avoid hazardous deterioration and enhance environmental and resource contributions to quality of life

HUMAN RIGHTS Extending elemental human rights to all people and developing better systems to protect such rights

The Impact of Change

Even the most superficial examination of accomplishment in each area, the true test of effective management, reveals serious deficiencies. Leaders of nations and their nationals have neither individually nor collectively responded adroitly to technological and political change during the last five decades, especially since World War II.

Technology has compressed the world. Transmission of infections—human disease, terrorism, or economic inflation—has accelerated. Indeed, local crises immediately become global concerns. Nations are more interdependent; human desires and aspirations are equalizing. In a physical sense, change has made the world one; no nation is isolated.

Technology has also had a direct, mostly negative, impact upon the maintenance of international peace and security. While nuclear bombs and other sophisticated weapons have made the magnitude of war's destruction intolerable, the rapid emergence of new nations and the widespread influence of military establishments have vastly increased the opportunities for armed conflict.

The world's economic order is bogged down. Economic interdependence and better technology have expanded trade, but the existing systems have not kept pace. Highly critical of unjust systems fashioned for developed countries, developing nations are frustrated.

The issue of economic and social development has been intensified by the collapse of Western colonialism after World War II. As newly independent countries have sought economic independence and rapid development, industrial nations have responded bilaterally and multilaterally to the call for external financial and technical assistance.

Resource/population balance—a new issue on the planet—is clearly the result of recent technological and political change. On the one hand, improved public health and medical care programs have ignited exponential population growth in developing nations. On the other, rising expectations of more people in both developed and developing nations create mounting demands on the earth's finite resources.

Advanced technology, industrial pollution, and ever enlarging resource demands burden the environment. Expanding populations and rising expectations add to this burden. Protection and enhancement of the biosphere become increasingly important.

Human rights progress has been stymied in many nations. Overgrown military influence, outright totalitarian and military regimes, and unstable national governments (many the result of economic forces) all tend to hinder human rights progress.

In the political area, world community efforts to manage the six critical issues are also hampered by changes. I will note six key factors. The PROLIFERATION OF NATION-STATES has placed many more actors on the world stage; UN membership is now 151 versus 51 Charter signers, and the diversity of experience and objectives complicates problem-solving. (This proliferation, however, is the result of desirable and long overdue political change.)

CONFRONTATIONS between major sectors of the world community are a second significant handicap. One such confrontation is longstanding but moderating; the other is more recent and as yet unpredictable. The East-West confrontation that crystallized after World War II has long hindered multilateral management efforts, particularly in the area of peace and security. The North-South or rich-poor confrontation, now in its infancy, has the potential to expand; it already interferes with international cooperation.

SHIFTS IN NATIONAL POWER are a third disturbing factor. Great Britain and France, although victorious, were seriously weakened after World War II: the collapse of colonialism further sapped their strength. Germany and Japan, mighty military powers of the defeated Axis, lost all semblance of power. The United States and the Soviet Union emerged as the most powerful nations. This bipolarity is still the major world political influence, but its dominance is waning with the emergence of other power centers. The People's Republic of China is a potential superpower, despite its disclaimer to such a role. Japan has regained influential position even without military strength. The European Economic Community has military and economic power surpassed only by that of the Soviet Union and the United States. Such nations as Argentina, Brazil, India, Indonesia, and Nigeria are gaining influence. Third World nations, when they cooperate, exert increasing political and moral power. The oil-rich members of the Organization of Petroleum Exporting Countries wield significant economic power.

NATIONALISM has been intensified, particularly in newly independent countries which subscribe easily to the nationalistic postures, prejudices, and practices of older nations. Carried to extremes, nationalism obstructs progress toward long-term interests and international cooperation.

It is paradoxical that another area of political change—the growing sense of INTERDEPENDENCE and emergence of international institutions—runs counter to nationalistic trends. Embryonic growth of global awareness is a positive political change beginning to influence the conduct of nations.

CHANGING ATTITUDES toward previously accepted establishments influence national decision-making. This positive political change finds activists in many countries challenging established policies and protesting against current systems. In the international arena, small nations band together to challenge the powerful.

Thus the impacts of technological and political change upon international affairs cannot be overemphasized.

Concepts of political science and international relations ingrained in the minds of today's national leaders 20 to 30 years ago are often archaic relics of the past. Governmental policies conceived a generation or a decade ago are often inadequate or totally obsolete. *Meeting the Challenge of Change*

Nevertheless, it is well to remember that change is not unique to recent decades; it is the very soul of history. For millennia human beings have encountered new conditions arising from natural phenomena or human events. Change has always demanded adjustment, and the price for failure to respond has often been high: death or subjugation for individuals, tribes, or nations. The rewards for seizing opportunities afforded by change have been equally great: profit, power, territory, improved quality of life, and expanded human rights.

The changing conditions confronting us today differ significantly, however, from those of the past. They differ in magnitude, scope, and complexity; they are of a new order. Moreover, they are extraordinarily interrelated, and responses to them have multiple consequences.

Failure to manage the changes of the last few decades is vastly more hazardous. The final repercussion of unrestrained international conflict and nuclear holocaust could be the destruction of civilization. The end result of environmental neglect could be an irretrievable upset in the delicate thermal and chemical balances of the biosphere. Failure to balance resources and populations could greatly deteriorate quality of life.

Another difference is the urgency of response required. So immediate are the probable consequences of failure that time becomes a primary factor. Slow, evolutionary response to problems over generations or centuries—the traditional human and political pattern—is untenable. Certain critical thresholds of no return may be passed.

Finally, the nature of change is so different that accumulated historical experience is of only marginal help as a guideline for the future; even extrapolations and projections of physical and economic data are of questionable value. Unfortunately, rational decision-making is not customarily an inviting process to the general public or to politicians who are particularly reluctant to move much beyond the safe limits of the known.

It takes wisdom, courage, and strength to recognize the inevitability of change, to adjust to it, and to grasp opportunities. A keen sense of timing and a willingness to innovate are needed.

Few national leaders today openly admit the magnitude, consequences, and urgency of current problems. Fewer still appear ready to do much about them. Obviously, a gap exists between performance and what is necessary to manage critical world issues. Until this gap is closed or significantly narrowed, efforts are destined to fall short of desired objectives.

In this book I address the challenge of achieving international attitudes and mechanisms capable of managing present and future global change in the context of greater interdependence. Facing this challenge will not be easy. There is no assurance of success, but failure by default is unacceptable.

2 MANAGEMENT

How should the world community attack the management of its critical world issues? Even a casual examination of progress in coping with global problems demonstrates the urgent imperative of different and more effective approaches. In the near-term, world leaders must find ways to aid and abet the cooperation of nation-states to manage international crises and solve global problems—a role that cannot be overemphasized. Today's stakes are high: avoiding debilitating war and assuring quality of life—and perhaps survival. The longer range, but equally important, task is fostering emerging world political and economic systems tailored for tomorrow.

Before examining the nature of different and more effective approaches to the management of global problems, it is well to examine one widely held view now hampering international cooperation: the pessimistic belief that world problems are irreparable. Doomsday prophets foresee early disaster. Some assert that war is inevitable, peace impossible; that the superpowers are on a collision course to nuclear holocaust; that ideological differences are so sharp that genuine cooperation is not attainable. Some anticipate disaster ranging from total famine to an environmental catastrophe. Many contend that nationalism is too intense and ingrained to be overcome. Pursuit of short-term national interests is seen as a certain path to deepening North-South conflict and ensuing disaster. Pessimists see no hope. Others, while not adhering to doomsday predictions, contend the point of no return has been crossed. At best, mankind is destined to continue in a deeply divided, feuding world.

It is not difficult to marshal evidence to support these gloomy outlooks. But rejection of a doomsday attitude is an essential prerequisite to proving it wrong. Fortunately, there are sound reasons to reject much of the counsel of pessimists while intensifying efforts to manage critical world issues.

Throughout recorded history, the human race has demonstrated a surprising will and ability to progress. As civilization has developed, mankind has recovered from widespread disaster, surmounted serious obstacles, and overcome threats. People have made the adjustments from the caves to the cities, from agricultural to industrial societies. The quality of life has ceased being marginal. Empires such as Babylonia, Egypt, Greece, and Rome have risen and prospered only to decline and sometimes disappear. As fortunes and powers have waxed and waned, man's progress has been forward, if at times undulating, toward a better quality of life and greater human rights. Although technological and economic advances have brought comparative affluence to only a sizable minority of the world's population, they hold the promise of improving the lot of all. National independence nears universality. Over the centuries institutions have evolved from tribes through city-states and feudal systems to today's nation-states and even to fragile regional and global international associations.

While the dangers of the past may seem less serious than today's, civilization's capability to deal with problems now exceeds that of the past. Wider education, more enlightened public opinion, advanced technology, and an arsenal of problem-solving and management tools are distributed widely; no nation or group of nations monopolizes them. Today's global chaos and peril result from the failure of the world community to rise above narrow nationalism and marshal adequate will and leadership. The latent capability to effectively manage critical world issues exists; the challenge is to use it. That is what this book is about.

The Path of Optimism   The most impelling reason for rejecting the counsel of pessimists is the inherent self-defeating nature of loss of hope. While realism about world problems and their resolution is essential, determination and cautious optimism are basic to any sustained rehabilitative effort.

But cautious optimism is not complacency. One school of thought, quite the opposite of pessimism, contends that current mechanisms and approaches are adequate; only time and patience are needed. Such advocates pin their hopes upon the evolutionary process. They believe traditional diplomatic processes and existing international organizations will adequately meet global threats and challenges. Some contend that the seriousness of today's critical issues is overrated and the need for urgent resolution is questionable. Optimism of this nature is hazardous and quite unwarranted by any demonstrated ability of the world community to deal with global problems. The record speaks for itself; different and more effective mechanisms and institutions are needed.

Many courses are enthusiastically advanced as keys to progress or as panaceas. Unfortunately, there is no simplistic approach. Some suggestions do, however, have merit and in the long run will contribute to global understanding. For example, dedicated followers of certain religions would rely upon broad acceptance and application of religious beliefs to change the world. They advance brotherhood as the best road to peace. Pacifists, contending that war is not justified under any circumstances, would shun all things military.

Another hope is building "community" among nations, community being interpreted to mean that nations will inherently seek common objectives because sufficient uniformity of interest exists. Proposed steps to achieve this condition are many. Some believe there must be similar economic systems throughout the world. Others would settle for greater understanding, better communications, and more common experiences. One school of thought considers language the primary barrier and advocates a universal language. Another segment contends there must be comparable educational levels; others feel only illiteracy need be overcome. Still others call for greater equalization of economic opportunity, and a few insist there must be equality of living standards and social status. At the extreme, some insist that only similarity of national political structures and a common ideology will achieve peace, security, and cooperation.

All who seek to improve relations and understandings among peoples and nations should be urged on. Those who work to enlarge concern for other human beings through the advocacy and practice of religious principles deserve encouragement. Those who challenge the necessity, the morality, and the credibility of war as a viable means of resolving international disputes should be applauded. All such efforts help to mold world opinion toward a more just and humane approach to global problem-solving. Likewise, efforts to build community should be encouraged and aided. Progress toward greater understanding, better communications, and common objectives would undoubtedly improve the political climate and stimulate international cooperation. But these processes are exceedingly slow due to great diversity of national interests, religions, and cultures. Unfortunately, the pressing critical world issues will not wait. They must be managed now.

Rule of Law   Rule of law on a global basis is one proposal for dealing with global problems, particularly peace and security. Supporters of this proposal believe that only world law will overcome anarchy, maintain justice, safeguard disarmament, peacefully settle disputes, and effectively manage global problems. World law would require supranational institutions with authority to enact, interpret, and enforce law within predetermined functional areas.[1] This calls for some form of world federation or world government.

Few objective scholars of world affairs doubt the ultimate need for government and law on the global level. For centuries states have sought to develop guidelines for the conduct of international affairs; laws governing conduct were promulgated as long ago as 2000 B.C. by Sumerians. Over the years certain principles—often termed international law—have crystallized, particularly pertaining to marine shipping and commerce. More recently, the League of Nations and the United Nations have standardized, by resolution and treaty, some norms or guidelines for national conduct in international affairs.[2] Since 1899 the International Court of Justice (ICJ), sitting at the Peace Palace in The Hague, has offered judicial resolution of controversies between national governments voluntarily accepting its jurisdiction.

Although these developments have been beneficial and generally favored, the world does not have a rule of law. The "laws" established by UN resolution are neither compulsory nor enforceable, and most UN conventions have escape clauses. Not only are nations not compelled to submit controversies to the World Court, but by passing the Connally Reservation, which denied the ICJ the right to judge any case involving the United States unless this nation voluntarily agreed, the United States Congress set a pattern for noncompulsory jurisdiction. No means except adamant world opinion exist to enforce the few decisions rendered by the World Court. The

1. Supranational institutions imply sovereign parliamentary bodies, with worldwide representation, empowered to legislate and set policies pertaining to predetermined functions on a global or regional level. Appropriate parallel organizations to administer, interpret, and enforce law are also implied. In the process of establishing supranational institutions, nation-states would delegate certain sovereign rights and thus forgo control or veto over the institutions' decisions and actions. Nation-states would influence supranational institutions' actions only through the initiatives of their representatives in the parliamentary body.

2. The terms "treaty" and "convention" are used interchangeably.

United Nations and its family of organizations must be recognized for what they are—voluntary associations of nation-states. The United Nations is not a world government; it is but a tool of nation-states, without independent authority.

Undoubtedly, some form of world law, and the supranational institutions required by it, are the inevitable but highly controversial next steps in the progress of civilization. We have progressed from tribes to city-states, from feudal dominions to nation-states. Government by law at the world level is next. Hence world organizations having authority greater than the United Nations are vital long-range objectives.

Unfortunately, today's international political climate and world opinion are not favorable to early action establishing supranational institutions with adequate authority. Nevertheless, the activities of organizations such as the World Federalists, Members of Congress for Peace Through Law, the American Bar Association's Committee on World Peace Through Law, the Commission to Study the Organization of Peace, the Institute for World Order, and others aimed at advancing the concepts of world law and supranational organization providing limited governmental authority on a world level should be applauded.

Pragmatically, if the world community is to learn to live with itself, the near-term management of critical world issues is an immediate undertaking to be approached in the present climate, using the existing political order and institutions. The nation-state system with all its inadequacies, the United Nations with all its contradictions, and the hodgepodge of other international organizations, regional and worldwide, are the framework for the immediate task. Greater coordination and control must be established over the manifold and interrelated activities of existing international organizations. The potential capabilities of this system and its institutions must be fully utilized; present institutions must be strengthened; and new organizations must be created to deal with matters beyond the competence or capability of existing ones. Some new organizations, established by treaty, will likely be given extranational or transnational authority to manage delegated functions better.[3] A few may even gain limited supranational authority.

3. Extranational or transnational institutions differ from supranational institutions in that they are established to perform specified functions within predetermined policy limits prescribed by the treaty creating them. Thus institutions granted extranational or transnational authority manage

What should be the response to the dual challenge of dealing with urgent current problems while assuring progress toward a governed world with political and economic institutions adequate for growing interdependence? How can nations get the most out of the United Nations and international cooperation? How can they lay the foundations for stronger transnational and supranational institutions? Obviously, greater determination must be demonstrated; stronger leadership must be exerted. Such will, determination, and leadership must be directed to developing and applying sound management processes.

What is management? It is the organization, implementation, direction, and control of activities to achieve desired objectives. Although not a cure-all, management is a prerequisite to solving problems. Historically, management has been little more than the art of getting things done. But in today's complex global community of myriad organizations and institutions, management processes have evolved into a modern science involving systems for dealing with people and ideas, and mechanisms for solving problems and achieving objectives. In capsule form, the management process consists of several sequential, but interrelated, phases:

IDENTIFYING PROBLEMS What is the issue? A case at point: The issue of resource/population balance is not yet broadly recognized as a global problem. Hence it receives little attention.

DEFINING OBJECTIVES What is the desirable, agreed upon longer range goal? Example: There is no agreement upon the type of security system needed as an alternate to the nation-state system. Without a long-range objective, little progress is likely.

ESTABLISHING A PLAN What programs of action will achieve near-term and longer range objectives? Illustration: No plan exists for the control and limitation of conventional armaments. Transfers of such weapons increase.

MARSHALING RESOURCES How are the human and monetary resources required to execute a plan to be provided? Example: Funds

and administer programs but lack the authority or parliamentary capacity to establish or alter basic policies. Extranational or transnational organizations, however, have a degree of independence superior to that of the United Nations, as now constituted. The United Nations and organizations like it are but vehicles for international cooperation; decision-making power remains with nation-states.

available for development are insufficient to accomplish a plan such as the UN Third Development Decade.

DELEGATING AUTHORITY How is responsibility assigned for executing established plans? Example: The UN Environment Programme lacks authority to fully cope with global environmental deterioration.

CONTROLLING PROGRESS How are programs, performance, and budgets to be monitored and controlled to assure desired results? Example: ECOSOC, as currently constituted, is unable to monitor and control the widespread, multilateral aid programs of UN agencies.

These management elements have wide acceptance in much of the world in business and industry and to a lesser extent in local, state, and national governments. But the embryonic world institutions lag far behind in the application of management techniques.

Appropriate management processes need to be selected and adapted to the nature of international decision-making and cooperation within the United Nations and regional organizations. In the remainder of the book, I discuss the application of management methods to global problems.

The next several chapters examine in some depth the six critical world issues. In each case the problem is defined and related to other critical world issues, and current progress in managing the issue is outlined. Using such material as a foundation, near-term programs are suggested to manage the problem and aid progress toward proposed longer range objectives. Finally, the posture of the United States is briefly stated.

I hope to provide sufficient understanding of each problem area and its likely solution to permit consideration of the procedures, mechanisms, and institutions required. Obviously, it is quite impossible in one book to discuss all substantive matters related to the solution of each of the critical world issues. The limited discussion of substantive matters will not satisfy specialists in any problem area; some may well challenge suggestions of likely solutions. But my intent is to emphasize the need and the path to progress in managing the issues, not to provide detailed solutions.

II THE ISSUES

3 PEACE AND SECURITY: THE SECURITY SYSTEM

The quest for peace has challenged mankind throughout all recorded history.

International peace is more than the temporary absence of war. To endure, peace must be secure. To be acceptable, peace must allow freedom, justice, and progress. An acceptable security system will have to provide methods to settle controversy peacefully, secure nations against external threats, discourage the use of armed force and intervention, and deal with the occasional would-be aggressor. Nations must be persuaded to relinquish the capability to use and threaten to use armed force; national military forces should not exceed those reasonably required for internal security. However, this will remain a utopian dream until the world community fashions effective mechanisms as alternatives to unilateral action of nations. Meaningful disarmament must be accomplished in concert.

Background

History clearly reveals that nations, acting either individually or through alliances, have been unable to maintain peace and security. After Napoleon's defeat, the 1815 Congress of Vienna proposed international peacekeeping machinery, including an international army and positive guarantees. A century later, at the close of World War I, peacemakers in Versailles again recognized the necessity of a world organization to enforce peace. The ill-fated League of Nations was a feeble effort to shift the responsibility from nations to an international organization.

Despite the demise of the League, steps to assure world security were again taken during the last years of World War II. The United Nations was designed with the primary responsibility for peace and security vested in the Security Council. Significant contributions have been made, but the United Nations has not maintained peace and security during the last 30 years. Although the world has been spared the holocaust of a nuclear World War III, the threat of force is constant and its use is frequent.

In the 30 years following World War II, 119 international or civil wars were fought; the territory of 69 countries and the armed forces of 81 nations were involved. Fatalities in these wars mounted to tens of millions, not far from the totals killed in World War II. In aggregate, a World War III has been fought without a single declaration of war.[1]

Nuclear and conventional arms races continue unabated. Localized war kills, destroys, and retards progress; today's sophisticated conventional weaponry possesses destructive capability far more massive than that of World War II. Nuclear war has the capacity to destroy cities and nations and endanger human survival.

Even though nuclear war has been avoided, our perceptions of the harmful effects of insecurity and our tenuous hold on peace are being dulled. The strident beat of today's military preparations drowns out reasoned pleas for greater international cooperation. Dissent, fear, hatred, and suspicion are generated. Attention is diverted from serious economic and social issues that cry for solution; the climate for resolving the other critical world issues remains unhealthy. Emphasis on military power encourages tension; it impedes cooperation to achieve nonmilitary approaches. Vast commitments to military activities (36 million active military personnel, 30 million military-related civilians, and $400 billion in 1978) absorb human, financial, and physical resources otherwise available for improving quality of life.[2] Many military activities detrimentally affect the environment. Preparation for war encroaches on human rights; war itself runs roughshod over them.

Objectives: Toward a World without War

Despite a near universal yearning for peace and a flood of rhetoric from national leaders, common understanding is lacking on how to implement the noble words of the Charter of the United Nations:

. . . to save succeeding generations from the scourge of war . . . to maintain international peace and security . . . to take effective collective measures for the prevention and removal of threats to peace, and for the suppression of acts of aggression or other breaches of peace, and to bring about by peaceful means

1. Stockholm International Peace Research Institute, *Armaments and Disarmament in the Nuclear Age*, Stockholm, Sweden, 1976, pp. 174 and 175.

2. Ruth Leger Sivard, *World Military and Social Expenditures* (Leesburg, Virginia: WMSE Publications, 1978), hereafter cited as Sivard.

. . . settlement of international disputes or situations which
might lead to a breach of peace. [Preamble and Article 1]

These quoted ideals are basic to the selection of global objectives
regarding peace and security. But greater specificity is needed. Proposed objectives must respond to the substantial technological,
political, and economic change that has occurred since the UN
Charter was drafted. Goals must look beyond current tensions, frustrations, and obstacles in order to lend encouragement and hope, but
they must also provide realistic guidance to near-term efforts. Com-
patibility with basic human desires for peace, security, freedom,
justice, and a higher quality of life is a fundamental requirement.

A world without war between nation-states, however distant its
achievement may seem, is the only objective fully meeting these
requirements. It makes sense because war is no longer an acceptable
ultimate tool of foreign policy. War has been made obsolete;
technology and economics have done what logic and morality have
failed to accomplish. It is broadly recognized that modern weaponry
has raised the costs of war beyond limits which most national leaders
will tolerate. Ministers of war speak only of defensive postures;
nuclear arsenals are called deterrents to war. The intolerable costs of
war preparation—human as well as monetary—become increasingly
burdensome as nations examine their priorities in the context of
economic stagnation and inflation. War has outlived its usefulness.

Achievement of the primary objective of a world without war
depends upon simultaneous progress in three areas:

PEACEFUL SETTLEMENT Assure peaceful resolution of controversies arising among nations and their nationals.

CONFLICT MANAGEMENT Deter imminent aggression and deal
effectively with breaches of peace, reflecting the common concerns
of the world community, even at the expense of encroachment on
national sovereignty.

DISARMAMENT Limit and reduce national armaments.

These three supporting objectives together provide an alternative
security system for a world without war. The first and second are
discussed later in this chapter; the third is examined in the following
chapter. But let us first examine assumptions regarding peace and
war.

This proposal to seek a world without war will draw a "yes, but" response from many opinion-shapers and most decision-makers. Yes, we all want a world without war; we are dedicated to peace. Yes, this is the very goal we are working for, the very purpose of our buildup of arms. But, realistically, isn't a world without war for the distant future? How can we do anything about it now? We want it, but adversaries aren't willing. They only understand force; so we must stay strong and await a better climate. How often we hear this rationale advanced to justify a reluctance to come to grips with the issue of peace and security.

The difference between a vague aspiration of peace and security and a working objective of a world without war is most significant. If the goal of a world without war were taken seriously, attention would be focused upon creating the required mechanisms and procedures. Action would replace the present attitude of wait and hope.

The proposed objectives are vital, urgent, and realistic. They boldly project action well beyond that deemed possible by today's conventional wisdom. They are realistic because they call for what is needed in today's world of change, rather than what timid political leaders consider practicable. They are urgent because time is of the essence. They are practical because they provide guidelines for near-term action.

Vulnerable
Assumptions   The objective of a world without war challenges several deeply entrenched assumptions regarding peace and security, the first being that war is inevitable—that humans, individually and collectively, are inherently belligerent. The contentions of innate human belligerency, as maintained by Konrad Lorenz [3] and others, have a wide following. But this theory is challenged by the extensive research and analysis of Erich Fromm [4] and others. Wars have occurred over the centuries because feudal rulers or national leaders have elected armed conflict to resolve controversies or to accomplish desired purposes. Wars between nations will continue as normal events only so long as the world community fails to provide and require the use of other suitable mechanisms to resolve controversy and deter aggression.

A second vulnerable historic assumption is that secure peace cannot be achieved until genuine community, as variously defined ear-

3. Konrad Lorenz, *On Aggression* (New York: Harcourt Brace Jovanovich, 1966).
4. Erich Fromm, *The Anatomy of Human Destructiveness* (New York: Holt, Rinehart and Winston, 1973).

lier, is created. Certainly prompt and adequate attention to global economic, social, and human rights problems deserves high priority; most of this book deals with such matters. But whatever validity the waiting-for-community concept may have, the urgency and serious-ness of current hazards and threats make it untenable. The common interest requires that a world without war be sought vigorously.

A third obsolete assumption is that nation-states can coopera-tively manage peace and security with little or no restriction upon the exercise of national sovereignty. Centuries of history, and par-ticularly the three decades of experience since World War II, clearly demonstrate nations' inability to maintain peace and security. Bur-geoning arsenals, power balances, alliances, and diplomacy—all exercises of national sovereignty—have failed repeatedly. The United Nations, carefully structured to avoid encroachment on na-tional sovereignty, has been less than successful in its efforts to maintain peace. Any serious effort to achieve a world without war requires some reasonable limits upon national right of action and some reasonable transfer of authority to global organizations. The institutions charged in the future with making judicial settlements, preventing breaches of peace, managing conflict, and administering disarmament need to act independently in the common interest of humankind. They require sufficient authority in clearly defined areas to prevent a small minority of nations to block progress. This is the sine qua non to managing peace and security.

Are the historic causes of war continuing as the world grows more interdependent? Are these causes susceptible to management by the world community in the common interests of peace and security? Wars have been precipitated between nations by the desires of na-tional rulers. Religious, racial, and cultural controversies have stimulated numerous conflicts. International wars have been launched to divert attention from domestic troubles, to avenge real or alleged affronts to national honor, to redress prior aggressions, and to wrest independence from colonial masters. The list goes on and on. *Causes of War*

Wars are man-made. Whatever the controversies, hatreds, fears, and differences among nations, wars occur because national leaders start them or permit them to escalate from border skirmishes or other incidents. They persist because conflicts are not resolved peace-fully.

A simple pattern for the start of war is a disagreement over some matter. Diplomatic efforts break down; third-party efforts to mediate or conciliate may be tried without favorable results; hard positions are taken, tempers rise, and injudicious threats are made; armies are mobilized and border skirmishes occur. Finally, one side or the other uses full-scale armed force and the war is on. The 1948, 1967, and 1973 wars in the Middle East; the 1949 and 1966 conflicts between India and Pakistan; the 1962 combat between India and China; and the 1977 conflict between Ethiopia and Somalia all fit this pattern. Whatever the underlying cause of the dispute, it is overshadowed by the decision of one or both parties to resort to armed force.

A second potential source of international war is a civil war that enlarges beyond national borders or attracts intervention by other nations. The outlook for protest and discontent is real in many countries, and factions are apt to take up arms. Once involved in a civil war, opponents seek arms and other help from the outside, raising the possibility that other nations may intervene directly. This was a factor in Vietnam, when the United States intervened to support the South, and the Soviet Union and China aided the North. Angola's civil conflict attracted troops from Cuba and South Africa, as well as supplies and equipment directly from the Soviet Union and indirectly via African countries from the United States.

The third potential source of war is a premeditated, unilateral decision by a nation to use military force to wrest certain advantages from others. The goal may be territory, resources, power, prestige, or merely the satisfaction of a whim or a desire of the rulers or decision-makers. This practice dates back to primitive days when adjoining tribes independently reached out for hunting grounds, campsites, or pastures. In modern times, when bluff, diplomacy, and maneuver failed, Adolph Hitler launched a blitzkrieg. Later Japan thrust into Manchuria, bombed Pearl Harbor, and stormed over Southeast Asia. And in 1950, North Korea invaded South Korea.

Fear of this type of aggression motivates the East-West, the Sino-Soviet, the Arab-Israel, the India-Pakistan, and other lesser armed confrontations around the world. It is at the root of the arms race between the Soviet Union and the United States.

Peaceful Settlement

A major source of war would be eliminated if nations could resolve their quarrels by peaceful means. The world community has understood this need and has endeavored to fashion suitable mechanisms, mainly under the aegis of the United Nations.

What is now called the World Court was integrated into the United Nations by the Statute of the International Court of Justice as the principal judicial organ of the United Nations. The ICJ is composed of 15 eminent justices from diverse geographical, cultural, and ideological backgrounds. Only nation-states may bring cases to it or may be parties in cases before it. The jurisdiction of the court is limited to referred cases and those matters specifically designated in the UN Charter or in treaties. The court applies international treaties establishing rules recognized by the ratifying states, international custom, general principles of law recognized by civilized nations, and judicial decisions and teachings of highly qualified publicists of various nations. (This guidance from the UN Charter reveals the primitive state of international law.) The ICJ lacks compulsory jurisdiction; all parties to a case must agree to its submission to the court. The court also renders advisory opinions upon the request of UN organs or agencies.

The caseload of the World Court is pathetically low, some forty cases in the last 25 years. Less than half of the UN members have accepted the jurisdiction of the ICJ, many of those with reservations such as the US Connally Reservation.

The Charter of the United Nations creates a second system to deal with disputes between nations, particularly those likely to endanger peace. Chapter VI, "Pacific Settlement of Disputes," authorizes the Security Council to "investigate any dispute, or any situation which might lead to international friction. . . ." The Security Council may recommend appropriate procedures or methods of adjustment and encourage parties to refer legal disputes to the ICJ. The Security Council may call upon nations to use negotiation, inquiry, mediation, conciliation, arbitration, resort to regional arrangements, or other peaceful means to settle their disputes. But its recommendations are nonenforceable.

Security Council involvement in pacific settlement of disputes has generally occurred after the rift has reached such a dangerous point that positions have hardened and settlement is difficult, if not impossible. Nevertheless, Security Council intervention, even at a late stage, has been fruitful in many instances. Within the last 30 years, more than 100 UN third-party interventions have been authorized, about 60 percent by the Security Council and 40 percent by the General Assembly. About half of those initiated by the Security

Council have dealt with disputes or conflicts between two or more countries. Thirteen have been peacekeeping operations related to cease-fires following armed conflict. Others have facilitated peaceful settlement. Such successful interventions include the avoidance of border conflicts in the Balkans in 1947, resolution of disputes between Cambodia and Thailand in 1958 and again in 1968, and disposition of Guinea's complaint of armed aggression by Portugal in 1971.

Regional organizations offer a third vehicle facilitating resolution of disputes between nations, albeit one marked more by potential than by accomplishment. For example, charters of the Organization of American States, European Economic Community, and the Organization of African Unity each contain procedures facilitating pacific settlement of disputes and breaches of peace.

Finally, individual nations, offering their good offices, can help disputants settle controversies. Obviously, the nation offering such help must be acceptable to both disputants, and the disputants themselves must be ready to negotiate. An example is the good offices role played in 1975 by Algeria aiding Iran and Iraq to resolve a long-standing, festering border dispute.

Thus mechanisms are available to promote the peaceful settlement of disputes between nations. But they have the common handicap that each involves some form of third-party intervention, an action seldom welcomed by sovereign nations. There being no compulsion, and some lack of confidence, nations are hesitant to turn to world organizations to settle controversies. How may we strengthen, improve, and augment the existing mechanisms and make certain that they are used? What plans should be pursued?

International Court of Justice

The ICJ provides a start to a judicial system for the world. But major improvements are needed to make the now fledgling system adequate for an interdependent and warless world.

Codification of international law is a first priority and should be accelerated to the fullest practicable extent. The International Law Commission, under the aegis of the Sixth Committee of the General Assembly, is making notable progress in this direction. As noted, international law is in a primitive stage and, until recently, nations have been reluctant to recognize any need to restrain their sovereignty. Some success has been achieved, including conventions ratified by many nations (for instance, the nuclear test ban treaty and various human rights conventions), resolutions of the General Assembly adopted by near-unanimous votes, decisions of the ICJ, and broadly accepted practices. Ratification of existing conventions and adoption of others pertinent to international relations can be pressed. Intensive UN sponsored research, with ICJ consultation, could reveal areas of broad agreement.

Another priority is to make compulsory the jurisdiction of the ICJ over certain kinds of disputes, for example, those listed in Article 36. They include "(a) the interpretation of a treaty; (b) any question of international law; (c) the existence of any fact which, if established, would constitute a breach of an international obligation; and (d) the nature or extent of the reparation to be made for the breach of an international obligation."

Another step is to assure the availability of the court for other kinds of cases, including those involving parties other than nations. The court also needs the authority to deal with a case presented by only one party to a dispute. Expanded ICJ capability will be invaluable as complex investment, economic, environmental, resource, and human rights controversies require adjudication. Amendments to the ICJ Statute are required to make such jurisdictional changes; the procedure is similar to amending the UN Charter. Pending such amendments, all nations should be encouraged to submit their legal disputes to the court and accept without reservation its jurisdiction in the Article 36 categories. National reservations to ICJ jurisdiction, including the Connally Reservation of the United States, should be repealed.

The need to expand and decentralize the world judicial system to make judicial settlement more available is becoming increasingly evident. Creation of regional courts with right of appeal to the ICJ would accomplish decentralization. But, if the needs of an interdependent world are to be well served, judicial processes will also be needed to resolve international disputes among citizens and corporations without involving their nations. A series of tribunals under the surveillance of the ICJ could be established to settle disputes not susceptible to decision on legal principles. Access to regional or other courts subsidiary to the ICJ could encourage adjudication of legal disputes. Prior to amending the ICJ Statute to make these changes, the ICJ itself can initiate decentralization. Its statute allows the court to divide into chambers and sit outside The Hague.

Other ways to improve the effectiveness and stature of the ICJ as a mechanism to resolve disputes include (1) further revision of rules of procedure to simplify and shorten trials and reduce costs (the ICJ-amended rules of September 1972 were a good start); (2) greater use of advisory opinions of the court upon request of UN organs and agencies (perhaps too upon request of member states); (3) greater assurance that the members of the court are free from national interference; (4) use of the ICJ to resolve disputes arising from existing treaties that do not provide adequate settlement methods; (5) granting in future treaties compulsory ICJ jurisdiction to decide treaty disputes; and (6) establishing a United Nations legal aid fund available to poor countries lacking in legal and monetary resources.

The crux of the matter, however, is the will of nations to use the ICJ instead of conventional diplomacy and threat of force. Strong leadership, including advocacy and exemplary use of the ICJ by the United States and other major powers, would speak louder than words.

Chapter VI
Settlement
Pacific settlement as authorized in Chapter VI of the UN Charter is available as a supplement to the judicial system. The Security Council now has authority in the area of pacific settlement; it also has considerable experience in the use of Chapter VI procedures.

More effective use of this method depends in large part upon Security Council alertness, initiative, and persistence. During cold war years, the East-West confrontation often hampered Security Council action; the troublesome Vietnam War was never dealt with by the Security Council; action in other conflicts was sometimes too late. Now with the waning of the cold war and with a larger membership, the Security Council can better perform its intended role. Several procedural and organizational changes would enhance its ability and willingness to do so.

The chances of successful pacific settlement would be greater were Security Council involvement to begin before conflicts intensify. Disputants themselves have the responsibility to bring developing controversies to the attention of the Security Council; any other member state may do so. The Secretary-General should be strongly encouraged to make greater use of Article 99 of the Charter, which permits him to bring to the attention of the Security Council any matter which, in his opinion, threatens maintenance of peace and security. The development of an information network utilizing UN staff members around the world and other sources would improve the Secretary-General's ability to perform this function.

Informal meetings of the Security Council, perhaps as a committee of the whole, to discuss developing disputes would facilitate more timely action. Appointed observers, fact-finding groups, and ad hoc committees all could aid this process.

Proceeding under Article 33, the Security Council could more persistently challenge the parties to disputes to fulfill their duty under the Charter to seek peaceful solutions. The Security Council needs to search constantly for independent initiatives in conflict settlement. Rigidity in procedure is unwise, as no two situations are alike. The good offices of the Secretary-General, mediators, task forces, and panels of experts are available whenever appropriate.

It is important, too, that the Security Council, perhaps in informal committee of the whole, follow through to final settlement of disputes; temporary avoidance or termination of armed conflict does not necessarily signal peaceful resolution of the controversy.

International convention could strengthen the capacity of the Security Council to achieve pacific settlement. Procedures and guidelines for mediation, conciliation, and other settlement methods under Article 33 would be helpful. To act on behalf of the Security Council, the Secretary-General needs increased availability of skilled mediators and other specialists, both within and outside the Secretariat.

In addition, the Security Council need not hesitate to use means of peaceful settlement available outside the United Nations, including regional organizations and the good offices of individual nations. Often these means may facilitate settlement, whereas formal presentation of the dispute to the Security Council may harden national positions.

The Chapter VI potential for pacific settlement has not been fully utilized. This is, in large measure, because of the unwillingness of the Security Council, particularly the permanent members, to act in the common interest. Fortunately, an improved climate of cooperation has been evident recently thanks to détente between the Soviet Union and the Unites States, cessation of US war involvement in Indochina, and effective leadership of several nonpermanent members of the Council.

Conflict Management

Because model behavior by over 150 nations is not likely even with improved mechanisms for peaceful settlement, the conflicts that occur must be managed in the common interests of all.

Drafters of the Charter of the United Nations tried in 1945 to provide mechanisms and authorities to manage conflict, but they did not anticipate the nuclear bomb, the end of Western colonialism, or the bitter East-West confrontation. The UN Charter lodges the responsibility for maintenance of peace and security with the Security Council on the presumption that its five permanent members— China, France, the Soviet Union, the United States, and the United Kingdom—remain united. The Big Five, having won World War II, are to deal with any nations that threaten war or aggression. The powers of the Security Council are prescribed in Chapter VI and in Chapter VII, "Action with Respect to Threats to the Peace, Breaches of the Peace, and Acts of Aggression."

The responsibilities and the authorities of the Security Council under Chapter VII include (1) determining the existence of any threat to the peace, breach of the peace, or active aggression, and making recommendations on what measures shall be taken; (2) calling upon the parties concerned to comply with any provisional measures deemed necessary or desirable; (3) deciding upon measures not involving the use of armed forces (economic and diplomatic sanctions) and calling upon UN members to apply such measures; and (4) taking action with air, sea, or land forces.

Under the terms of the Charter, members of the United Nations commit themselves to contribute to the maintenance of international peace and security by making available to the Security Council, on its call, armed forces and other assistance in accordance with special agreements. Members further agree to hold immediately available national air force contingents for combined international enforcement action.

A Military Staff Committee (Article 47) was established to advise and assist the Security Council on all questions relating to military requirements, the employment and command of forces placed at its disposal, and the regulation of armaments and possible disarmament.

The United Nations has employed the collective security method envisaged in Chapter VII only once—when North Korea invaded South Korea in 1950. United Nations forces, composed largely of US troops, but with contingents from other nations, successfully resisted the invasion. The action was cloaked with UN authority by the famed Uniting for Peace Resolution passed by the General Assembly at the time of a Soviet walkout.

Since then, when preventive measures fail and combat starts, UN observers, mediators, and missions are withdrawn. UN efforts during conflicts are limited to resolutions and behind-the-scenes activities encouraging a cease-fire. The peacekeeping role, not specifically covered in the Charter, is often referred to as a Chapter VI½ function: a thin blue line of UN forces, consisting of contingents from various member states exclusive of the superpowers, is interposed between the combatants with their consent. More symbolic than powerful, UN peacekeeping forces separate the combatants and allow them to proceed with peacemaking, if they are willing. Such UN emergency forces have been used on several occasions: UNEF (1956) to separate Egyptian and Israeli forces; ONUC (1960) to stabilize the former Belgian Congo (now Zaire); UNFICYP (1964) to separate Turkish and Greek Cypriots in Cyprus; the current UNEF (1973) in the Sinai Desert; the UNDOF (1974) on the Golan Heights; and the UNIFIL (1978) in Lebanon.

While UN peacekeeping actions have, on balance, served a temporarily useful purpose, UN efforts following cease-fires have been notably unsuccessful. Throughout the life of UNEF (1956–1967), the Arab-Israeli controversy remained unsettled; and Egypt's request for withdrawal of UNEF forces in 1967 paved the way for the Six-Day War. Despite UN mediation efforts and resolutions by the Security Council, no solution followed and hostilities were renewed in October 1973. The outcome of present UN peacekeeping in the Golan Heights and Lebanon remains uncertain. The UN forces in Cyprus kept the Greek and Turkish populations separated from 1964 until 1974 but neither UN nor other peacemaking efforts resolved the basic controversy or prevented the Turkish invasion of 1974. The controversial UN action in the Congo was perhaps the most successful of all; a civil war was ended and stability restored to the newly independent nation.

The lack of success of UN peacemaking action results in part from inadequacy of mechanisms and authority and in part from a tendency to forget a situation once active combat has ceased. Two areas require attention: prevention and restoration.

The opportunities for preventive action available under the current UN Charter are limited. Even though the basis for action by the Security Council is implied in Chapter VII, collective security as practiced in the Korean War is not the likely pattern to be followed. How then can the will of the whole be exerted upon would-be transgressors?

Preventive Measures

Focusing the heat of world opinion upon would-be combatants is one alternative. The Security Council may do so under the authority of Chapter VII. Concurrent economic and diplomatic sanctions by most nations could have significant impact. To try out this approach, the Security Council has to be alert to potential aggression and to move in time to prevent it.

In short, nation-states must delegate to the United Nations, or other organizations, the authority to quarantine disputant nations and to take other steps compelling peaceful resolution of disputes. Possibilities are a UN peace force interposed between quarreling nations; UN observers on land, sea, or air; observation satellites to monitor declared economic sanctions or communications embargoes; and judicial action against all parties involved in a dispute. Thus volatile situations might be cooled.

Before the United Nations or an alternate organization can exercise authority in any of these ways, carefully structured safeguards and appropriate mechanisms and procedures are required. Peace forces—permanent, multinationally balanced, and directly recruited by the United Nations—must be established, equipped, and stationed around the world, giving the globe the equivalent of a domestic police force.

Nations must become convinced of the need to strengthen the hand of the world organization so that it may act in the common interest. This can occur through revision of the UN Charter or by a treaty creating a new organization. Preferably, if the United Nations is strengthened to perform the suggested role, the Security Council—perhaps with some modification of the veto and restructuring of its membership—can be given responsibility for decisions and surveillance over a peace force managed by the Secretary-General. The United Nations needs the right to intervene along national borders and at strategic communication centers. An assured source of revenue will be necessary. Traditional concepts of national sovereignty and superiority must give way.

The achievement of such goals will take time and effort. Nevertheless, realism demands constant striving and the relating of interim steps to the longer range view. Substantial progress in the reduction of national armaments, discussed in the next chapter, is a parallel need.

Restorative   Breaches of the peace and aggression are likely to be fairly fre-
Measures   quent in the near-term and occasional in the longer range despite the best efforts to prevent them. Hence, peacekeeping and peacemaking, the current UN mechanisms to restore peace, deserve continu-

ing attention and improvement. The following six proposals were discussed at an international conference in 1973.[5] They expand upon the preceding suggestions.

AUTHORIZATION OF ACTION The Security Council should have the primary right and responsibility to authorize peacekeeping actions. The General Assembly should retain the power to act under the Uniting for Peace resolution if the Security Council is unable to act. In most situations, peacekeeping can now be done only with the consent of the parties to the dispute and the permanent members of the Security Council.

OPERATIONS The Secretary-General should have operational responsibility for peacekeeping after authorization by, and under principles established by, the Security Council. He should be an operations officer rather than a commander-in-chief. The Security Council may wish to establish a special committee to oversee the Secretary-General's execution of peacekeeping, but the committee should not become involved in operations. A more balanced and representative composition of the Secretariat staff should be sought.

FORCES AND SUPPORT Recognizing the ad hoc nature of most peacekeeping operations, forces and logistic support must be arranged in advance to the maximum possible extent. Earmarked and thoroughly trained national units should be immediately ready when needed. A headquarters staff and other specialized United Nations units should exist and be available at all times. Agreements reached under Article 43 of the Charter should also provide for supplying forces for peacekeeping. Peacekeeping forces should come from nations not involved in the conflict, including those with differing political and social systems. Model agreements on designating, training, and furnishing forces for peacekeeping should be drafted promptly.

WITHDRAWAL OF FORCES In all future peacekeeping, it must be made clear that after a nation has consented to a peacekeeping operation on its territory, the UN forces will not be withdrawn without the approval of the Security Council, even if demanded

5. Eighth Conference on the United Nations of the Next Decade, sponsored by The Stanley Foundation, Muscatine, Iowa, June 1973.

by one or both parties. Withdrawals like that in the Middle East in 1967 must not be repeated.

MEDIATION Whenever the Security Council authorizes peacekeeping, it should simultaneously appoint a mediator or take other appropriate action toward peaceful settlement of the dispute. Peacekeeping is not a substitute for peacemaking and both should be used to resolve conflicts. The Security Council should insist upon continuing negotiations by the parties and should regularly review the situation.

FUNDING A United Nations special fund for peacekeeping should be established. This could allow the advance accumulation of voluntary contributions so that funds would be available for peacekeeping whenever needed. This fund should not be the sole source of money. Peacekeeping should be financed primarily through the general budget and from independent sources of revenue.

The capacity of the United Nations to restore peace can be enhanced in several other ways. First, by reaching agreement upon the guidelines for peacekeeping now deadlocked by US-USSR confrontation in the Special Committee on Peacekeeping Operations of the General Assembly (Committee of 33). Second, by reactivating the dormant Military Staff Committee to advise the Security Council and consult with member states regarding their making available forces specially trained for peacekeeping operations. Third, by making advance arrangements with various UN members for use of bases, facilities, and logistic support.

Looking ahead to strengthened UN capability for both preventive and restorative measures, it seems obvious that a permanent UN peace force is needed. The headquarters staff and other specialized UN units—communications, transport, and supply—could be created and maintained at the present time in cadre form without Charter change. This would be a significant beginning toward the establishment of a permanent UN peace force.

How Far to Go   In the longer range, creation of an adequate security system depends upon specific delegation of both authority and responsibility to the organs of the United Nations or to a substitute organization. Action for peaceful settlement and conflict resolution must be neither dependent upon voluntary cooperation nor subject to veto by any nation.

Civil war is an especially difficult problem. Ultimately, the world community will need to do more than quarantine civil war. It will need authority and capability to effect a cease-fire, maintain peace, and assure peaceful self-determination. To obtain agreement on any significant UN role in civil wars, it may be necessary to limit UN intervention to situations involving requests for UN help from existing national governments. But the United Nations dare not merely prop up an existing government. Guidelines for UN civil war intervention require some kind of free election before UN forces are withdrawn. United Nations authority to deal with overt and covert intervention into domestic controversies, including movement of weapons and mercenaries across national boundaries, is certain to be resisted by many nations as being itself interference in domestic affairs. Care is needed lest UN action thwart legitimate self-determination. Police-like force should be used only as a last resort.

The problem of world community influence and authority over the major powers remains. Currently, this influence is limited to public opinion and persuasion, and the situation will not change soon. No UN peace force is likely to have enough strength to restrain a powerfully armed country, nor should it have this capacity. The creation of such a powerful UN force would encourage, rather than reduce, current emphasis on military strength. The great powers are not ready to relinquish their veto power in the Security Council. While they will retain overwhelming power in the foreseeable future, it is increasingly desirable and in their self-interest to use power responsibly. The pressures of growing interdependence, economic factors, and world opinion tend to foster greater willingness to use the ICJ and other means to settle controversies. As tension lessens and progress is made toward arms reduction and disarmament, this willingness increases.

The ultimate objective, however, remains a rule of law prohibiting both war and the possession of military forces beyond those reasonably needed for internal security. This rule of law requires delegation of supranational authority to a world institution, either a restructured United Nations or a new organization. Until this rule of law, enforceable upon individuals as well as nations, becomes a reality, the management of international peace and security will remain troublesome and confused.

Where does the United States stand with respect to the proposed overall objective of a world without war? How are we contributing to the management of international peace and security?

United States Posture

Ambivalent is perhaps the best one-word description of the US posture; a dichotomy exists between our rhetoric and practice. World peace under a rule of law has long been enunciated by US leaders as a fundamental aspiration of our foreign policy. Intervention, covert as well as overt, has been decried as an unhealthy and hazardous invasion of the internal affairs of nation-states. We strongly advocated a world organization and played a key role in the drafting of the Charter of the United Nations. On paper we have a sound record supporting world community effort to maintain peace and security.

Our actions, unfortunately, add up to a less impressive record. We have made no use of the International Court of Justice. Neither our example nor our Connally Reservation have encouraged other nations to use the court to resolve disputes.

We have supported all UN peacekeeping operations and floated a $100 million bond issue to fund UN debt arising from the Congo venture in the early 1960s. But our disastrous involvement in Indochina and revelations of CIA dirty tricks in many countries create the impression that we do not hesitate to intervene in the affairs of other nations. Nor does our recent pattern of personal diplomacy— avoiding the United Nations—strengthen the role of the United Nations in making and keeping the peace.

Our emphasis on military power, our obvious dedication to power balance, and our strong support of national sovereignty do not provide leadership toward the objective of a world without war. We have adamantly opposed proposals to revise the Charter or to develop ways whereby the United Nations is trusted with the power it needs to maintain international peace and security. In summary, our failure to practice what we preach has weakened the role of the world community in this important field.

4 DISARMAMENT

Peaceful settlement of disputes and effective management of conflict will do much to bring closer the goal of a world without war; the third supporting objective is disarmament.

Disarmament alone will not guarantee peace; war can be waged with any level of weapons: primitive, conventional, or nuclear. Reduction of national armaments and armed forces to a reasonable level for internal security, however, lessens the ability and the temptation to threaten or to use force externally to achieve national interests.

Disarmament progress is partially a by-product of a more adequate security system. The reverse applies too: disarmament progress can contribute to a climate more conducive to the development of an adequate security system.

Since World War II, efforts to control, limit, and reduce national armaments have produced very limited results: never have so many nations been so heavily armed with such destructive weapons. Disarmament has been approached multilaterally under the aegis of the United Nations, regionally in Latin America and Europe, and bilaterally by the United States and the Soviet Union. What has been accomplished? *Efforts and Accomplishments*

The United Nations' responsibility for disarmament is established by the Charter.

The Security Council shall be responsible for formulating, with the assistance of the Military Staff Committee . . . plans . . . for the establishment of a system for the regulation of armaments. [Article 26]

There shall be established a Military Staff Committee to advise and assist the Security Council on all questions relative to . . . the regulation of armaments, and possible disarmament. [Article 47]

The General Assembly may consider the general principles of cooperation in the maintenance of international peace and security, including the principles governing disarmament and the regulation of armaments, and may make recommendations with regard to such principles to the Members or to the Security Council or to both. [Article 11]

While the Security Council, thwarted by the US-USSR confrontation, has scarcely discussed disarmament, neither has the dormant Military Staff Committee, but the General Assembly has repeatedly debated and adopted disarmament resolutions. The long inactive, but recently reactivated, United Nations Disarmament Commission created by the General Assembly and consisting of all member states also adopted resolutions urging action. As neither the General Assembly nor the Disarmament Commission has been an appropriate body for arms negotiations, encouragement has been given to the Geneva Disarmament talks—Conference of the Committee on Disarmament (CCD)—comprised initially of 18, and later 31, nations. Since 1962, the principal forum for multilateral negotiations has been the CCD—replaced in 1979 by the Committee on Disarmament. Several treaties limiting extension of arms have been perfected and recommended to the General Assembly.

Treaties adopted by the General Assembly include the Antarctica Treaty (1959); the Treaty Banning Nuclear Weapon Tests in the Atmosphere, in Outer Space, and Under Water (1963); the Treaty on Principles Governing the Activities of States in the Exploration and Use of Outer Space (1967); The Treaty on the Non-Proliferation of Nuclear Weapons (1968); the Seabed Arms Control Treaty (1971); the Convention on the Prohibition of the Development, Production, and Stockpiling of Bacteriological (Biological) and Toxic Weapons and on Their Destruction (1972); and the Convention on the Prohibition of Military or Any Other Hostile Use of Environmental Modification Techniques (1976). These seven treaties are now in force. The CCD worked for several years on a treaty dealing with chemical weapons, but agreement has been blocked by the United States.

The May–June 1978 Special Session on Disarmament of the UN General Assembly (SSOD) sought to strengthen the determination of member states to deal with disarmament and to improve UN machinery for this purpose. The session involved six weeks' work by the UN member states, following five meetings of a preparatory committee dating back to March 1977. The end product of SSOD was its Final Document containing sections entitled Declaration,

Programme of Action, and Machinery. This Final Document, unprecedented in the disarmament history of the United Nations, together with the formal statements and information discussions, may have created a turning point in UN efforts and capability to make disarmament progress. Various of the SSOD proposals are discussed later in this chapter.

Not all disarmament efforts have occurred on a global basis. The nations of Latin America, acting multilaterally, perfected the 1969 Treaty for the Prohibition of Nuclear Weapons in Latin America (treaty of Tlatelolco) and established as a control mechanism the Organization for the Prohibition of Nuclear Weapons in Latin America (OPANAL). For more than five years, 18 nations have been negotiating in Vienna to develop a treaty on Mutual Force Reduction (MFR) between NATO and Warsaw Pact nations. The outcome of MFR negotiations remains uncertain, but recent progress appears to have narrowed the differences between the two sides.

While efforts to date have not yet reduced armaments, the several treaties have prevented extension of nuclear armaments to Antarctica, outer space, the seas, and Latin America—all areas of limited strategic interest to the superpowers. Other treaties have forced nuclear testing underground, advanced the concept of nonproliferation of nuclear weapons, and outlawed bacteriological and environmental weapons.

Since the early 1960s, the United States and the Soviet Union have sparred with each other over disarmament matters, maneuvering for propaganda advantage. Independently, but with eyes on each other, they have adopted important arms control measures increasing the stability of mutual nuclear deterrence and lessening the chance of inadvertent nuclear attack. Examples include submarine-based missiles, hardened missile launchers, early warning systems, and the hot-line between Moscow and Washington.

Finally, in November 1967, the superpowers began serious Strategic Arms Limitation Talks (SALT). These negotiations culminated in the 1972 SALT I Treaty setting limits on numbers of nuclear equipped intercontinental ballistic missiles (ICBMs)—well above then current levels—and limiting each nation to two antiballistic missile (ABM) installations. Subsequently, the 1974 Vladivostok agreement tentatively set new, but higher, ceilings on ICBMs and other delivery systems and new limits upon missiles equipped with multiple independent reentry vehicles (MIRVs). Agreement was also reached to limit ABM installations to one each. Before

SALT I expired in October 1977, the United States and the Soviet Union began negotiating SALT II, a process started by the Ford administration but delayed during the 1976 presidential campaign.

The Carter administration resumed negotiations and proposed significant reductions and stricter limits concerning strategic nuclear delivery systems which the Soviet Union promptly rejected. Subsequently, SALT II was negotiated and signed by Brezhnev and Carter and is before the US Senate for ratification as this book goes to press.

In 1976 President Ford and Premier Brezhnev signed a bilateral treaty setting a ceiling of 150 kilotons—the force of 150,000 tons of TNT—for single nuclear devices exploded underground. But the treaty allows a total yield from an explosion involving more than one device of up to 1,500 kilotons. Advance notification is required and on-site inspection is permitted for explosions exceeding 150 kilotons.

Like the multilateral arms limitation efforts, bilateral negotiations between the Soviet Union and the United States have not produced arms reduction. So far, they have only established higher ceilings on delivery systems for strategic nuclear warheads.

Weapons Unlimited

Meanwhile, the arms race continues: $107 billion in 1960; $138 billion in 1965; $201 billion in 1970; $356 billion in 1976; and undoubtedly over $400 billion now (all in current dollars). World military expenditures in constant dollars (1975) have increased from $242 billion in 1965 to $331 billion in 1976; developing nations' military expenditures in constant dollars have increased by a factor of 2.67 to 1.00, from $27 billion to $72 billion in this period.[1]

Recently the Soviet Union and the United States have compounded the strategic arms race by adding qualitative improvements to weapons and delivery systems. Both sides are busily expanding delivery systems to the Vladivostok ceilings, increasing their holdings of MIRVs, perfecting improved guidance systems and other apparatus. Research, including underground nuclear tests, continues unabated. Each government voices fear that the other may score a breakthrough or acquire first strike capability. Both propose and introduce new weapons systems—cruise missiles, neutron bombs, B1 and Backfire bombers, larger missile launching submarines, and mobile land-based ICBMs—ostensibly for security but possibly to bargain from a position of strength. Such actions are

1. Sivard, 1978, p. 20.

incompatible with current overkill levels, with the basic concept of mutual nuclear deterrence, and with the expressed determination of both countries to avoid nuclear war.

Well-intended efforts to control the proliferation of nuclear weapons have been only marginally successful, though the Tlatelolco treaty is likely to come into full force at an early date. Long-time holdouts Brazil and Chile have ratified the agreement, and Argentina has indicated its intent to ratify.

The Nuclear Non-Proliferation Treaty (NPT) adopted in 1968, in force since 1970, and reviewed in 1975 reflected the superpowers' idea of restraining nuclear weapon proliferation. While formalizing a desirable concept and stimulating the International Atomic Energy Agency to important advances in safeguard technology, the treaty has not achieved fully its objectives. India exploded a nuclear device and joined the nuclear club in 1974; Israel is believed to have a few nuclear weapons. Others are expected to join soon. Despite endorsement in 1968 by the UN General Assembly (95 yes, 4 no, and 21 abstaining), the NPT was never popular, particularly with the targets of its restrictions—the potential nuclear weapon states. The treaty has been ratified by 104 nations. But the nonratifying nations include nuclear weapon states China, France, and probably Israel; India, the latest nation with nuclear capability; and such potential nuclear weapon states as Argentina, Brazil, Egypt, Indonesia, Pakistan, South Africa, Spain, and Turkey.

Conventional Weapons

Limitation and reduction of conventional weapons has been almost completely ignored as arms controllers have concentrated upon nuclear weapons and strategic delivery systems. Yet all armed conflicts since 1945 have been fought with conventional weapons and some 80 or 85 percent of the world's annual military expenditures support conventionally armed forces. In recent years, the international traffic in armaments through sales, gifts, and military assistance has been substantial; $8.0 billion in 1967; $8.3 billion in 1971; and $12.8 billion in 1976 (all in constant 1975 dollars).[2] New military equipment, weapons, and ammunition are manufactured and exported from many countries. But of $88.3 billion exported from 1961 through 1975, over 94 percent was supplied by nine major exporters, ranked in order of sales: the United States, the Soviet Union, France, the United Kingdom, China, West Ger-

2. US, Arms Control and Disarmament Agency, *World Military Expenditures and Arms Transfers 1967–1976*, pub. no. 98.

many, Czechoslovakia, Poland, and Canada.[3] A limited market for used military equipment is supplied by various nations and brokers.

Except for the Mutual Force Reduction (MFR) negotiations, no official action looking to limitation or reduction of conventional armed forces is currently under way. Major and lesser powers alike, with few exceptions, modernize and enlarge their conventional armaments for prestige as well as security reasons. As cease-fire agreements stop hostilities, combatants rearm; witness the flow of arms into the Middle East, India, and Pakistan following recent wars. Armed confrontations continue in such hot spots as the Sino-Soviet border, the 38th Parallel in Korea, the India-Pakistan border, and the Golan Heights, Lebanon, and elsewhere. Suggestions to control the arms traffic or reduce stockpiles of conventional weapons are brushed off with the argument that control of nuclear weapons must come first.

The Disarmament Objective   The limitation and reduction of national armaments must be examined against this discouraging background. Disarmament's urgency is emphasized by the following quotations from SSOD's Final Document:

> Mankind today is confronted with an unprecedented threat of self-extinction arising from the massive and competitive accumulation of the most destructive weapons ever produced. Existing arsenals of nuclear weapons alone are more than sufficient to destroy all life on earth.
>
> Mankind is confronted with a choice: We must halt the arms race and proceed to disarmament or face annihilation.

Is substantial arms reduction, as distinguished from arms control and ever higher nuclear ceilings, achievable or is it merely a pipe dream? Will nations, particularly the key nuclear states, see the light and act in common self-interest?

While answers to these questions are obscure, a guarded affirmative seems logical, given the growing interdependence of the world. The need to reduce armaments is generally accepted, economic pressures are growing, and few nations feel more secure despite enlarged military capabilities. But, there is no assurance that logic will prevail or that the strong influence of emotional nationalism and strident militarism upon national decision-making will be broken.

Determined action must be substituted for lofty rhetoric if disar-

3. Sivard, 1977, p. 9.

mament progress is to be made. The vital prerequisites to action are (1) a clear and bold statement of long-range disarmament objectives; (2) effective disarmament machinery; (3) specific near-term arms reduction programs achievable in the current world climate; and (4) determination of nations, particularly the overarmed, to make disarmament progress. All are needed if the world community is to free itself from the burdens and hazards of a war-prone world.

General and complete disarmament (GCD), under effective international control, is proposed as the longer range objective, even though its attainment may seem far removed. The usual case for GCD is a simple one; if the implements of war are removed, nations will be unable to wage war. Unfortunately, such a stereotyped conception is too simple to withstand scrutiny. Disarmament alone will not assure peace: an adequate world security system, as already discussed, is also necessary to make disarmament safe.

GCD, however, offers several advantages. If certain types of armaments are prohibited, the detection of any indicates violation. On the other hand, if nations are permitted to maintain certain armaments at arbitrary levels, it becomes more difficult to assure compliance. Thus GCD would simplify verification and inspection problems. GCD would yield maximum savings; tremendous expenditures of men, money, and materials now going into armament programs would end. Finally, and most fundamentally, national offensive armaments would be unnecessary if the responsibility for national security were lodged with an effective world organization. Pie in the sky? By no means. Difficult? Certainly, but what other objective offers any real hope for long-term peace and security?

GCD is not a new idea. Both the Soviet Union and the United States proposed GCD to the United Nations in the early 1960s. Just prior to the US proposal, John L. McCloy of the United States and Valerian Alexandrovitch Zorin of the USSR reached certain agreements related to disarmament principles.[4] The late President John F. Kennedy presented the US proposal to the General Assembly on September 25, 1961. A month later a conference of US citizens from a wide spectrum of opinion and belief carefully scrutinized this proposal and found it a credible beginning warranting further development and serious negotiation.[5] These proposals,

4. Joint Statement of Agreed Principles for Disarmament Negotiations, approved by the 16th UN General Assembly.
5. Third Strategy for Peace Conference, sponsored by The Stanley Foundation, Muscatine, Iowa, October 1961.

never seriously examined by the United Nations, became casualties of the cold war. Undoubtedly, both were intended more as cold war polemics than as serious documents. Nevertheless, the Soviet and US proposals had much in common and were credible starting points for serious consideration of GCD.

The Final Document of SSOD clearly reconfirms and restates GCD as the world's ultimate disarmament objective. Its Declaration and Programme of Action include numerous references to GCD. One of the concluding sections (126) reads:

> In adopting this Final Report, the States-Members of the United Nations solemnly reaffirm their determination to work for general and complete disarmament and to make further collective efforts aimed at strengthening peace and international security.

Taking the First Steps   Regrettably, the SSOD document is vague about how GCD is to be accomplished. Before GCD stops being a mere rhetorical aspiration and becomes a working objective, there is need to affirm certain principles. These include (1) establishing criteria regarding permissible levels of nonnuclear arms for internal national security; (2) creating a suitable world organization, perhaps an International Disarmament Organization affiliated with the United Nations, to administer GCD treaties; (3) reducing both conventional and nuclear armaments and armed forces on a staged basis over a period of years; (4) balancing scheduled arms reductions to assure that no nation's security is jeopardized; (5) applying arms reductions universally or at least to those nations of appreciable military strength; and (6) establishing reliable verification procedures to monitor agreed reductions of armed forces and destruction of weapons. Were the United Nations to strengthen its SSOD statement by developing such concepts, flesh would be put upon the GCD framework.

Serious attention to GCD, however, depends upon a vastly improved political climate. Hence the importance of initiating and continuing disarmament activities aimed at lesser goals. The following near-term programs are suggested as areas of emphasis; each is itself beneficial and each would help to lessen tensions and improve the international climate: (1) establishing effective UN machinery to deal with disarmament matters; (2) halting and reversing the nuclear arms race between the superpowers; (3) limiting the proliferation of nuclear weapons; (4) developing procedures to limit and reduce conventional weapons and armed forces; and (5) stimulating research, study, and discussion of the many technical, economic, and political facets of disarmament.

Appropriate organization and procedures are fundamental to the management of any program once overall objectives are established. This need has been frequently disregarded in international affairs as nation-states engage in running debate to score points with world opinion-makers or the public back home. Such disregard of basic management techniques, characteristic of disarmament matters since the origin of the United Nations, is partly responsible for today's minimal progress. The lack of adequate mechanisms has been a continuing handicap to disarmament efforts.

UN Machinery for Disarmament

Recognizing that the United Nations under its Charter has a central role and primary responsibility regarding disarmament, SSOD urged a more active role, calling upon the United Nations to "facilitate and encourage all disarmament measures—unilateral, bilateral, regional and multilateral—and [to] be kept duly informed . . . of all disarmament efforts outside its aegis without prejudice to the progress of negotiations."

No particular machinery is required for independent disarmament initiatives by any nation. (The salutary potential of unilateral action is discussed later.) International machinery, however, can aid vitally important bilateral negotiations, like those between the United States and the Soviet Union. Such negotiations usually have resulted in a draft convention submitted to the Conference of the Committee on Disarmament for review and modification and then to the UN General Assembly for final action. While multilateral negotiations regarding nuclear-weapon-free zones or zones of peace are likely to take place in existing or ad hoc regional organizations, they may be encouraged by the United Nations, and resulting treaties may be referred to the General Assembly.

Perhaps SSOD's major contribution will prove to be the decisions incorporated in the "Machinery" section of its Final Document.

SSOD reaffirmed that the General Assembly will remain the main UN deliberative organ for disarmament matters. Its annual agenda will now include an item dealing with review of the implementation of SSOD recommendations and decisions; and it will continue to monitor disarmament progress and to review and act upon proposed international disarmament conventions.

Two changes adopted by SSOD are likely to strengthen the General Assembly's capacity to perform these functions. The First

Committee of the General Assembly is henceforth to deal only with questions of disarmament and "related international security questions." This will allow more adequate time for the numerous disarmament resolutions that are presented at each General Assembly. The other important action is agreement to convene a Second Special Session on Disarmament on a date to be set by the General Assembly, presumably within the next three or four years. Such a session, or alternatively a World Disarmament Conference as proposed by the Soviet Union and others, could again focus world attention upon disarmament. Occurring at regular intervals, these sessions could prod nations to greater progress; stimulate educational, research, and political activities; contribute to a better understanding of complex issues; and reinforce universal disarmament responsibility. The General Assembly subsequently scheduled a second SSOD for 1982.

SSOD also improved disarmament machinery by resurrecting the dormant UN Disarmament Commission. This commission will serve as a deliberative body of the whole, subsidiary to the General Assembly. It will consider and recommend to the General Assembly various disarmament issues and monitor and follow up SSOD decisions and recommendations. In taking this action, delegates to SSOD recognized the time restraints of the General Assembly and its First Committee: regular sessions are not conducive to relaxed consideration of disarmament matters. The Disarmament Commission met in 1979 and, presumably, annually thereafter and will report each year to the General Assembly. Its initial focus is upon the elements of a Comprehensive Disarmament Programme. It will function on disarmament matters somewhat as ECOSOC functions on economic and social matters.

Modification of the world community's smaller disarmament negotiating body, CCD, was another SSOD initiative. A smaller body is necessary to deal with complex disarmament details and to negotiate treaties for adoption by the UN General Assembly and ratification by member states. CCD has been a useful mechanism, but has been criticized for the permanent US-USSR co-chairmanship and insufficient liaison with the United Nations. While France and China both abstained from CCD participation, France announced during SSOD that it would participate in a restructured successor to CCD.

During the SSOD discussions, agreement was reached to create a new Committee on Disarmament (CD) by January 1, 1979, to replace CCD. The membership of this new committee includes all nuclear weapon states, all members of CCD that desire to partici- pate, and a few other member states chosen in consultation with the president of the 33rd General Assembly. The intent is to involve nations most interested in disarmament matters with due regard for regional and political balances. The chairmanship of the CD is to rotate among all members on a monthly basis; it is believed that this change will encourage the participation of France and China.

Liaison with the UN General Assembly is to be strengthened in several ways: (1) the secretary of the CD will be appointed by the Secretary-General of the United Nations and will act as his personal representative; (2) the CD will report to the General Assembly at least annually and provide documentation of its activities to all members of the United Nations on a regular basis; and (3) arrange- ments will be made for interested noncommittee member states to submit proposals and to express views to the committee regarding their particular disarmament concerns.

The existing Centre for Disarmament of the UN Secretariat is a fourth disarmament management mechanism. SSOD recognized that the Centre for Disarmament needs strengthening and that its research and information functions need broadening. The center is directed to examine the disarmament information and potential as- sistance of all institutions and programs within the United Nations system. The center is also encouraged to increase its contacts with nongovernmental organizations and research institutions in view of the valuable role they play in disarmament.

Finally, SSOD requested the Secretary-General to appoint an ad- visory board of knowledgeable and qualified eminent persons with equitable geographical representation. This board is to advise the Secretary-General on various aspects of disarmament and arms lim- itation studies.

The machinery established by SSOD substantially strengthens the capability of the United Nations to be involved in multilateral disarmament matters. As these mechanisms begin to function, pro- cedures can be improved in a number of ways, including (1) eliminating duplication of general debate in the First Committee and the General Assembly; (2) preparing for the General Assembly one omnibus resolution each year reaffirming past years' resolutions; (3) utilizing semipermanent appointees and staff for the First Com- mittee and the Disarmament Commission; (4) making greater use of subcommittees for in-depth consideration of complex disarmament matters; (5) placing the Centre for Disarmament under the supervision of a deputy secretary-general; and (6) making greater use of nongovernmental organizations, research institutions, and independent experts.

If properly used, disarmament machinery created by SSOD has the capacity to provide much more effective management of multilateral disarmament efforts. The conduct of essential bilateral negotiations between the United States and the Soviet Union can be eased, and unilateral and regional arms reduction measures can be stimulated. But nations must use the machinery.

Nuclear Limitation   While it is too late to put the nuclear genie back in the bottle, the real turning point to break the political logjam and improve the climate for serious consideration of arms reduction must be checking and reversing the nuclear arms race.

The responsibility to initiate nuclear restraints rests upon the two nuclear giants. Only they can break the self-imposed chains shackling them to the powerful momentum of a competitive build-up started long ago. The world community may prod and encourage, but the United States and the Soviet Union must take the crucial first steps and then provide leadership.

Charting a course to halt and reverse the nuclear arms race would not prove exceedingly difficult were the nuclear powers determined to do so. The Soviet Union and the United States have both expressed the intent that once SALT II (with its lower limitations on delivery vehicles) is negotiated, SALT III will address nuclear reductions.

To stop expansion of the nuclear arms race, target objectives need to include (1) cessation of production and additional deployment of nuclear weapons and their means of delivery; (2) cessation of production of nuclear materials for weapons purposes; (3) cessation of qualitative improvement and development of nuclear weapons; (4) cessation of nuclear weapons testing by moratorium and/or a Comprehensive Nuclear Test Ban Treaty; and (5) cessation of development of anti-satellite or other devices capable of threatening verification systems.

Reversal of the arms race means reduction and, ultimately, elimination of nuclear weapons. This calls for a comprehensively phased program with agreed schedules for progressive and balanced reduction of stockpiles of nuclear weapons and their means of delivery. Reduction involves destruction or conversion of nuclear weapons and delivery systems. Such a comprehensively phased reduction program would require assured verification.

The challenge is to negotiate balanced agreements that implement cessation and reduction without jeopardizing national security. While the programs need to start with the United States and the Soviet Union, other nuclear weapon powers must be brought into the process at an appropriate time; nuclear disarmament must become universal.

Joint action to curtail the nuclear arms race is a logical outgrowth of détente. The documents formalizing détente reveal its meaning: realization that the two superpowers have no alternative to peaceful coexistence. Both nations know that a nuclear exchange is too devastating to risk. Their huge nuclear arsenals and numerous delivery systems have but a single security function: deterring each other from doing what they both know each dare not do. Such is the Alice in Wonderland illogic of mutual nuclear deterrence in a time of nuclear stalemate. The two nations, whether they like it or not and despite diverse ideologies and goals, are compelled to prevent mutual confrontations from escalating into war.

Why then are the two countries so reluctant to act boldly, contain the nuclear threat, and end their senseless competition for greater overkill? Relations between the Soviet Union and the United States are colored by more than a half century of distrust and fear, arising basically from conflicting ideologies but heightened by post–World War II events. (Soviet-American relations are further examined in a later chapter.) Beyond this primary element, several secondary factors handicap progress despite common commitment to controlling nuclear weapons and avoiding nuclear war.

One factor is the sheer momentum of each nation's system for developing, manufacturing, and managing its strategic armed forces. Amply funded and warmly encouraged for three decades, the nuclear arms movement is now an extensive and intricate organism with a life force of its own—embracing scientists, manufacturers, armed forces, managers, workers, and decision-makers. Vested interests are great among those involved, civilian as well as military. The inertia of the massive complex, plus both deliberate and inadvertent resistance by its managers, handicaps the political leaders of both countries in their stated efforts to achieve nuclear disarmament.

Another major handicap is the dominating influence of the military establishment on disarmament matters. Most military officers have both a personal career conflict of interest and a philosophic approach to security that impede objective consideration of disarmament. The militarily trained mind, with few exceptions, assumes the worst possible set of circumstances, adds a few contingencies, and cautiously plans to deal with the problem. This may be the proper posture to prepare for war, but it is a poor approach to arms reduction. Dominant military influence stifles objective consideration of disarmament proposals and overshadows important political, economic, and humanitarian factors.

Legitimate and imagined concerns regarding verification constitute still another handicap. Each side, fearful lest the other fail to carry out treaty commitments, relies upon its own satellite and seismographic verification systems. The Soviet Union has generally opposed on-site inspection, a likely essential to verification of conversion or destruction of nuclear weapons and delivery vehicles. Neither side has looked with favor upon an international verification system such as that recently proposed by France. Both fear their satellite verification systems could be threatened by anti-satellite weapons or systems. (Fortunately, discussions have begun between the United States and the Soviet Union regarding anti-satellite weapons; they may lead to an agreement to ban these weapons, perhaps as an extension to the Outer Space Treaty.)

One important measure to strengthen the will of the two superpowers is to broaden the range of views among disarmament advisors and decision-makers. Generalists of vision, judgment, independence, and broad outlook are needed; technical experts, disassociated from the military establishment, could be involved in decisions regarding weapons, verification processes, and risks. Disarmament matters are much too vital to allow veto power to remain with overly cautious generals.

A second measure is intense study of all aspects of disarmament and its relationship to an adequate security system. Certain once-valid assumptions regarding mutual nuclear deterrence—still the "peace of terror" that Winston Churchill labeled it—need to be tested. Are we preparing for situations that no longer exist, a common mistake of generals? Does mutual nuclear deterrence continue to make the superpowers more secure? If deterrence is needed, what level of overkill is warranted? What impact do current levels of superpower nuclear armament have upon China's decisions regarding its nuclear capability? Will improved nuclear weapon quality add more security than weapon reduction and nonproliferation?

How good are nuclear guarantees? Such questions focus on the heart of the nuclear arms race.

A third measure is to expand bilateral negotiations and discussions. SALT talks, supplemented by ongoing diplomatic exchanges, are the principal bilateral negotiation mechanisms. Periodic Committee on Disarmament meetings are an additional forum. While expanded use of these mechanisms is desirable, other vehicles are needed to encourage informal discussion well in advance of consideration of specific treaty drafts. Scientists could get together to examine verification technology; political scientists and politicians to explore disarmament in the context of adequate security. SALT could broaden its agenda to include examination of general and complete disarmament, starting with the 1961 proposals by the United States and the Soviet Union.

Nongovernmental organizations (NGOs) and research institutes should be encouraged to play a greater role in promoting unofficial discussions. The Pugwash conferences have enabled scientists from both countries to gain a better understanding of many nuclear matters. Joint US-USSR and United Nations Association policy studies, Dartmouth conferences, some Stanley Foundation meetings, and other NGO activities generate discussion on a wide range of peace and security concerns. At the 24th Pugwash Conference on Science and World Affairs in 1975, representatives of 31 nations urged a world meeting on disarmament and expanded research on the hazards of nuclear power programs.

The immediate test of will, however, centers upon SALT II and SALT III. Ceilings, even higher than desirable, are better than nothing. But SALT negotiations will do little to advance disarmament until they also set a schedule for staged reduction of nuclear armaments.

The objectives of the Nuclear Non-Proliferation Treaty (NPT) remain valid. More nuclear buttons within reach of more hands add to the hazard and destabilize the present nuclear balance of terror. More sources of plutonium without proper safeguards increase the probability of nuclear theft. More nuclear installations of whatever type multiply the potential for accidents. Efforts to limit these hazards should not be abandoned because the NPT has failed to accomplish fully its intended purpose.

Nonproliferation

The NPT will continue in its present form at least until the next review conference scheduled for 1980. Additional ratification by nonnuclear weapon states should be actively encouraged. This effort would be significantly enhanced if the Soviet Union and the United States would deal positively with their commitments under Articles IV and VI of the treaty.

The nuclear giants, with the participation of the nonnuclear nations, should plan and execute a workable international program assuring availability of peaceful nuclear technology to nonnuclears. Participation by the beneficiaries of the plan is essential to allay suspicion that the nuclear powers have no intention of living up to the commitments of Article IV.

Compliance with Article VI is a different matter; only the Soviet Union and the United States are involved. Bilateral agreement and implementation of measures to limit and reduce nuclear arsenals, to curtail new weapon introduction, and otherwise to halt and reverse the nuclear race would demonstrate good faith. Superpower vertical "deproliferation" would then match the horizontal nonproliferation demanded of would-be nuclear weapon states by the NPT.

A Comprehensive Nuclear Test Ban Treaty (CTB), prohibiting all tests of nuclear explosives, would help limit proliferation and is generally considered an important disarmament priority. The treaty, once adopted by the UN General Assembly and upon ratification by the required number of nations—including the United States and the Soviet Union—should be made operative even if other present nuclear weapon states are not prepared to ratify. The CTB could have been adopted long ago if the United States and the Soviet Union had not squabbled over verification and on-site inspection. Advances in seismographic and space satellite observation technology have simplified verification procedures. The May 1976 bilateral agreement incorporated a provision for on-site inspection of explosions exceeding 150 kilotons.

Even if parties to the treaty act in good faith to increase its credibility, there is no guarantee that the NPT will achieve its purpose. Hence other measures are needed to cope with proliferation. One possibility is to subject all nuclear installations to agreed safeguards, to reduce the danger of theft or diversion of fissionable materials. Spent fuel from nuclear power reactors contains plutonium which, if separated, may be used for explosives or as a fuel for the breeder type reactor now being developed. Safeguarding the removal, transportation, and storage of spent fuel and separation of the plutonium it contains are crucial to preventing diversion. Control of plutonium will become more difficult if breeder reactors for electrical power generation are introduced commercially. These reactors require plutonium for start-up; once the power plants are in operation, the additional plutonium they breed will vastly increase the total supply that must be safeguarded.

The International Nuclear Fuel Cycle Evaluation (INFCE), now in progress, brings together representatives of over 50 nations to study technical aspects of use, processing, and management of nuclear fuels. Its forthcoming report is expected to establish a foundation for future progress on nonproliferation in the 1980s.

The International Atomic Energy Agency (IAEA) has pioneered the development of safeguards in response to requirements of the NPT. Supplier nations that design and construct nuclear facilities—the United States, the Soviet Union, Great Britain, France, West Germany, and Canada—could cooperate by insisting that recipient states agree to appropriate IAEA safeguards. Supplier nations have sufficient leverage at the time of contract to require contractual commitment by purchasers.

Nuclear-weapon-free zones offer another approach. Areas without serious confrontations between nations and containing no nuclear weapon states offer the greatest opportunity: Sub-Saharan Africa, Scandinavia, Central Europe, the Middle East, the Mediterranean, the South Pacific, Southeast Asia, and South Asia. The Tlatelolco treaty and its Organization for the Prohibition of Nuclear Weapons in Latin America have pioneered this approach.

Colocation of key nuclear process facilities is another potentially useful method to deter plutonium theft or diversion. Were uranium enrichment, plutonium separation, fuel fabrication, waste treatment, and disposal facilities located together, perhaps with multinational ownership on a regional basis, surveillance and accountability would be simplified. Colocation of key facilities could have great appeal in nuclear-weapon-free zones.

It would be a tragic error for the world community to give up on nonproliferation efforts. The NPT established a sound standard. Limiting proliferation is a vital link in disarmament progress.

The scoreboard for efforts to limit conventional weapons and armed forces is nearly blank—no successes, a few failures, and really no broad effort since World War II. The single exception is the current slow-moving Mutual Force Reduction negotiations. The proper questions are how and where to start on the gigantic task of bringing the conventional arms race under control and setting the

Conventional Weapons

stage for ultimate reduction to levels reasonably required for internal security.

The problems related to conventional armaments and forces are quite different from those of nuclear weapons. Tradition and emotion are on the side of conventional armaments. Nation-states have long maintained conventional forces armed with the weapons of the day, ranging from bows, arrows, spears, and catapults to machine guns, tanks, missiles, and jet fighters, and have used them for offensive as well as defensive purposes. Long taken for granted, the increasing sophistication and destructiveness of conventional weapons do not generate the awesome fear of the atom bomb. Conventional force limitation touches every nation rather than the few involved with nuclear weapons. These differences contribute to the lack of concern about conventional disarmament. Reduction of conventional armaments is needed, according to many nonnuclear states, but only when the nuclear arms race is brought under control.

Nevertheless, conventional disarmament is overdue for serious attention. Conventional arms and forces absorb between 80 percent and 85 percent of global military expenditures. In 1976 the military expenditures of the developing nations aggregated $81 billion (current dollars).[6] This is a significant amount compared to the external nonmilitary aid they received (see chapter 7).

While conventional weapons disarmament warrants high priority for economic and security reasons, there is another persuasive reason: the extreme difficulty of separating nuclear disarmament from conventional. Neither can be adequately dealt with alone. Progress would be more likely if all nations were involved in disarmament and the whole range of weaponry were tackled together. Can anyone imagine the Disarmament Commission successfully pressuring the nuclear powers without calling upon other nations to deal with conventional disarmament?

Until future agreement on permissible levels of national armaments is reached, what progress can be sought? Because most conventional arms, and particularly the more sophisticated, are imported, control of transfers from supplier to recipient nations is a key opportunity. As measured in 1975 constant dollars, the value of world arms trade rose from $8 billion in 1967 to $12.8 billion in 1976. Transfers in 1976 into the Near East were $4.2 billion, to

6. Sivard, 1978, p. 20.

East Asia $1.1 billion. Imports by developing countries rose from $5.4 billion in 1967 to a peak of $11.7 billion in 1973, declining to about $9.4 billion in 1976.[7]

Do such transfers promote peace and security or do they fuel the fires of future armed conflict? No one can answer with certainty about any specific area. Arms transfers may temporarily balance forces among enemies and delay armed conflict, but long-term security is seldom enhanced. The presence of tools of war stimulates competition to acquire more to keep ahead of perceived enemies. It also increases the temptation to seek military solutions to controversies. The sad fact is that over the years most arms races have ended in war.

Arms transfers could be controlled by any of three alternatives. First, supplier nations could agree to ban or limit arms transfers of certain types or to certain areas. This was done by France, the United Kingdom, and the United States in the Middle East from 1950 to 1956, until an arms deal between Egypt and Czechoslovakia upset the arrangement. Soviet efforts in the late 1950s and US proposals since 1967 to embargo arms to the Middle East proved unsuccessful. But no supplier can be effective alone. Were the nine nations exporting over 95 percent of arms transfers in agreement formally or tacitly, arms traffic could be quickly curtailed.

Agreement by recipient nations, a second path to check arms transfers, would seem practical only on a regional basis. Such agreements would be most likely in areas free of bitter ongoing controversy and with comparatively low levels of armaments and military spending. Latin America, Sub-Saharan Africa, and Southeast Asia have been suggested as potential areas—especially would this be logical in Latin America where a nuclear-weapon-free zone has already been created. The 1974 Declaration of Ayacucho by eight Latin American countries is a hopeful move of this type. In Southeast Asia this approach would be consistent with the expressed intent of the five-nation Association of Southeast Asian Nations (ASEAN) to neutralize their area. Agreements to limit arms imports would most likely ban certain types of sophisticated offensive weapons but might also place limits on aggregate imports.

Thirdly, conventional weapon transfers could be controlled by a worldwide treaty prohibiting specific types of weapons and establish-

7. US Arms Control Agency, *World Military Expenditures* 1967–1976, p. 115.

ing limits on aggregate transfers to any nation-state, according to a suitable formula relating factors such as population, area, and length of borders. Negotiation of such a treaty would depend, in part, upon creation of an adequate verification system. Verification, however, would not be an insurmountable problem because the number of supplier nations is small and each has the ability to monitor and control shipments.

Reporting arms transfers to the United Nations would be a useful first step to shed light upon the magnitude of the problem. This has been proposed by Malta (1965), Denmark (1968), and the United States (1969, pertaining to the Middle East only). The UN Centre for Disarmament or a Security Council subsidiary body established under Article 29 could receive these reports by arms suppliers, monitor the arms trade, and publish an annual summary.

Neither supplier nor recipient nations have yet demonstrated the desire to limit arms transfers, contending that restrictions would handicap achievement of national objectives. While recipients are concerned with security and prestige, suppliers have a variety of concerns. Militarily they may want to help friends or allies or to balance forces in some volatile area. Economically they want income, improved balance of payments, or reduced weapon costs for their own forces through greater production volume.

In addition, regional agreements such as MFR could be used to limit the level of deployed, if not standing, conventional forces. In zones of peace, as proposed in the Indian Ocean, arms build-up could be prevented. Certain types of more sophisticated weapons could be banned and limits placed upon annual military expenditures as related to gross national product.

Continued development of treaties by the CD is desirable. The pending treaty banning chemical weapons, the main topic of discussion at the 1973 CCD session, deserves early adoption and ratification. The same applies to modification and ratification of the treaty concerning meteorological warfare, hardly conventional but nonnuclear. Continued study and research would likely indicate other beneficial treaties.

Attitudes toward conventional disarmament should be closely watched. The world community as a whole will not be seriously involved in disarmament matters until it comes to grips with conventional armaments. Castigation of the nuclear weapon states by nonnuclears is appropriate but every nation needs to attend, at the same time, to the limitation and reduction of conventional armaments. Disarmament dare not be left to the nuclear weapon powers alone.

To achieve disarmament, the world must break new ground and move far beyond conventional wisdom and experience. Major, bold, and innovative measures must be adopted. Time will not permit cautious waiting periods between steps to test their efficacy. National and international decision-makers need the help of extensive research to chart the way, aid opinion-shapers, and generate public support.

Disarmament Research

Current research devoted to disarmament and an adequate security system is minuscule, particularly as compared to military and weapons research. At The Stanley Foundation's first Strategy for Peace Conference in 1960, it was reported that the United States, then spending $40 billion annually on its military establishment, had less than twenty people devoting full time to arms control and disarmament research. That conference, by recommending creation of a US research unit, helped stimulate the subsequent establishment of the Arms Control and Disarmament Agency (ACDA). This agency, supplemented by a few people in the Pentagon and at other desks in the State Department, constitutes the US disarmament research staff. ACDA's paltry 1979 budget of $16.5 million is totally overshadowed by the US Department of Defense fiscal year 1979 budget of $12.5 billion for research, development, test, and evaluation.[8] The United States situation is not dissimilar from that of other governments. Few have adequate ongoing disarmament research: most have none. And the UN Centre for Disarmament currently has only 34 staff members.

An adequate agenda for the research needed would be very lengthy. It would include development of a comprehensive disarmament plan for achieving GCD, together with study of nuclear limitation, nonproliferation, and conventional weapons. Important investigations should deal with peaceful settlement and conflict management, the interrelationship of an adequate security system and disarmament, and the economic aspects of disarmament.

Who should undertake this research? Everyone. It is a global responsibility. Specifically, four theaters for research activity are suggested.

The first is the United Nations. The Centre for Disarmament

8. US, Office of Management and Budget, *Budget of the US Government 1978/79*, p. 329.

needs to be given broader responsibilities for coordinating and dis-
seminating research undertaken by others; it should undertake limited research specifically related to matters under consideration by
the Disarmament Commission and the Committee on Disarmament.
The United Nations University, with its Planning and Coordinating
Center in Tokyo, might be encouraged to stimulate multidisciplin-
ary research in the areas of conflict management and disarmament,
in addition to its three first-stage priorities: world hunger, human
and social development, and the use and management of natural
resources.

A second highly desirable institution would be an independent
global Disarmament Research Center staffed by outstanding scientists, statesmen, and researchers and financed by adequate funds
from governmental and private sources. This institution would need
to be sufficiently prestigious that its recommendations would be
respected and that it could remain free from the political influence of
any nation or group of nations. Utilizing international experts, task
forces, and panels addressing specific research topics, such an institution could do much to develop the concepts and ideas needed to
advance toward a world without war.

Third, every nation, especially if it is a member of the Committee
on Disarmament, needs its own research organization, however
small it may be. Such units should report directly to the prime
minister (or equivalent) to avoid subordination to either foreign
ministers or ministers of defense.

The last, but by no means least, recommendation is for increased
research by nongovernmental organizations (NGOs), including research institutes. Currently, NGOs in the aggregate may be doing
more research and promoting more discussion of disarmament than
are governments. Nevertheless, substantial enlargement of NGO
activities is desirable. Because NGOs are financed by private funds
and by contracts with governmental units, they have an independent
viewpoint that is useful and an outreach to opinion-shapers that is
essential.

Paralleling theoretical and practical research, there is need for
expanded communication, discussion, and debate within and between nation-states involving opinion-shapers as well as decision-
makers.

Obstacles   With rare exceptions, national leaders are sincere when they call
for peace, decry war, and describe their military establishments as

defensive. Why then is the world community so reluctant to take the necessary steps to manage the critical world issue of peace and security? From among the many obstacles, three are selected for comment: one peculiar to peace and security and the others common to the management of all critical world issues.

Tradition is the mighty barrier to innovative progress toward management of the peace and security issue. Nation-states are deeply locked into the security concepts of the centuries-old nation-state international political system. Military power is perceived as the only force that will be respected; alliance-ridden power balances preserve the status quo; military threats are normal support to diplomacy; and, as a last resort, war is an acceptable device to settle international controversies. Leaders are imbued with the belief that responsibility for security has always and must always rest upon the military power of nation-states.

The second obstacle, which applies to all critical issues, is the myth that sovereignty rests with the nation-state rather than the people, a concept prevalent in the minds of most national leaders and their constituents. This myth is intensified by today's strong worldwide spirit of nationalism and by the numerous ideological, racial, and economic confrontations that continue to generate fear, hatred, and suspicion. There is a great reluctance to delegate even minor and controlled authority to any regional or world organization. This attitude leads to continued reliance upon national power for security.

Lack of dynamic and progressive leadership is the third handicap to managing peace and security, as well as the other critical world issues. Strong, effective, and innovative leadership is essential if the hurdles of tradition and sovereignty are to be overcome. It is needed to cope with the vested interests—the military-industrial complexes with their labor and governmental associates.

Regrettably, the posture of the United States toward disarmament must be rated as strongly negative. We maintain the world's most powerful military force and are constantly adding more sophisticated weapons, conventional as well as nuclear. Our nuclear arsenal possesses overkill far beyond any reasonable need. Our presidents repeatedly declare that we will be second to none. Our secretaries of defense call for constantly expanding Pentagon budgets and press arms upon Japan, Iran, Saudi Arabia, and other nations. We are the world's major exporter of conventional arms. Our failure, along with

United States Posture

the Soviet Union, to comply meaningfully with the arms reduction commitment of Article VI of the NPT has undermined that document. Suspicion remains that, despite our ill-fated involvement in Vietnam and the beginning of détente with the Soviet Union, we expect one day to be called upon to defeat a communist giant. Such impressions overshadow our efforts to negotiate bilateral nuclear ceilings with the Soviet Union and to continue our support of treaties developed by the CD.

Despite our rhetorical aspirations to a world without war under a rule of law, we have not provided strong leadership toward either disarmament or the development of the adequate security system that must accompany it.

5 WORLD ECONOMIC ORDER: BACKGROUND

Smoldering questions about the fairness and adequacy of the world's economic order were inflamed by the oil crisis during the 1973 Arab-Israeli War. The 13 nations of the Organization of Petroleum Exporting Countries (OPEC)—including the non-Arab states of Indonesia, Iran, Nigeria, and Venezuela—challenged the economic dominance of the industrialized world with a fourfold increase in petroleum prices and accelerated expropriation of foreign-owned oil facilities within their borders. Arab members of OPEC challenged the political dominance of the great powers with an embargo and injected oil diplomacy and oil money into the volatile Middle East conflict.

The impact of OPEC action echoed and reechoed around the world. Political and economic conditions changed: domestic economies of oil importing nations were strained, traditional balances of payments upset, and national monetary systems disturbed. New markets now flourish as OPEC nations expand development plans, arm themselves and friends, invest in developed countries, and dispense foreign economic aid.

But the most lasting impact of the 1973 embargo may prove to be greater emphasis upon reform of the world economic order. OPEC's successful challenge to traditional economic and political establishments encouraged developing nations to demand change. Their mounting discontent and frustration were dramatically focused upon the industrialized developed world. These forces will be felt long after the world community has adjusted to higher fuel prices and diminishing petroleum supplies.

Attention was focused on the economic order none too soon; alarming symptoms of distress and systems overload have been evident to developed, as well as developing, nations for some time. Although national currencies have been devalued, gold standards abandoned, and exchange rates altered and floated, monetary problems continue. Negotiations on duties and tariffs end in frustration. Controversies arise over the operation of multinational corporations. Programs for economic and social development falter. Developing nations have long contended that the world economic order was tilted against them. Thus despite the ensuing discomfort, the developing world has brought the world economic order to the forefront as a timely and serious issue.

Relationships   Progress in managing economic issues is closely tied to peace and security. The lack of economic progress causes political unrest: although most recent coups have been rapid and reasonably bloodless, civil war always looms as a possibility, inviting intervention and threatening to spill over national borders. Angola and Lebanon provide recent examples. Fear of instability encourages national leaders to maintain high levels of armaments and increases the temptation to use them, whereas tolerable economic progress lessens internal pressures and allows governments to be more attentive to external relations.

Likewise, the quality of life is largely determined by economic and social factors affecting living standards, human relations, and human rights. Economic, social, and human problems intrude constantly upon all peoples and all nations. Little progress toward individual liberty occurs in countries plagued with stagnant economies or the resulting unrest and instability.

The recent clamor for a new world economic order has dramatized the close connection among the workings of world economic systems, the well-being of more advanced economies, and development in poorer nations. Although development has been considered a global problem for several decades, it has been viewed erroneously as an isolated matter—charitable assistance from rich to poor nations or handouts to win friends. Resources and population are obviously key factors, even though the linkage between them is not widely accepted. While present concerns about the biosphere focus largely upon quality of life, the serious longer range impact upon the resource productivity of the biosphere has been underrated as a critical problem in world economics.

Thus world economic order, development, resource/population balance, and biosphere are intricately related. Although it is difficult to discuss them as separate issues, it is necessary to do so to avoid utter confusion.

The Sixth Special Session of the General Assembly (April 1974), convened originally "to study the problems of raw materials and development," became a forum for vigorous confrontation between developing and developed nations, with the United States as special target. Developing nations attempted to document the parameters of the new economic order they demanded. A Declaration on the Establishment of a New International Economic Order and a Programme of Action on the Establishment of a New International Economic Order were drafted. These documents, adopted by consensus but with major reservations by the United States and other industrial nations, outlined extravagant aspirations well beyond the near-term financial and managerial capabilities of the world community.

Action at the United Nations

The volatile 29th General Assembly (1974) adopted a Charter of Economic Rights and Duties of States. The purpose of the charter, proposed by former President Luis Echeverría of Mexico, is "to promote the establishment of a new international order, based on equity, sovereign equality, interdependence, common interest, and cooperation among all states irrespective of their economic and social systems . . ." While this purpose is both noble and desirable, the charter contained a number of provisions unacceptable to industrial nations. Nevertheless, the developing nations, having the votes, adopted it (120 yes, 6 no, and 10 abstentions). Significantly, the nays and the abstentions included the United States and most of the industrial nations looked to for financial, technological, and other development aid. (Belgium, Denmark, West Germany, Luxembourg, the United Kingdom, and the United States voted no; Austria, Canada, France, Ireland, Israel, Italy, Japan, the Netherlands, Norway, and Spain abstained.)

The confrontation continued; discussions on oil prices by OPEC and the Organization for Economic Cooperation and Development (OECD) failed when the oil producers insisted upon including other commodity pricing in the deliberations. This 27-nation North-South dialogue, officially called the Conference on International Economic Cooperation (CIEC), resumed in late 1976. The industrialized nations finally agreed to discuss two agenda items—debt relief and the linking of oil prices to the cost of industrial goods imported by the OPEC countries—but did not come to any agreement. The proceedings of governing bodies such as the United Nations Educational, Scientific, and Cultural Organization (UNESCO) and the

Economic and Social Council (ECOSOC) were politicized by discussions of the new economic order. As the September 1975 Seventh Special Session of the General Assembly neared, the stage was set to turn the stated agenda, Development and International Economic Cooperation, into bitter controversy.

Unexpectedly, the scene changed quickly as former US Secretary of State Henry Kissinger presented sensible proposals to deal with many of the economic problems affecting the developing nations. The atmosphere cooled; serious discussion replaced polemic diatribe. The moderates of the Third World were heard above the extremists. Resolution 3362 (S-VII), Development and International Economic Cooperation, reflecting many of Kissinger's proposals, was adopted by consensus with but limited reservations on the part of the United States. This final Seventh Special Session resolution changed nothing in the world's economic order, but it did highlight the need for equity and reconciliation. No problems were solved, but a sounder basis was established for constructive dialogue and cooperative approaches to economic reform.

The Seventh Special Session of the General Assembly established an ad hoc committee on the Restructuring of the Economic and Social Sector of the UN System. The dialogue between developed nations and those developing nations with moderate positions continues despite interruptions such as the 1975 Arab-backed resolution equating Zionism with racism and the flamboyant and vitriolic interventions of former US permanent representative Daniel Patrick Moynahan. Subsequently, the Nairobi meeting of the United Nations Conference on Trade and Development in May 1976 continued the dialogue, concentrating upon programs to stabilize commodity prices and promote debt relief for developing countries.

Since then, there has been a greater willingness to negotiate substantive matters and avoid nonproductive confrontations. Some progress has been made toward a common fund to finance buffer stocks of commodities produced by developing nations. Some action has been taken to cancel debts of those poorest countries facing crushing balance-of-payment problems. Both the North and the South have undoubtedly gained a better understanding of each other's problems and postures. No major breakthroughs have occurred, however, nor even modest reform of the present systems.

There is hope, though, that conditions are right for long overdue examination and reform. The developing world demands a new order. The United States and certain developed nations appear ready to deal with reforms. But the postures of certain socialist states remain uncertain. Operating largely outside the economic order of the free world, these states have minimal involvement with its systems and mediocre records as dispensers of technical and economic aid. Siding with the developing nations in criticism of long-time ideological enemies has cost socialist states little. But, with or without their cooperation, serious negotiations toward reform can proceed.

The General Assembly has taken steps aimed at stimulating negotiations. A Committee of the Whole (COW) has been established to carry on the North-South dialogue earlier undertaken by CIEC; thus permitting all nations to participate. A special session of the General Assembly has been scheduled for 1980 to deal with proposals for a Third Decade of Development. A preparatory committee has been established to draft an International Development Strategy (IDS) for adoption at the special session.

What is the existing economic order? There is no clear-cut and accepted concept. Broadly, the world economic order embraces the many systems, institutions, and practices related to international trade, commerce, finance, transportation, and communication. Its scope is broad, its elements numerous, its relationships intricate, and its control fragmented and tenuous.   *Existing Order*

The beginnings of the world economic order long predate today's nation-states. The Egyptians carried on a flourishing barter trade with Crete, Phoenicia, Palestine, and Syria soon after 2000 B.C. Today's economic systems evolved gradually in the following millenniums. Merchants and traders searching for profits fashioned trade practices. Monarchs, city-states, and, later, nation-states encouraged trade, levied tariffs to gain wealth, granted monopolistic privileges to trading companies, and promoted exploration in search of new markets and dominions. Currencies and exchange mediums were created, allowing trade to move beyond the barter stage. Exchange mediums encouraged speculation in gold and silver and stimulated growth of transnational banking and credit. As free enterprise flourished and national wealth grew, nations became concerned about trade balances and about precious resources within their borders. Tariffs were juggled to reduce imports, and manufacturers were encouraged and subsidized to increase exports.

Until World War II, the world economic order operated largely within the private sector. The role of most national governments was limited to establishing and collecting tariffs, stimulating exports, and establishing import policies. Only socialist governments were more directly involved in international commerce. No global entity had a significant part in the world economic order until after World War II.

Meeting at Bretton Woods, New Hampshire, in 1944, the United Nations Monetary and Fiscal Conference representatives from 44 nations changed this pattern and charted modifications of the economic order to make it more adequate for anticipated postwar conditions. The conference established the International Monetary Fund (IMF) and the International Bank for Reconstruction and Development (World Bank) and prepared the way for the 1948 General Agreement on Tariffs and Trade (GATT). Complexity grew as the United Nations took over or created a number of international and regional organizations. Meanwhile, nations in several regions established economic organizations independent of the United Nations. The roster of transnational elements of the economic order continues to increase.

Private sector elements include myriads of businesses and individuals of every nationality involved in all types of ventures across national boundaries: exporting, importing, lending, borrowing, manufacturing, extracting, servicing, transporting, communicating, and granting aid. Public sector elements include the parliaments, ministries, departments, and quasi-public units of nations as they manage national monetary systems and author and administer national policies regarding international economic affairs. In socialist states, governmental units rather than private elements conduct most international business. In addition to the IMF, the World Bank, and GATT, worldwide international elements include the International Finance Corporation (IFC), International Development Association (IDA), and United Nations Conference on Trade and Development (UNCTAD).

Regional international elements of an official nature include the European Economic Community (EEC); Economic Commission for Africa (ECA); Economic Commission for Europe (ECE); Economic Commission for Latin America (ECLA); Economic Commission for Western Asia (ECWA); Economic and Social Commission for Asia and the Pacific (ESCAP); regional development banks in Asia, Africa, and Latin America; and other permanent and ad hoc groups concerned with trade and economic matters. In addition to governmental organizations, many ad hoc and permanent private sector groups, with members from several countries, are involved in the economic order.

The amorphous nature of the world economic order compounds the problems of reform and improvement. Instead of a compact whole, it is comprised of several complex systems: (1) monetary, (2) trade, (3) transnational enterprise, (4) multilateral aid, (5) bilateral aid, and (6) development banking. The first three systems are the historic sectors of the world economic order. The monetary system provides the credit and exchange facilities needed to operate the world economy. The trade system services both developed and developing nations and has important impacts on their economies. The transnational enterprise system transfers capital, technology, and management for business enterprises across national boundaries, even as it benefits the home nations of the enterprises.

The last three systems, which relate directly to economic and social development, are of recent origin. The multilateral and bilateral aid systems extend technical assistance and economic aid to the governments of developing countries or to their subdivisions. The bilateral aid and development banking systems transfer capital to them.

While the systems are closely intertwined, each presents a different set of problems with its own institutions, constituencies, and managers. Each system must be reformed and managed accordingly, but with due regard for interlinkages; no single set of solutions is possible. Management is complicated further by the diversity of national economies ranging from complete state ownership to nearly free enterprise, from centralized planning to near laissez-faire.

Additionally, a vast network of transportation and communication links the various systems throughout the world. Despite its importance, I will not discuss this system, since its management is less directly related to that of the critical world issues.

The basic segments of the present world economic order were *The Problem* fashioned for a colonial world. Although systems to extend assistance to developing countries have been added, the order remains strongly oriented to the needs of the developed nations. Feeling shortchanged by today's systems, the developing nations register three basic concerns. Change to accelerate economic and social development is first and foremost—they need and want more help; second, greater autonomy in managing their own economic affairs, because they fear economic imperialism; third, greater participation in the decision-making and management of the world economic order. These concerns are as much political as economic.

The developed world also criticizes the performance of present systems. Dissatisfaction with the monetary system is widespread. Multinational corporations are under fire at home as well as abroad. The supply of investment capital and credit is insufficient for the needs of the world economy. Trade restrictions and procedures satisfy no country. Multilateral aid is cumbersome and inefficient.

Although the need for reform is generally recognized as urgent and justified, no consensus exists on how to change the present systems. Without agreement on specific objectives, proposals for coordinated change focus largely upon the near-term; objective consideration of the future is muddled. Resolving conflicting interests, overcoming traditional patterns, developing clear-cut proposals, and making positive decisions will be an exceedingly difficult, complex, and sluggish process. Reform of the world economic order is likely to be more evolutionary than revolutionary; the array of actors and the absence of adequate institutional structures to manage the process hinder rapid progress.

*Toward
Economic
Order*

Four objectives are proposed for world community efforts to reform the world economic order. The first is agreement upon principles. As the developing nations correctly contend, economic order is more than merely the systems, procedures, and practices employed by the private, public, and international sectors. These may be the bones and the muscles, but the economic principles applied to managing them are the all-important heart, pumping life blood through the whole.

Creating and maintaining a global climate more conducive to compromise and progress is the second proposed objective. More than goodwill and encouragement are needed; cooperation and negotiation, with mechanisms to assure ongoing constructive dialogue, must replace confrontation and diatribe. Nations already developed have to be persuaded that greater involvement in development is in their interest; developing nations, that achievable goals will attract more support than grandiose ones; and both, of the advantages of simultaneously dealing with a package of interests— some more important to developing nations, others to developed, and some to every nation.

The third objective is ongoing research into the numerous aspects and interfaces of the systems singly and together. I offer no apology for frequent reference to research in connection with the management of the critical world issues. Decision-makers need every help that intensive and futuristic research can provide.

The fourth, and ultimate, objective is the reform and restructuring of the six systems of the current world economic order. Whether changes are termed a new order—as developing nations demand—or modifications of the present one is immaterial; the needed changes are the same in either case.

Several precepts seem appropriate to structure an economic order that fairly, efficiently, and effectively serves the needs of an increasingly interdependent world community.

Guiding Precepts for Economic Reform Structure

RIGHTS AND FREEDOMS Fundamental principles stated in the Charter of the United Nations or properly inferred from it should be fully respected. These include the right of every nation to choose its economic system, to engage in international trade and other forms of economic exchange, and to enjoy freedom from outside interference in its economic affairs.

NATIONAL RESPONSIBILITY Each nation-state is primarily responsible for its own development and, therefore, can be expected to establish desired objectives and to implement programs to achieve them.

COOPERATION Both developed and developing nation-states have an enlarging responsibility to cooperate and avoid actions harmful to the economies of other nations.

INSTITUTIONAL FRAMEWORKS The world community has a responsibility to establish and maintain institutional frameworks to better manage the world economic order and assure a climate conducive to tolerable economic and social development progress.

ECONOMIC GROWTH The magnitude of the world economy needs to be enlarged to accommodate developing nations; the more affluent nations are certain to resist redistribution of their wealth. A positive sum rather than a zero sum approach is desirable: the bigger the pie, the more to distribute.

DECISION-MAKING Adequate participation by all groups of nations in the decision-making and management of the world economic order is a prerequisite to cooperation.

JUSTICE Last, but most important, fairness and justice are fundamental principles governing economic reform. No nation should be deprived of the opportunity to make economic progress.

How can the world community reach agreement upon such principles and express them in a suitable governing doctrine? The Charter of Economic Rights and Duties of States was such an attempt. Although most of its general principles were acceptable, 16 nations, mostly industrialized, did not vote for it, primarily because of the charter's detailed interpretation of principles. Debate revealed wide differences in economic philosophies. Developing nations sought to place guilt and responsibility for their plight upon former colonial masters and alleged economic imperialists. The Soviet Union supported the developing nations' attack upon Western Europe and the United States but avoided acceptance of responsibility to aid them.

Obviously, further debate, negotiation, and compromise are required to develop governing economic principles. While debate on doctrine is bound to continue within the UN General Assembly, its standing committees, UNCTAD, smaller working groups, and ad hoc task forces are more likely to facilitate negotiation and compromise. As a practical matter, this process might best be focused upon amendments to challenged interpretive provisions in the present Charter of Economic Rights and Duties of States.

The process of persuading nations that implementing such a doctrine is in their own self-interest will be tedious and time-consuming. But even as debate rages about economic principles, much can be accomplished. Nations may find it easier to reform and strengthen systems than to formalize economic doctrine; reform may facilitate agreement on doctrine.

Climate   A world climate conducive to economic development and more equitable and effective systems cannot be legislated by the General Assembly. Developed nations will not be forced to transfer capital, technology, and management.

The desired climate is more likely, nevertheless, to evolve through action than oratory. For example, the multilateral aid system warrants high priority as a channel for direct transfer of development assistance, particularly technology and management. Moreover, its lack of reform is often cited as a reason for meager funding of multilateral, bilateral, and development banking systems. The United Nations, however, can restructure the system:

because the developing nations have strong majorities in the General Assembly, in ECOSOC, and on the governing boards of agencies, they have the power to put the system in order and favorably influence the development climate. It is important, on the other hand, that the developed nations also be intimately involved in reform, for they are the major sources of aid financing.

Reform of the other world economic systems would improve the climate by favorably affecting the financial strength of both developed and developing nations and enlarging the capability to transfer capital, technology, and management. These systems, however, are less responsive to direct UN action; reform efforts call for the use of other forums and mechanisms.

Despite the importance of action, the critical prerequisite for a climate more conducive to development progress is the constant use of open channels of communication between developing and developed nations. Neither the developing nations, with overwhelming voting power in the General Assembly, nor the developed world, with financial and technological strength, can design or dominate reform, but either can block it. As the participants in a 1974 conference summarized:

In endeavoring to harmonize their views, member nations must recognize that there is a constellation of issues of varied importance to different members. Harmonization will be achieved when it is recognized that few, if any, of these issues can be resolved independently of the others. Cooperation, coupled with conscientious efforts towards mutual understanding and accommodation between nations, is essential.[1]

A vast research program on the economic order is required. It *Research* needs to be innovative and comprehensive, but practical, with adequate input from all sectors of the world community. Investigations must be based on accurate data, partially provided by the UN Secretariat data system proposed in chapter 7. Programs need not duplicate the substantial research now under way regarding agriculture, industry, health, and education. Attention should be focused upon the economic, political, and social aspects of the world economy and development.

The agenda for a thorough, flexible research program would be

1. *Decision-Making Processes of the United Nations*, report of the Ninth Conference on the United Nations of the Next Decade, The Stanley Foundation, Muscatine, Iowa, June 1974.

lengthy. The impact of global changes upon the world economy needs to be better understood. The development process itself is not adequately understood. Intensive study could result in ways to improve each of the six complex systems comprising the world economic order. Attention to the interrelated impacts of resources, population, environment, and disarmament upon the world economy and development would be worthwhile, as would analysis of the benefits accruing to developed nations from more rapid economic progress in the developing world. A study of the benefits of greater socialist state participation in the world economic order would also be useful. Other topics would suggest themselves.

Who should undertake this research? The answer, as with disarmament research, is *everyone*; it is a world responsibility. More specifically, three locales are suggested.

The first is a Center for Economic and Development Research. Like the Disarmament Research Center suggested earlier, it should be established outside the United Nations. This would achieve better coordination of the trade, transnational enterprise, monetary, and development banking systems which are not fully within the managerial framework or competence of the United Nations.

Responsibility for coordination could rest with the recently appointed director general for development and international cooperation. This individual might direct Secretariat development activities and the Secretariat unit supporting ECOSOC's expanding planning and policy formation; he could provide coordination with research units of national governments and the private sector, including NGOs. The center would also work closely with the United Nations University in Tokyo.

The center should be governed by a board of eminent persons and staffed with competent research personnel from all parts of the world. Its staff need not be large in size, but high in quality. Its primary function should be formulation of desired research programs and stimulation and coordination of research. Financing for the center could be sought partially from the United Nations, partially from nation-states, but to the fullest extent practicable from private sources. Success of the center will depend on its being as free as possible from political and ideological special interests.

Secondly, every nation needs its own research organization, however small it may be, to advise its leaders. Such units would best report directly to the highest levels of government decision-makers.

Third, research by NGOs and other private sector organizations could be further stimulated. The private sector not only has a stake in the future, but is more likely than government to emphasize innovative and futuristically oriented approaches and outreach to opinion-shapers.

Lastly, the results of economic investigations must be shared among nations to stimulate opinion-shapers and decision-makers to pay greater attention to the needs of the world economic order.

The basic and historic elements of the world economic order, the monetary, trade, and transnational enterprise systems, are in need of restructuring. They are dominated by the private and national sectors. International institutions, created in most cases since World War II, have growing importance but lack the authority to manage the widespread elements comprising these three systems.

Monetary System

Whatever the shape of the future world economic order, a sound and manageable monetary system is essential, including not only currencies but also the mechanisms and institutions controlling or influencing exchange rates, reserve assets, credit, and liquidity.

Today's fragmented monetary system is characterized by continuing crises. Euro currency—and now oil money—compete with the rising and falling values of national currencies. Although the debt service payments of most developing, and a number of more developed, countries are becoming oppressive, the demand for more credit continues. Private banking institutions are reaching their limits. Money power is shifting as a handful of oil-rich nations challenge the long-established dominance of the industrialized countries. Reform of the archaic system is urgent.

Objectives: Toward a Single Currency   Creating a global single-currency monetary system would serve the long-term interests of all nations: it would eliminate problems of convertibility, provide a common basis for reserve assets, and greatly reduce the impact of national economic variables. Entities with global roles similar to those of national banks and other agencies now functioning could manage the expansion of reserves and liquidity. But to develop the specifics of an adequate system, extensive study and negotiation will need to compromise the wide differences of national interests and attitudes.

The stability of a single-currency system would generate confidence, and its simplicity would stimulate trade and development. Reform of the world's monetary system, however, is destined to prove more difficult than the reform of other systems of the world economic order because it challenges the sovereign right of nations to use monetary policies to manage domestic economies, increase employment, and dampen inflation. These rights are exercised now with little regard to their impact upon the world economy.

Current efforts of Western Europeans to establish a European Monetary System (EMS) emphasize the need for progress toward a single-currency monetary system. Their frustrations in doing so, even on a regional basis, indicate the difficulties of creating a global currency.

Pending the creation of a truly global monetary system, the world community has no alternative but to struggle with the existing non system.

The Non System

Today's world monetary system is far from systematic. Dissatisfaction is widespread. For example, inflation and other domestic ills are too readily transmitted among nations, and speculative flow of funds from one currency to another is encouraged. As a result, the hazards of international trade and transnational investment are increased. Maintaining optimum reserves, credit, and liquidity to support an expanding world economy without undue inflation is difficult.

Presently, world financial operations involve numerous national currencies, and nation-states manage domestic currencies through their national banks or other designated agencies. The convertibility of any domestic currency, therefore, depends greatly upon national economic and political decisions. Governments decide whether or not to balance their budgets, control imports within the limits of exports, or run printing presses to enlarge money supply. The number of national currencies has more than doubled since World War II (some 130 versus about 60). Separatism prevails; for example, members of the British Commonwealth and former British colonies have substituted their own currencies for the once powerful pound sterling. Upon achieving independence, nearly every country, however small, promptly exercises its sovereignty to establish a national currency. A few years ago in Nairobi, Kampala, and Dar es Salaam, I personally observed the confusion that occurred when the East African currency, once used by Kenya, Uganda, and Tanzania, was replaced by three new coins of the realm, a backward step indeed.

Because every economic transaction across national boundaries, excepting barter deals, involves exchange rates, mechanisms have evolved to facilitate exchange. In contrast to official exchange rates, actual exchange rates reflect the judgment of the world's financial community, banks, and money managers. Many currencies float independently, but some are pegged to other currencies. Black market exchange rates, less favorable to a certain nation's currency, frequently result from improper exchange rate management.

Until World War II, the monetary system was controlled by the major industrial nations acting through their central banks or agencies. They managed the principal currencies and influenced exchange rates. Private banks and other private sector organizations made loans, extended credit, and transacted business; national governments did not grant or loan money to other nations, except to finance the costs of war. The Bank for International Settlements in Basel, Switzerland, facilitated exchange adjustments. There was growing recognition, however, of the need for some degree of international influence, surveillance, and direction of the monetary system.

Well aware of this need, the conferees at Bretton Woods adopted basic rules to guide the post–World War II monetary order and created the International Monetary Fund (IMF) to oversee operations, stabilize international exchange, and promote balanced international trade. They did well. The design worked satisfactorily for two decades. The US dollar emerged as a strong international currency and provided stability. United States balance of payments deficits met the world's need for liquidity quite tolerably. IMF functioned well, using its resources and expertise to stabilize exchange rates, provide short-term credit to members, and assist financially troubled nations.

Reliance upon a national currency (even the US dollar) to serve as an international one is only viable, however, so long as that national currency is viewed with confidence, is convertible, and affords increased credit and liquidity commensurate with the needs of an expanding world economy. By the later 1960s, confidence in the US dollar began to deteriorate. Disequilibriums among national currencies grew, world liquidity became less adequate, and convertibility was threatened. The Euro currency system was developed by private monetary institutions to meet partially the need for enlarged credit and liquidity.

In 1969 IMF created the new form of reserve assets called special drawing rights (SDR). Their value is determined in terms of a weighted "basket" of the 16 currencies of countries whose 1968–1972 exports were one percent or more of world exports. As of June 1978 one SDR equaled $1.20635 (US 1960 dollars). Official holdings of foreign exchange in billions of SDRs rose from 45.4 in 1970 to 201.2 in 1977. Of this total, 103.8 were official claims on the United States. During this period, identified holdings of Euro currency deposits, all beyond the control of national monetary authorities, rose from SDR 10.9 to 70.3 billion.[1]

SDRs were created as a tool to acquire convertible currencies for participant nations in need of reserves. Predesignated IMF member nations were obliged to accept SDRs under certain conditions. The total quota of SDR 39 billion is allotted to the members of IMF in proportion to their membership quotas. Under certain circumstances and subject to stipulated conditions, members apply to IMF for purchase of necessary foreign currency to adjust balance of payments, thus avoiding resort to unilateral action that might depreciate domestic currency or impose arbitrary trade or exchange restrictions.

The Bretton Woods order collapsed in August 1971 when the United States ended convertibility of the US dollar into gold or other reserve currencies. Financial chaos followed, despite the determined efforts of the Group of 10 (finance ministers from countries with major currencies). Only temporary relief resulted from the 1972 stopgap Smithsonian Agreement forced by the United States. Soon, the fixed exchange rates gave way to floating rates. The inadequacies of mechanisms for adjusting disequilibriums among surplus and deficit nations became more evident.

The oil crisis beginning in 1973–1974, together with recession in industrial nations, created other problems. The higher petroleum prices established by the Organization of Petroleum Exporting Countries (OPEC) and reduced exports to industrial nations altered unfavorably the balance of payments for many countries and occasioned extreme hardships for numerous developing countries already burdened by heavy external debt. Several of the OPEC nations with revenues exceeding their domestic needs and development capabilities have difficulty investing huge surpluses.

1. Data regarding the monetary system are compiled, unless noted otherwise, from the *Annual Report 1978* of the International Monetary Fund, Washington, D.C.

Since 1975, IMF has administered the Subsidy Account for loans to nations classified as those most seriously affected (MSA) by recent world economic conditions. IMF loaned $3.5 billion through its oil facility and monitored the UN emergency operation of $4 billion in loans to MSAs in 1974. The private banking system has accepted deposits of petro money and recycled them as loans to hard-pressed countries. IMF has continued to encourage adjustments of disequilibriums among national currencies, assist developing countries to reschedule external debt, and aid ailing national economies.

Total international reserves increased from SDR 123.2 to 262.8 billion in the six-year period 1971–1977. The 1977 reserves were held 53 percent by industrial countries, 6 percent by other more developed countries, 24 percent by major oil exporting countries, and 17 percent by other developing countries. Inadequacy and imbalance of reserves resulted. Reserves, as ratios of imports, except for OPEC countries, decreased sharply from 1971 to 1975: from 33 percent to 22 percent for industrial countries, 33 percent to 26 percent for the more advanced developing countries, and 28 percent to 23 percent for the other developing countries.[2] Greater total reserves are desired to facilitate expanding trade, and developing nations want greater access to reserve assets.

In 1974, the Group of 10 gave way to a Group of 20 charged with developing a negotiated basis for improvement of the international monetary system, a most difficult and controversial task. Officially designated as the Twenty-Nation Interim Committee of the International Monetary Fund, the Group of 20 consists of Argentina, Australia, Austria, Brazil, Canada, France, Germany (Federal Republic), India, Iraq, Italy, Japan, Mexico, Morocco, Netherlands, Nigeria, Norway, Thailand, United Kingdom, United States, and Zaire. The effort is encountering resistance from numerous specialized interests. Despite growing support within the Group of 20 for fundamental change, IMF's initial response has not yet been adequate.

The Second Amendment of the Articles of Agreement of the Fund became effective April 1, 1978. This amendment (1) permits members to choose exchange arrangements for their currencies, subject to IMF surveillance; (2) reduces the role of gold, including disposition of part of IMF's holdings; (3) facilitates greater use of SDRs as

2. International Monetary Fund, *Annual Report 1977*, Washington, D.C., p. 40.

reserve assets; (4) simplifies and expands IMF's financial operations; (5) permits establishment of a Council as a new IMF organ to replace the present Interim Committee of the Board of Governors; and (6) improves the organization and administration of IMF. An increase of quotas from a total of SDR 29.2 billion to 39 billion recently became effective. Another review of quotas is in process. Although hailed by some as reform of the monetary system, these changes are, at best, palliatives.

Recent events encourage IMF to increase its loan capacity and extend maturities. The private banking system is reaching the limits of its ability to recycle the huge surpluses of Saudi Arabia, Kuwait, the United Arab Emirates, and other OPEC countries. International debt, particularly of poorer countries, rises dramatically as oil-importing nations are reluctant to cut back on expenditures and risk political instability. Non-OPEC countries run trade deficits aggregating over $50 billion annually, while OPEC nations accumulate comparable surpluses. IMF is now seeking oil money and other funds in substantial amounts to increase its facility to finance hard-pressed developing nations and to help manage their debt. But IMF's expanding role does not relate solely to developing nations; large credits were extended to the United Kingdom in 1976 and to Italy in 1977.

Clearly, the present non system falls far short of what is needed in a growing and ever more interdependent world economy.

Near-Term Changes: What Can IMF Do?

The existing system would better serve the world community if procedures and mechanisms were altered to increase the probability that (1) convertibility of national currencies at reasonably stable, but flexible, exchange rates is maintained; (2) disequilibriums among national currencies resulting from the surpluses of oil-producing countries, balance of payments fluctuations, or other situations are adjusted more promptly; (3) reserve assets are created at a rate assuring adequate credit and liquidity for expansion of world trade and development on a reasonably noninflationary basis; (4) expanded reserve assets become more beneficial to the economic and social development of developing nations; (5) transmission of inflationary or recessionary influences from one nation to others is dampened; and (6) decision-making in international organizations dealing with monetary matters remains balanced and credible to the several affected groups of nations.

One issue is recycling the huge surpluses now accumulating in oil-producing countries. These surpluses will continue until certain OPEC countries greatly increase imports or significantly expand development transfers to other nations. Because recycling should be accomplished increasingly on a long-term investment basis, IMF, structured for extending short- and intermediate-term credit, cannot assume the full recycling burden. Private banks must carry the major role; but the World Bank could be an important vehicle, particularly if some petro money becomes available on concessionary terms. Nevertheless, IMF has an important function. Enlarged lending facilities, such as IMF is considering, will be needed to provide short-term credit to nations in financial stress and to continue the relief already given by the stopgap IMF and UN emergency loans.

Secondly, looking beyond the recycling of petro money, we need to review the historic role of IMF regarding stabilization of exchange rates. This already difficult function will become more complex as nations choose alternate exchange arrangements for their currencies. Improved procedures are required to assure appropriate alteration of exchange rates and to correct disequilibrium in balances of payments. Timely rate changes by surplus, as well as deficit, countries would lessen the opportunity for disruptive flow of speculative funds. Economic sanctions of some type might be imposed against countries which refuse to make indicated changes. Such steps would increase the stability of exchange rates and encourage relatively constant, but readily adjustable, floating rates.

Improved short-term lending procedures could counter speculation and disruptive and destabilizing capital markets. The large and potentially destabilizing US dollar and petro money balances now hanging over the money market need to be decreased.

Nations with critical debt problems present a third challenge to IMF. A series of crises is pending; a substantial part of the more than $200 billion of external debt of nations may need readjustment. Private banks and national governments, as well as international agencies, are involved. Rescheduling of maturities, consolidation of existing obligations, and new loans are used to fashion adjustments acceptable to the creditor and the debtor nations. IMF's crucial role in such situations extends far beyond extension of short-term credit to adjust disequilibriums. As an international organization, it collects data, analyzes the troubled nation's ability to pay, suggests solutions, and coordinates the approach of the several creditors. These functions bring stability to the readjustment process. As a "third party," IMF has both the opportunity and the stature to prescribe for the debtor nation conditions and procedures for sound fiscal management. Once the readjustment is accomplished, IMF has a continuing surveillance function to assure that imposed conditions are met.

IMF has already moved in the direction of increased use of SDRs as reserve assets by changing the status of gold, increasing IMF resources, and agreeing to sell a portion of its gold reserves to benefit the poorest countries. Greater use of SDRs as reserves would tend to reduce the use of national currencies, as well as gold, for this purpose. It could be an important step toward a single world currency.

If fairness is to prevail in a reformed world economic order, developing nations need greater access to expanding international reserves. This calls for jointly agreed objectives on the use of these assets, changes in their management, and restraint on the part of nations so as to minimize actions with potentially unsettling impact upon exchange rates and convertibility.

The International Monetary Fund is the appropriate vehicle to advance reform of the monetary system, at least in the near-term. IMF's performance over the years has won widespread acceptance by nation-states. Its membership has global range, except that socialist states other than China, Romania, and Yugoslavia are absent by choice. *Reform Mechanisms*

IMF is already seeking to reform the monetary system through its Interim Committee (the Group of 20). For this Interim Committee—made permanent, and its functions enlarged to reach beyond near-term to the longer range objectives of a single-currency world monetary system—to serve as an ongoing negotiating unit, it needs reasonable continuity and enough flexibility of membership to reflect changes in the world's monetary power structure.

IMF, including the Interim Committee, could work closely with the proposed Center for Economic and Development Research and take advantage of research and study by national governments and nongovernmental organizations. Periodic examination of facets of the monetary system by ad hoc groups of experts should become a regular process.

Some changes in IMF's decision-making process will be needed. Members of IMF now hold shares and vote in proportion to their capital quotas. The powers of IMF are vested in a board of governors, one appointed by each member nation, who meet annually and deal with broad policy matters. Major decisions, such as amendments to the articles of the fund, require favorable vote of 60 percent of the members having 80 percent of the quotas. Most powers are delegated to 20 executive directors: 5 appointed by the members having the largest quotas, the others elected every two years by the governors of the other members. Votes of the executive directors are weighted by the total of the voting power, or quotas, of the country or countries they represent.

While there have been some changes, today's capital subscriptions ratios and voting powers largely reflect the money power structure of 1944. Neither Germany nor Japan has voting power commensurate with their economic status. Saudi Arabia, now looked to as a major source of funds, has no vote of its own. The OPEC group now has about 5 percent of the voting power; a proposal to increase to 10 percent is pending. Increased voting power for the countries supplying future funds may prove a precondition to expanding IMF loan activities.

On the other hand, many developing nations advocate a system resembling the one-nation/one-vote system of the General Assembly. They are unhappy with the weighted voting structure that now permits control of decisions by the countries contributing most of the capital. This controversy highlights the basic question regarding the validity of decision-making processes. Credibility in the eyes of the various groups of nations most affected by its operation is an important criterion. In the case of IMF, this means both the nations contributing financial resources to IMF and debtor nations.

IMF's present decision-making pattern has maintained credibility. Developing nations have had input through their governors and executive directors. The richer nations, with controlling voting power, have supported and encouraged IMF's role and have advanced funds. Whether or not major changes should be made now in IMF decision-making is a pragmatic question. Will the industrial and oil-rich nations provide the desired funds and respect, support, and enlarge IMF's activities if poorer nations with debt and exchange problems have the authority to control the operation? Any significant change in the voting formula of IMF would probably reduce support from the wealthier nations. As long as IMF's capital comes largely from these nations, major changes in voting formula would seem unlikely.

Efforts to make the existing monetary non system more workable and more responsive to global needs are destined to be frustrating and disappointing. The benefits of foreseeable reforms are likely to be temporary and more in the nature of stopgaps than solutions.

In summary, then, it is urgent to accelerate efforts to develop an adequate global monetary system and to adopt and ratify a suitable treaty. Such a treaty would establish a single world currency—perhaps SDRs—to be used for reserve assets and, ultimately, as the means of exchange; it would create a central institution to perform global functions similar to those of central banks within nation-states. By amendment of its charter, IMF might become this institution. The treaty would also formulate an acceptable decision-making process for the institution and designate certain mechanisms for governing the monetary system, including the settlement of controversies.

Trade System

International trade is vital to the economic life and development of any nation not content with subsistence existence on the periphery of the world economy. Trade creates jobs at home and markets abroad, moves raw materials and finished goods from producer to user, and generates foreign exchange to finance purchases on the world market. Trade is undoubtedly more important than aid to the longer range financing of economic and social development. International trade grows in importance with increasing interdependence.

Currently, the world's trade system is in trouble. Pressures for reform result not only from the system's deficiencies but also from the economic plight of many nations. Trade balances of most nations, excepting OPEC countries, suffer from combinations of mounting external debt, higher costs of petroleum and other imports, and weakened prices of commodities and other exports. Historic commitments to freer trade are challenged by both producer and consumer groups, by developed as well as developing nations. Reform is essential.

Stated simply, the world community needs a trade system that adequately and fairly serves its composite needs. With expanding interdependence, this means a freer flow of materials, goods, and services. *Criteria for Reform*

Specification of the details of tomorrow's trade system is quite impossible; it must reflect compromises between widely divergent views. But reform of the system should be judged against the following criteria: (1) open access to markets for all exporters and importers, (2) greater stability of commodity prices, (3) enlarged capacity consistent with the expanding volume of international trade, (4) simplified mechanics, (5) participation of socialist states, and (6) shared management of the system in a manner assuring credible decision-making.

Initially, these objectives must be sought in the context of existing institutions. A longer range objective, however, would be the establishment of stronger institutions more able to administer global trade matters. Further, a reformed trade system could, in the future, generate some portion of the revenues needed for world community matters, including economic and social development.

Trade
Agreements

The trade system has grown haphazardly and, until after World War II, largely without benefit of official international guidance or influence. The 1948 General Agreement on Tariffs and Trade (GATT) and the 1964 United Nations Conference on Trade and Development (UNCTAD) were the first institutions to deal with trade on a global basis.

GATT, a multilateral trading arrangement, was adopted as a temporary measure when the proposed more ambitious International Trade Organization (ITO) failed to receive approval from a number of governments, including the United States. The GATT document outlines principles of conduct calling for nondiscrimination, protection of domestic industry by tariffs only (not quantitative or other restrictions), tariff reductions through multilateral negotiation, and consultation among member countries to overcome trade problems. One chapter deals with trade and development. Six major negotiating conferences—the Kennedy Round of 1964–1967 being the latest—brought a number of reductions in tariffs and other trade barriers. The lengthy Tokyo Round of negotiations, started in 1973 and completed in 1979, will reduce some tariffs and establish regulations further limiting non-tariff barriers. The Tokyo Round has again revealed developing countries' demands that GATT be tailored more to their needs.

But GATT has its limitations. It has not been able to deal with agricultural trade. Article 35, called the great loophole, gives members the option of not applying GATT rules to new members. For example, the EEC has denied Japan full access to its markets. Violations of the provisions, as well as the spirit of GATT, have been commonplace.

UNCTAD was established upon the recommendation of the first

UN Conference on Trade and Development, where the North-South split first became apparent, and is a permanent organization of the UN General Assembly, reporting to it through ECOSOC. It is larger than the United Nations itself because some specialized agencies belong. UNCTAD places emphasis directly upon the link between trade and development. Its principal functions are to (1) promote international trade, particularly between countries at different stages of development; (2) formulate and implement principles and policies on international trade and related problems of economic development; (3) review and facilitate the coordination of other institutions within the UN system regarding trade and development; (4) cooperate with the General Assembly and ECOSOC in matters of coordination; (5) initiate action for negotiation and adoption of multilateral agreements in the field of trade; and (6) act as a center for harmonization of trade and related development policies of governments and regional economic groups.

Dominated by the developing nations, the four UNCTAD conferences have adopted many proposals, serving more to draw attention to problems than to solve them. UNCTAD III, held in Santiago in 1972, urged concessions on interest rates, longer loan repayment schedules, preferences on technology transfers, larger allocations of SDRs, a link between SDRs and development aid, preferential aid for the 25 poorest countries, and greater participation by developing countries in negotiations on trade and monetary policies. UNCTAD IV, held in Nairobi in 1976, placed primary emphasis upon the price stabilization of some 18 commodities now comprising between 55 and 60 percent of all raw material exports, exclusive of petroleum. Little was accomplished at UNCTAD V, held in Manila in 1979. Typically, the key issues were not resolved, despite progress toward understanding and commitments to further study. Once again the seriousness of the North-South split was revealed.

The International Trade Center (ITC), established by GATT in 1948, is now operated jointly with UNCTAD. This center provides information, advice, and assistance on trade matters, principally to developing nations.

On the regional level, nations have fashioned several trade and tariff pacts aimed at stimulating trade and developing larger markets. The European Economic Community (EEC) is a prominent example. Others include the Central American Common Market (CACM), the Latin American Free Trade Association (LAFTA), the East African Community (EAC), and the European Free Trade Association (EFTA). Such pacts benefit participants and encourage larger and more efficient manufacturing plants serving common markets. But they do not lessen the need for stronger global mechanisms to manage international trade.

World trade expanded 6.0-fold from 1960 through 1975, when it totaled $878 billion. The growth of exports from the developing countries, excepting members of OPEC, and from centrally planned economies has fallen behind the developed market economies: 5.2- and 5.8-fold increases versus 6.8. Exports from OPEC members roughly paralleled those of other developing countries until 1973, but nearly trebled in 1974. (table 1)

Table 1
EXPORTS BY COUNTRY GROUPS
Billions of Dollars (US)

Group	1960	1975	Ratio 1960/1975
Developed market economies	85.0	580.2	6.8
OPEC	8.5	113.9	15.7
Non-OPEC developing market economies	18.9	97.3	5.2
Centrally planned economies	15.0	86.8	5.8
World	127.4	878.5	6.9

Source: Overseas Development Council, *The United States and World Development—Agenda 1977*, Praeger, New York, 1977, pp. 206–207.

Confrontation   The issues discussed by UNCTAD and other conferences dominated by developing nations are broader than trade; they include matters related to the monetary system and to development. Developing nations in critical need of foreign exchange want to increase the value of their exports. They want (1) freer access to markets in other countries, particularly the affluent; (2) higher and less volatile prices for the raw materials and commodities they export; and (3) the opportunity to add greater value to what they export by processing commodities and manufacturing goods. The third is a development matter requiring transfers of capital, technology, and management, often with the participation of transnational enterprises. Industrial countries, on the other hand, have a different set of goals, including

(1) access to raw materials and commodities at reasonable costs and (2) access to foreign markets for the export of goods and products.

Both developed and developing nations employ tariffs, quotas, and other trade restrictions to protect domestic industry from foreign competition. They also apply duties to imports to raise revenue. These restrictions are not evenly applied to all nations; politicization is common. Nations have bilaterally and multilaterally negotiated agreements favoring each other and their friends: examples include agreements within the British Commonwealth, the EEC, or regional groups, and the US most-favored-nation policy. The United States, certainly not alone, has used these methods, particularly against socialist nations. We have long banned exports of critical materials to the Soviet Union and China, and have established quotas against Polish hams, Argentine beef, and other products. These discriminatory practices reflect the protectionist wave of the 1930s and the Cold War psychology and provide a response to domestic pressures.

OPEC's success in raising petroleum prices has stimulated interest in supplier cartels, while producers of commodities less adaptable to cartels press for price stabilization and buffer stocks. The spirit of protectionism is rising, both globally and within the United States and other industrial nations. Trade policies are affected by inflation, unemployment, shifts in labor intensive industries, and the need to adjust to less rapid economic growth.

Greatly expanded research—as for all issues—would improve current management and prepare for more effective institutions in the future. The Center for Economic and Development Research already proposed would be a proper vehicle.

Near-Term Action

Multilateral and bilateral negotiations should proceed at an increased pace and focus upon reducing discriminatory tariffs and other trade restrictions, upon simplification and standardization of trade procedures, and upon mechanisms to enlarge the trade system's capability. Despite the difficulties of accomplishment, freer trade remains a valid goal; growing interdependence demands it. Impediments against importation of Third World manufactured and semimanufactured products need to be removed. Such steps would reduce the current discrimination of the system.

Lessening the extreme price volatility of commodities and raw materials is a near-term need. Developing nations, highly dependent upon income from sale of such commodities and raw materials, are seriously hurt when prices fall. Dependent upon imported materials, developed nations react negatively to rising prices. Planners recognize the need to stabilize commodity and raw material prices, but do not agree on how to accomplish it. Supplier nation cartels, similar to OPEC, are one answer where the number of producer nations is limited and the product has low price-use elasticity. Producer-consumer accords like the International Coffee Organization are another route. Price indexing, controlled reserves, and stockpiling are other possibilities. Currently, attention focuses upon creating a sizable fund to acquire buffer stocks of a number of raw materials as a means of balancing supply and demand.

Enlargement of the capacity of the trade system is vitally needed to handle trade expansion expected in the 1980s and the 1990s, given current population growth, development trends, and resource distribution. Simplification and standardization of trade procedures would help enlarge the system's capability. Trade restrictions now vary greatly from nation to nation, as do procedures regarding permits for imports and exports, inspection, valuation, and collection of customs. Red tape is complicated and frustrating. Such confused situations handicap trade and add to its cost.

Greater trade activity by Eastern Europe and China may be expected in the 1980s and 1990s. Their isolation is breaking down as they find need for commerce with the rest of the world. But even though their increased participation may create problems within the system, it is to be encouraged.

Managing the Trade System   The existing institutions for managing the trade system are completely inadequate. While GATT and UNCTAD were properly viewed as improvements when created, their inability to bring about the needed changes in the world trade system is quite evident. UN General Assemblies have adopted resolutions and charters enunciating principles to govern international trade, but these have produced little change.

As with the disarmament area, periodic meetings of all nations are needed to establish and update objectives and priorities and review progress. Such meetings, occurring at regular intervals of two or three years, need to be of sufficient length to allow serious consideration of substantive matters, and thus warrant attendance by high level representatives of government. Currently, UNCTAD conferences, held every four years, only partially meet this need. Between conferences, the 68-member Trade and Development Board meets semiannually. The board's staff, the main committees (Commodities, Manufactures, Invisibles and Financing, Shipping, and Transfer of Technology) and other subsidiary bodies carry on the work of the organization.

If UNCTAD were effective, its parent, the UN General Assembly, would find it less necessary to deal with trade matters both in regular and special sessions. This duplication could be eliminated by discontinuing UNCTAD's quadrennial conferences and using special sessions of the General Assembly to deal with trade matters at two- or three-year intervals.

Many of the ongoing functions of UNCTAD deserve continuation. Some belong with the proposed Center for Economic and Development Research. Some, such as the ITC, might be shifted to the UN Secretariat. Others, related to the functions of GATT, could be combined with it.

Good management practice suggests smaller bodies to deal with the complex trade details and to negotiate treaties. GATT has proposed a 20-member body for negotiation purposes. An ongoing unit combining certain UNCTAD and GATT functions could deal with tariffs, restrictions, and other matters. Alternatively, under the direction of the special sessions of the General Assembly, task forces or work groups of moderate size could be assigned specific areas of negotiations. In which case, the UN Secretariat would need enlarged capability to provide adequate support to the special sessions of the General Assembly and to negotiating bodies.

Nevertheless, the reform suggestions I have presented are only stopgap measures. The world community needs a strong, permanent organization with authority and resources to manage trade matters within established policy guidelines and to facilitate world trade treaties. I propose, therefore, that a World Trade Administration (WTA) could (1) serve as an international center for information (now a function of ITC), (2) cooperate with the Center for Economic and Development Research regarding trade matters, (3) convene ad hoc groups to negotiate tariffs and other trade relations, (4) investigate violations of trade agreements, (5) arbitrate controversies, and (6) initiate action before the ICJ or other appropriate tribunals when arbitration is unsuccessful.

Such a World Trade Administration would have many similarities to the ill-fated ITO of the 1947 Havana Charter. To avoid repeated deadlocks, all groups of nations—exporting as well as importing, agricultural as well as industrial, and developed as well as developing—must be fairly represented. The structure of a WTA might incorporate many of the organizational arrangements that have proven workable in the World Bank and IMF; namely, a board of governors with one governor per member and an executive board of perhaps 20 directors. A first task could be to reach the difficult compromise on allocation of voting power.

Another opportunity lies in using the trade system itself as a source of independent revenue for world community needs. A one percent global tariff upon current volume of international trade ($878 billion in 1975) would produce $8.78 billion of revenue which could go far toward financing such operations as multilateral aid and development banking.

Transnational Enterprise System

The private sector performs another key role in the world economic order. Private companies serve as active and useful vehicles for transferring capital, technology, and management capability—basic elements of development—from one nation to another. This transnational enterprise system consists of business organizations of one country (the base nation) operating productive, extractive, or service functions in another country (the host country), a definition which excludes simple export operations from one country to another. Transnational enterprises (TNEs)—the designation used here rather than multinational corporations because it is more descriptive—usually conceive, organize, finance (in whole or in part), construct, and operate industrial, extractive, or service ventures.

Objectives   The primary objective regarding TNEs should be the structuring of policies and procedures to assure the continuing availability of TNEs as development mechanisms to countries desiring them. This must be done in a manner that maximizes benefits and minimizes abuse or hazard to the host country, and is fair to TNEs and their base countries.

Steps required are (1) preparation of a code of conduct governing TNE operations to guide both host countries and TNEs; (2) expansion of research and collection of information pertaining to TNE operations to provide a sounder basis for decisions regarding TNE operations; (3) provision of objective technical assistance to host nations, particularly developing countries, regarding contractual relations with TNEs; and (4) development of appropriate processes for resolving controversies between TNEs and host countries.

As the world community moves toward a rule of law, it will face two longer range alternative objectives regarding TNEs. The first is the development of a body of law established by suitable conventions to govern TNE operations. The alternative is a world mechanism to regulate TNEs. The basis of regulation could be either the licensing of national corporations undertaking TNE operations or the chartering of global corporations.

The development of TNE law seems more desirable because it maintains the direct one-on-one relationship between the TNE and the host country, avoids interference from a remote global institution, and provides greater stimulus to the private sector. In either case, procedures to resolve controversies about TNE operations are required.

TNEs fall into two categories, one operating between developed nations and the other operating from developed to developing countries. The first category is illustrated by the presence of companies like General Motors and IBM in the European Economic Community, Fiat in the Soviet Union, and Unilever and Toyota in the United States. Examples of the second category include Shell producing oil in Nigeria, Dunlop manufacturing tires in Kenya, Republic Steel mining iron ore in Liberia, Sears pioneering US type merchandising in Venezuela, or my company, Stanley Consultants, providing professional services in Malaysia.

Operation of Transnational Enterprises

Most organizations that undertake transnational ventures are corporations owned by private investors. A limited few are quasigovernmental agencies or authorities; oil complexes of Italy (ENI) and of Indonesia (Pertamina) are examples. Many TNE ventures in developing nations are partially owned by host governments or private investors within the host nation, usually with representation upon the venture's board of directors. Some are wholly owned by the host country, with the TNE providing technology, management, and perhaps some capital on a contractual basis; this practice is common in socialist countries.

Private banking institutions that make loans to foreign countries or to industrial or commercial enterprises in foreign countries are an additional category of TNEs providing capital transfer. Their operations are less complex than those of industrial or commercial enterprises. Yet they make important contributions to countries and enterprises whose economies are sufficiently sound to support borrowing of funds in the world money market.

The magnitude of TNE input to developing nations is partially indicated by 1975 statistics of capital transfer: $21.96 billion from private sources versus $16.61 billion official development aid transfers from national governments through bilateral or multilateral channels. Transfers of applied technology and management skills are also substantial, although not easily quantified.

Most base nations have encouraged TNEs to go abroad; many have even subsidized them through tax or other incentives in order to expand exports, help balance of payments, and produce taxable income. Most host countries have welcomed TNEs as a means of developing resources and advancing industrialization. Without TNEs from Europe, Japan, and North America, few developing nations would have been able to exploit oil and mineral resources, initiate industrialization, and build essential infrastructure.

Despite important contributions, the TNE system is controversial. Criticism comes from developed as well as developing countries, from base as well as host nations. From developing host countries, criticisms focus upon such claims as: (1) TNE profits are too high, (2) TNE ventures are too capital intensive, (3) TNEs are inadequately controlled by their hosts, and (4) TNEs interfere with domestic politics. Indeed, some host countries have taken punitive action against TNEs: expropriation of facilities, forced renegotiation of concession agreements, increased taxation, restrictions on work permits for expatriates from base nations, and legislation calling for set percentages of local facility ownership. Criticism by the more developed host nations, on the other hand, reflects fear that TNEs will unfairly compete with local industry and syphon profits from the country. Some interested groups in base nations, particularly the United States, are concerned that in reaching out from their shores TNEs are exporting jobs, reducing income tax revenues, weakening the industrial economy, and evading domestic control.

TNEs, in turn, often criticize the countries in which they operate, charging unfair treatment, expropriation without equitable compensation, and interference with management. They contend that many host nations do not understand the importance of TNEs' contributions to development through expansion of productive capacity. TNEs also criticize base nations, particularly the United States, for enactment of punitive tax policies and failure to recognize the contributions they make to the domestic economy and the balance of payments.

In the face of rising dialogue about TNEs, an international Group of Eminent Persons to Study the Role of Multinational Corporations on Development and International Relations was appointed by the UN Secretary-General upon authority of the General Assembly. It submitted a significant report in 1974. This report recognizes the operation and regulation of TNEs as a global problem and comments upon their important contributions. The report does, however, reflect many of the biases of developing nations. It contains a number of recommendations, but places the primary responsibility for action upon national governments. It comments upon the absence of suitable international institutions as a handicap toward harmonization of national policies and laws regarding TNEs and establishes a framework for global strategy concerning TNEs. The report also lists as a Programme of Work the following topics: code of conduct, information and reporting procedures, technology, employment and labour, consumer protection, competition and market structure, capital transfer, pricing, and taxation.

Deciding that new institutions were not required, the Group recommended (1) full discussion of TNE-related issues in the Economic and Social Council (ECOSOC) at least once a year, (2) establishment of a 25-member commission on TNEs under ECOSOC to fulfill its functions regarding TNEs, and (3) establishment of an Information and Research Centre in or closely linked to the Secretariat and under the guidance of the commission.

Spurred by this report, ECOSOC established a Commission on Transnational Corporations in December 1974. The commission was charged to act as a forum within the United Nations system to consider TNE-related issues, to promote intergovernmental exchange, to assist ECOSOC in recommending a code of conduct, and to develop a comprehensive information system on TNE activities. ECOSOC also created a sparsely staffed Information and Research Centre on Transnational Corporations. Along with providing research and staff work for the commission, it has the responsibility of supplying information to nations seeking to develop expertise in this area.

At the 48-member commission's first meeting in March 1975, the struggle to agree upon a code of conduct began. The current lack of even a preliminary draft reflects the difficulty of developing a fair code, plus fundamental differences between proponents of private versus state ownership. Nevertheless, work on the code is proceeding, and international accounting standards are under review. The Information and Research Centre on Transnational Corporations is gathering information and giving assistance to developing nations.

Unfortunately, UN efforts to establish acceptable guidelines for TNE operations are handicapped by the injection of irrelevant political issues. TNEs are very critical of the commission's procedure, claiming it is unsympathetic to private business, and TNEs are skeptical of the Centre's proposed information system.

Meanwhile, the Organization for Economic Cooperation and Development (OECD) has made progress on guidelines for TNE operations on behalf of its 24 developed and mostly Western countries. A Declaration on International Investment and Multinational Enterprises by OECD in June 1976 contains guidelines for TNEs, a recommendation that member nations treat foreign enterprises operating in their territory no less favorably than they treat domestic enterprises, and proposals on incentives and disincentives to be extended by member countries for international direct investment. The OECD continues to review the TNE guidelines and other portions of the declaration and consider possible revisions.

The Governing Council of the International Labor Organization (ILO) approved a Tripartite Declaration of Principles concerning Multinational Enterprises and Social Policy in November 1977, supporting such principles as freedom of association and equality of treatment in employment and embodying a number of principles contained in the OECD declaration.

ECOSOC is dealing with the problem of illicit payments. A working group of experts is preparing a draft treaty for consideration of a diplomatic conference now planned for 1980. The Conference on International Economic Cooperation (CIEC), concerned with North-South economic relations, discussed codes for TNE operations and indicated its intention to deal further with this matter.

Dichotomy   The sharp divisions of opinion regarding the role and the performance of TNEs reflect divergent appraisals of potential benefits and abuses, particularly of TNEs operating in developing nations.

Under proper conditions, TNEs do aid the economies of developing nations by (1) creating and upgrading employment, (2) producing goods or rendering services for domestic consumption, (3) generating foreign exchange from exported commodities and products manufactured to offset imports or exports, and (4) aiding the creation of national wealth through savings.

The capital transferred by TNEs is capital not available through governmental channels. The technology transferred is usually technology not possessed by governments and only partially available through official channels. The management capability transferred by TNEs is a unique results-oriented type, little recognized and less practiced by governments and international organizations. Management capability is transferred through early assignment of base nation professionals; installation of proven methods and processes; and, above all, through ongoing, on-the-job training of host nation workers, supervisors, and managers. No official bilateral or governmental aid program can begin to match the TNEs' capability to make these three types of transfers.

Successful TNE operation depends upon several factors that must be given careful attention in planning, implementing, and operating. Abuses occur, and host nations and TNEs suffer, when these factors are not handled properly.

In the beginning, each project must be properly conceived. The starting point is negotiation between a TNE and a host country. Both parties are thereby involved in determining the type of operation, its orientation toward domestic or export markets, its level of capital and labor intensity, and its selection of technology. During this process, the host country can make certain the proposed project is compatible with and contributory to the objectives of its development plan.

Second, the TNE and the host government need to negotiate an acceptable contract dealing with such matters as investment, ownership, waiver of taxes, level of taxes, division of profits, recovery of profits and investment by the TNE, waiver of import duties on equipment and materials, protection from imports, competition, use of base nation nationals, training of host nation personnel, protection regarding expropriation, etc.

Effective management and exemplary conduct on the part of the TNE are the third component of success. Political interference is off limits for the TNE guests. They must recognize and abide by the laws of their hosts.

On the other hand, host countries have a responsibility to understand the nature of the TNE operation and to assure reasonable cooperation. As private enterprises, TNEs are entitled to profits compatible with the cost of organizing and financing the venture and the degree of risk, and to freedom from operational interference as long as contractual agreements are honored.

Concern over the presence of TNE plants, owned at least in part by gigantic corporations whose total annual revenues possibly exceed the host country's gross national product is to be expected. Such fears often stimulate already antagonistic attitudes toward private enterprise. Some national leaders—from their education, experience, or ideology—disapprove of any enterprise not owned by the state. However, the risk of properly structured and managed TNE operations subverting political independence is minimal; TNEs can neither enter nor operate within a host country without its approval. Host countries enact the laws governing foreign business ventures within their territory. They participate in the negotiations determining the nature of the venture and the contractual conditions governing it. And, as a last resort, host countries enjoy the right of expropriation.

Although properly utilized TNEs contribute to economic development, they are not a panacea. Rather, they are an important tool supplementing other development activities, aimed at providing basic needs. Failure to make effective use of this important segment of the world economic order would be a serious setback to many nations in critical need of increased transfers of capital, technology, and management capability. I admit to a bias toward the private sector, arising from lifetime experiences and widespread observations in developing countries. Private enterprise, given fair incentives and reasonable regulation, offers an effective path to accelerated industrial and agricultural production. Developing countries that maximize the use of TNEs can be expected to make the greatest progress.

Improving the TNE System   There is no overall international institution governing transnational ventures. The system consists of numerous informal bilateral relations between TNEs and host nations, with but limited involvement of base nations and no official regulation at the global level.

Nevertheless, the United Nations has a role to play, a role already recognized and initiated. To this end, the UN General Assembly can contribute by continuing ECOSOC's Commission on Transnational Corporations, expanding the functions of the Information and Research Centre on Transnational Corporations, and providing the Secretariat with more adequate capacity for technical assistance to host nations considering contractual relations with TNEs.

The United Nations and the private sector can jointly accelerate the development of guidelines. The ensuing codes for conduct of TNE operations would facilitate contract negotiations and might address such factors as division of investment in the venture between the TNE and the host nation; provision for the investment of some share of TNE profits in the host nation; minimization of risks to TNEs; basis for expropriation of TNE capital and share of profits; basis for expropriation of facilities, including reasonable compensation; representation of host nation on TNE governing bodies; freedom of management; training of host nation personnel; use of base nation nationals; settlement of disputes; transfer of technology; and adequate reporting.

Nongovernmental organizations also have a continuing, important role regarding TNE operations. Their recommendations may prove useful to TNEs and host nations long before international guidelines are established. NGOs and ad hoc groups representing TNEs can stimulate education and understanding among host and base nations, as well as among TNEs, regarding their mutual responsibilities.

The possibility of a regional approach to TNE codes and guidelines should not be overlooked. Similarity of circumstances and needs might minimize polemics and speed agreement.

To facilitate resolving controversies arising from TNE operations, agreements between TNEs and host countries could contain provisions for arbitration. The International Court of Justice would be the appropriate body to settle major legal differences and to serve as a court of appeal. Special tribunals, however, would be more logical for controversies over economic or operating matters. When the need arises, the United Nations and ICJ will have to establish such tribunals by amendment to the UN Charter.

As with disarmament, US posture regarding the world economic order has been ambivalent. Our advocacy has been forward-looking; we have urged free trade; substantial aid to developing nations; transfer of capital, technology, and management capability through TNEs; and remedial action on the world monetary system. But our deeds have not always measured up to our words. *United States Posture*

We played a positive role at Bretton Woods and in the creation of the World Bank and IMF. We contributed greatly to the development of the Havana Charter and GATT. At times we have played a strong role in efforts to stabilize the monetary system.

But at times, perceived short-term interests, as presented by the political pressures of labor and industry and the economic pressures of unemployment and inflation, have prevailed and our posture has been less than positive. We failed to support the Havana

Charter that would have created the ITO. We have handicapped our corporations operating as TNEs. We have often resorted to selective protectionism and trade restriction.

Along with other nations, we too have guarded jealously our national sovereignty. Recognition that interdependence requires the delegation of authority to extranational or supranational organizations has not yet sufficiently influenced our policy.

Yet on balance US efforts have been more positive than negative. When compared to the other major powers, we have done more to lead than to hinder progress toward a sounder world economic order.

7 DEVELOPMENT

In the face of the bitter schism between rich and poor and the North-South conflict, accelerated economic and social development is vital to the people of the developing nations and the health of the world economy. Economic development will be the most valid measurement of the success of world economic reform efforts, at least from the perspective of the developing nations.

Nowhere are the inadequacies of managing global problems more starkly revealed than in the areas of economic and social development. Objectives are poorly defined; plans, where they exist, are confused and conflicting; committed resources are insufficient; authority is lacking; and control of the systems involved is poor. Development offers a life-sized case study of management processes on the global level.

Prior to World War II development was considered a national responsibility; each nation was on its own. Business, industrial, and governmental leaders set the pace and pattern. While many nations obtained financial and technical assistance from outside, they did so on a commercial basis. Nineteenth century expansion of the United States was aided by investment from Europe, particularly England, and by technology brought in by immigrants and entrepreneurs. Railroads were built, industries started, and commercial ventures launched. But no government-to-government economic aid was involved. The Soviet Union, too, even with its different ideology, made use of European and American experts and entrepreneurs in the late 1920s and early 1930s. Lenin, recognizing the need, imported Western know-how even while predicting and promoting collapse of the capitalist system from whence it came. Again, no government-to-government aid was involved; the United States government did not recognize the Soviet Union at the time. Currently both the Soviets and the Chinese are arranging joint enterprises with Western industries, again through private channels.

Development: A Global Issue

The Charter of the United Nations broke new ground in Article 55 of Chapter IX, "International Economic and Social Cooperation."

With a view to the creation of conditions of stability and well-being which are necessary for peaceful and friendly relations among nations based on respect for the principles of equal rights and self-determination of peoples, the United Nations shall promote:

a. higher standards of living, full employment, and conditions of economic and social progress and development;

b. solutions of international economic, social, health, and related problems . . .

The Charter vested the General Assembly with responsibility for these functions and established the Economic and Social Council to coordinate and manage them.

Although the UN Charter legitimized world community concern for development, three subsequent events made it truly a global issue. After World War II, resources for reconstruction and rehabilitation of devastated European countries were not readily available. Fear grew that the seeds of communism would sprout quickly in the rubble of bombed-out cities. Stalin was busy consolidating the Soviet grip on Eastern Europe, certainly as a buffer zone, perhaps to overrun Western Europe. At this juncture, the United States proposed the imaginative European Recovery Program, better known as the Marshall Plan. Nearly $12 billion poured into war-torn Western Europe (1948–1951). Rehabilitation was rapid and the communist threat was thwarted. Regrettably, Poland and Czechoslovakia, under Soviet pressure, withdrew from the program. Through the highly successful Marshall Plan, financial and technical aid in generous amounts were given from government to government; precedent for bilateral aid from the prosperous to the needy was established.

Next came the collapse of Western colonialism in Africa and Asia. Most of the new nations were poor and lacking in technical, managerial, and financial capabilities. Joined by older, but no more affluent, countries, they charted ambitious development programs. Determined to catch up quickly, they sought technology and capital from industrial nations. Their united voices called for multilateral aid through UN agencies. The United States and several other developed nations, including former colonial powers, initiated bilateral aid programs and supported UN multilateral activities.

The cold war was a third factor influencing attitudes toward world community responsibility for economic and social development. The superpowers offered bilateral aid to the new nonaligned nations, seeking neutrality, if not friendship, among them. Some developing nations pyramided development assistance by skillfully playing the Soviet Union against the United States. The cold war stimulated the flow of assistance and led more industrial nations to accept some responsibility for helping the newly labeled Third World.

Development sufficient to assure survival is the all-consuming concern of the 1.5 billion inadequately fed people of whom half a billion are severely malnourished.[1] The great majority of the world's people do not willingly tolerate living standards incompatible with human decency. Nor should the industrialized nations tolerate these conditions. Festering poverty in any part of the world sooner or later impinges upon the well-being of the whole.

The three decades of development efforts have produced mixed results, some commendable but most disappointing and frustrating. Developing nations, in most instances, have made some economic progress as measured by gross national product (GNP) but too often scarcely enough to keep up with population growth. Most have registered some gains in health and education, only to intensify other problems: shortages of schools and teachers; inadequate agricultural production; unemployment and underemployment; and urban housing for hordes of migrants to the cities. *Accomplishment*

Statistically, the record is poor. The First UN Decade of Development (1960–1969) projected an average per capita GNP growth target of 5 percent; the Second, beginning in 1970, targeted 7 percent. Against these targets, the weighted average per capita GNP growth rate (1965–1974) for 123 developing countries with a total 1976 population of 2,957,000,000 was only 3.2 percent.[2] For the group of 49 Low Income countries with a total population of 1,341,300,000, the weighted average growth rate for the same period was but 1.7 percent.

The 123 developing nations include 49 classified as Low Income

1. Population Crisis Committee, *Population*, briefing paper no. 1, Washington, D.C., 1976.
2. Data on GNP and growth rates used in this chapter, unless otherwise noted, are based on material in *The United States and World Development— Agenda 1977* by the Overseas Development Council (New York: Praeger, 1977). The updated information in the 1979 version of this document does not alter appreciably the overall picture of GNPs and growth rates.

countries (1974 per capita GNP below $300 US), 39 Lower-Middle Income countries ($300 to $700), and 35 Upper-Middle Income countries ($700 to $2,000). These 123 countries approximate the so-called Third World. The 49 Low Income countries correspond roughly to the most seriously affected (MSA) as designated in 1975 by the Seventh Special Session of the UN General Assembly. They are sometimes referred to as the Fourth World. The majority were formerly colonial dependencies, nearly half in Africa. Other characteristics include low endowment of resources; subsistence farming or nomadic herding; inadequate infrastructure; unemployment in towns through migration from country to city; and dependence on the outside for manufactured goods. The crux of the distinction of countries as MSA or Fourth World is the inadequacy of present means for generating momentum from the sum of available domestic and external resources; impetus for growth is dependent upon still further measures that need to be taken by the outside world.

Of the total 123 developing nations, only 19 had per capita GNP growth rates of 5 percent or more. Happy exceptions, with growth rates of 6 percent or higher, included Botswana (6.2%), Brazil (6.3%), China (Taiwan) (6.9%), Gabon (6.4%), Iran (7.7%), South Korea (8.7%), Malta (8.4%), Nigeria (8.4%), Oman (19.2%), Portugal (6.5%), Romania (6.8%), and Swaziland (6.1%). Most of these exceptions reflect special situations: major exports of oil or other extractive resources, substantial support from the United States, or economic progress advancing the country to the threshold of developed status. At the other extreme, 15 of the 123 countries had zero or negative GNP per capita growth for the period 1965–1974, and another 14 ranged between 0 and 1 percent.

The magnitude of donor nation contributions to bilateral and multilateral aid is another important indicator. Many years ago the late Paul Hoffman boldly proposed a world development program calling upon developed nations for annual contributions by national governments of 0.75 percent of their GNP. The Second UN Decade of Development and the 1975 Seventh Special Session of the UN General Assembly urged a 0.7 percent level. Such contributions, identified as Official Development Assistance (ODA) in the analyses of OECD and the World Bank, consist of multilateral contributions and bilateral loans and grants to developing countries and multilateral institutions. Eighteen Development Assistance Countries (DAC) account for 95 percent of development assistance; they are Australia, Austria, Belgium, Canada, Denmark, Finland, France,

Italy, Japan, the Netherlands, New Zealand, Norway, Portugal, Sweden, Switzerland, the United Kingdom, the United States, and West Germany.

As shown in table 1, such official development assistance from national governments as a share of their GNP was only 0.36 percent in 1975. Total resource flow from DAC to developing nations, including official and private assistance, is summarized in table 2. Thus resource flow from private sources in the DAC now exceeds both ODA and total official flows ($23.3 billion in 1975 versus $13.6 billion ODA or $16.6 billion total official).

Resource flows from socialist countries to noncommunist developing nations are not large: only $1.852 billion in 1975. The Soviet Union committed $65 million to Turkey, $437 million to Afghanistan, and $177 million to other noncommunist developing countries. Bulgaria, Czechoslovakia, East Germany, Hungary, Poland, and Romania committed $319 million, and the People's Republic of China committed $269 million.

The physical quality of life, although difficult to measure, is a further indication of development progress. The Overseas Development Council (ODC) has recently proposed a physical quality of life index (PQLI) based upon three factors: life expectancy, infant mortality, and literacy. The PQLIs for the four groups of countries, as computed by ODC, together with 1974 average per capita GNP, are shown in table 3. The correlation between physical quality of life and development progress as measured by GNP is evident. Both

Table 1

OFFICIAL DEVELOPMENT ASSISTANCE (ODA)
FROM DEVELOPMENT ASSISTANCE COUNTRIES (DAC)

	Year		
	1960	*1970*	*1975*
ODA ($ billions)			
Current prices	4.6	6.8	13.6
1975 prices	11.0	11.5	13.6
GNP ($ billions)			
Current prices	900	2,000	3,800
ODA as % of GNP			
Current prices	0.52	0.34	0.36

Source: Adapted from Overseas Development Council, *The United States and World Development—Agenda 1977*, p. 231.

cause and effect come into play; a low PQLI handicaps development; poor development progress deters improvement of physical quality of life.

Since 1974, sharp increases in petroleum prices, worldwide recession, and excessive inflation have further handicapped the in-

Table 2

NET FLOW OF RESOURCES FROM DAC
TO DEVELOPING NATIONS ($ BILLIONS, CURRENT)

Source	1964–66 Average[a]	1970[a]	1975
Official development assistance (ODA)	5.91	6.79	13.59
Other official[b]	0.24	1.14	3.02
Total official	6.15	7.93	16.61
Private (at market)	3.93	6.87	21.96
Grants by private voluntary agencies	n.a.	0.86	1.34
Total private	3.93	7.73	23.30
Total	10.08	15.66	39.91

a. Excludes New Zealand and Finland.
b. Official export credits, debt relief, etc.

Source: Adapted from Overseas Development Council, *The United States and World Development—Agenda 1977*, p. 236.

Table 3

PHYSICAL QUALITY OF LIFE INDEX

Group of Countries	Number	PQLI	Average GNP per Capita
Low Income	49	39	$ 152
Lower-Middle Income	39	59	338
Upper-Middle Income	35	67	1,091
High Income	37	95	4,361

Source: Overseas Development Council, *The United States and World Development—Agenda 1977*, p. 150.

adequate pace of development and revealed the fragility of the economies of most developing and some developed nations. The inadequacy of development progress can be fully supported by analyses of specific elements touching people: employment, housing, education, and medical care. Much has been accomplished but far more remains undone.

A nagging sense of frustration matches the disappointment with development progress: no light shines at the end of the tunnel. Many developing countries see no way to cope with mounting unemployment and underemployment, runaway inflation, urban blight, and expanding debt service, to say nothing of hunger and starvation. Countries vent their frustrations upon the industrial nations, particularly the United States. Donor nations are equally dissatisfied that their sincere efforts to help have not produced intended results. Incensed by polemic charges of some developing nations and facing internal economic problems, most of the donor nations have become less sympathetic and less generous.

Two concepts accepted by development dilettantes are really *Myths* myths. One has it that there is a standard approach to development. Unfortunately, a uniform approach won't work: the variety of dilemmas is too great. As described earlier, what is commonly considered a somewhat homogeneous Third World of developing nations breaks down into three subgroups. The 49 Low Income countries are hard pressed to avoid starvation and, despite development efforts, unable to make appreciable economic progress. At the other end of the scale, the 35 Upper-Middle Income countries, with few exceptions, are making tolerable progress; most have the resources to support continuing development. With the 39 Lower-Middle Income countries, it is touch and go. Twelve are considered as MSAs; all but a few have a low level of physical quality of life. The 13 oil-rich OPEC members, which range across the four income categories, enjoy substantial near-term revenues exceeding, in some cases, their own development needs.

Obviously, development needs, objectives, and courses of action in each subgroup are different. Moreover, within each subgroup no two nations are at the same stage of development or have the same combination of human, monetary, and natural resources, to say nothing of comparable leadership. If development programs are to succeed, they must be tailored to each nation's particular situation.

Too often talk is of closing the gap between rich and poor nations, and doing it quickly. This too is a myth, as shown by the simple mathematical computation summarized in table 4. Starting with 1974 per capita GNP, growth rates for the four income level groups of nations have been projected using assumed annual compounded growth rates, which may be compared to actual 1965–1974 growth rates. The growth assumptions for Low Income and Middle Income groups are optimistic, while that for the High Income group is pessimistic.

Table 4

ECONOMIC PROJECTIONS FOR COUNTRY GROUPINGS

	49 Low Income	39 Lower-Middle Income	35 Upper-Middle Income	37 High Income
Growth Rate (%)				
1965–74 [a]	1.7	4.4	4.7	4.0
Projected	3.0	6.5	7.0	2.0
Per Capita GNP (1975 dollars)				
1974 [a]	$152	$ 338	$1,091	$4,361
1980	182	493	1,637	5,208
1990	244	926	3,221	6,998
2000	328	1,738	6,336	9,405

a. Computed from data in Overseas Development Council, *The United States and World Development—Agenda 1977,* Table A-3, pp. 160–171.

Careful analysis reveals the stark magnitude of the development task. The prospects of the Upper-Middle Income nations are good. By 1983 the projected 7 percent growth rate (1½ times the present rates, and at the level of UN targets) could bring this group to $2,000 annual per capita GNP, the current threshold of the High Income group of countries. Most of these nations have resources to achieve this projected growth, given good management and adequate use of external monetary and technological assistance. Even so, the gap between this group and the High Income countries widens by 1980 and narrows only slightly by 2000.

The outlook for the 49 Low Income countries, on the other hand, is dismal. Even with near doubling of their projected growth rate (3.0 percent versus 1.7 percent), they would little more than double GNP per capita by 2000. Not until near the end of the century would the average per capita GNP of these 49 nations reach $300, the current base of the Lower-Middle Income countries. Achievement of the projected 3.0 percent growth rate by Bangladesh, Ethiopia, India, Upper Volta, Yemen, and other poverty-stricken nations would be a phenomenal accomplishment.

The outlook for the 39 Lower-Middle Income nations is marginally hopeful. The 6.5 percent annual growth rate (half again that of 1965–1974) should be achievable with reasonable increases in transfer of capital, technology, and management. If the rate is maintained, the average per capita GNP of this group will pass the $700 threshold of the Upper-Middle Income group by 1986, and by 2000 will increase fivefold over 1974. Even so, the gap between this and the High Income group will widen, as will the gap relative to the 35 Upper-Middle Income countries.

While this projection is speculative, it does support the conclusion that the gap between the composite 123 developing nations and the developed world will not be closed in the foreseeable future, although individual nations will certainly forge well ahead of the averages. A number of nations will move upward, but the criteria for determining the success of development efforts would better relate to improved quality of life within each nation than to quantitative comparisons with others. The basic need, particularly in Low Income countries, is to close the gap between poverty and a decent life by a steady increase in per capita income.

Nongrowth of High Income countries, sometimes proposed as a method of narrowing the gap, is not likely to be a viable way to improve the lot of poorer countries. Few developed nations will voluntarily reduce their economic growth. Future economic and resource conditions are likely to compel life-style changes, but these will come slowly. Lower growth rates in High Income countries would tend to stagnate economies, curtail imports from developing nations, and increase the reluctance to support bilateral and multilateral aid. Developing nations would be hurt, not helped. More realistic approaches to aiding the developing nations are needed.

Development is a national process; people working together and through governments. Outsiders can help, but only national governments and their peoples can create the political stability and economic climate essential for continuing development. National governments must make development decisions, implement development programs, and accept or reject proffered assistance. They

Roles and Responsi- bilities

deal with such important related policies as land reform, population stabilization, taxation, fringe benefits, conduct of trade and commerce, and stimulation of private savings and enterprise. Nations establish the all-important priorities for production (agricultural, industrial, resource extraction) and for infrastructure (education, health, transportation, communication, utilities). And most importantly only the citizens of a nation can provide the will, determination, and hard work required for development.

No nation, however poverty stricken, is willing to abdicate these vital functions to global institutions. Hence their development role must be secondary, but supportive, to the efforts of nations in need. This does not preclude the use of forums such as the UN General Assembly to express and document development goals and to persuade and encourage developed, as well as developing, nations to intensify participation in the processes. But most General Assembly pronouncements on this topic are general and often lofty expressions of aspiration. Setting achievable near-term objectives would better encourage real progress. Developing nations need to define clearly their own responsibilities as they demand assistance.

Toward Higher Levels of Development

The minimal short-term objective, even for the poorest and least able nations, should be steady progress toward tolerable standards of human decency measured in terms of food, shelter, and health. Many Low Income nations have yet to reach such minimum standards. Nearly all nations contain pockets of population deficient by these standards. But any lesser targets would be intolerable.

Pessimistic observers, advancing the lifeboat theory, contend that since available resources won't meet the needs of all, some nations should not be helped. They liken developing nations to shipwrecked victims clamoring to board overcrowded lifeboats; some must be left behind or the boats will be swamped. The question is which nations will sink and which stay afloat. Another pessimistic view suggests applying triage, a French term derived from battlefield practice of medical doctors faced with more wounded than they can attend. Some wounded will survive in any case; some will succumb even if given aid; medical assistance goes to those in the middle group for whom prompt attention is the vital element. The question is how to decide which developing nations to abandon as unlikely to survive even with aid. But applied to development, any form of triage or selection is morally repugnant. Proper use and management of available technology and resources should allow most developing nations that are determined to help themselves to progress at least to tolerable standards of human decency. A few countries, nevertheless, are so lacking in resources that even this minimal target is unreachable. Others, though better endowed, will not succeed because they misuse resources, they do not stabilize their population, or they do not take other necessary stern measures. Nations that, for any reason, fail to make progress impose an enormous burden upon the international community. Their repeated calls for help may not always be answered; the lifeboat and triage theories may tragically come into play.

Optimum longer range targets should, of course, be much higher than rising above abject poverty. Every nation deserves the opportunity to develop economically and socially in order to achieve a quality of life consistent with its potential, culture, national goals, and national effort.

What are the world community's development responsibilities in a secondary and supportive role? A general principle is provided in the preamble of Resolution 3362 (S-VII) adopted by the Seventh Special Session of the General Assembly (September 1975) entitled "Development and International Economic Cooperation":

> Believing that the overall objective of the new international economic order is to increase the capacity of developing countries, individually and collectively, to pursue their development, . . .

The objectives proposed in chapter 5 for the international economic order—agreement upon governing precepts, creation and maintenance of a more conducive climate, expansion of research, and reform of the six systems comprising the world economic order—are intended to help increase the capacity of developing countries.

Finance and technology are normally considered the prime elements of successful development programs. Equally important is management, including entrepreneurship, often considered as a part of technology but better listed separately. *Successful Development Programs*

Application of more capital, with appropriate management, technology, and effort, accelerates development. Capital can be generated by public sectors and, where they exist, by private sectors whenever income exceeds costs of operation and debt service. Public sectors have two internal sources of revenue: various taxes (property, sales, income, licenses, export and import duties) and receipts from ownership or participation in industrial or commercial enterprises and concessions granted for the exploitation of natural resources or other services. Public sectors also obtain grants or loans.

Private sectors generate development funds through personal savings and retained earnings of business ventures. Domestic or transnational private enterprises finance plants, projects, and businesses with internal or external loans and investment.

Appropriate technology in such diverse areas as agriculture, industry, communications, transportation, health care, population stabilization, and education is equally important, if suited to local conditions and consistent with development goals. Modern technology may or may not be the proper answer; substantial unemployment or underemployment calls for labor intensive industry at least for products intended for local consumption. Methods of health care, education, and similar activities must be adapted to local conditions.

Public sectors supplement their own technology through grants of services from multilateral and bilateral aid sources, employment of expatriates, and use of foreign consulting services. Private sectors obtain technology through licenses, patents, expatriates, and foreign consulting services. Transnational enterprises are a major source of technological expertise in many developing nations.

Capability to manage the development process from inception to completion is the third essential, and it cannot be overemphasized. Decision-making will be much improved if planning has been well managed and objective attention has been given to alternates and obstacles, as well as to needs and desires. How many five-year plans have failed because they were loaded with politically inspired targets, almost without realistic appraisal? Political leaders too often fail to distinguish between leadership, decision-making, and the management of organizations and programs.

Most developing nations lack both adequately experienced personnel to execute major operations and internal training opportunities. Broad-based managerial competence and entrepreneurship are developed by a pattern of education and experience quite different from that which produces political expertise. Management training for nationals can be an important by-product of policies encouraging a strong private sector. Until indigenous management competence is developed, outside managerial resources needed by most developing countries can be provided through the same channels as technology.

For over twenty years my consulting firm has handled engagements in some thirty developing nations in Africa, Asia, and Latin America. Our numerous projects and personal travel have given me many opportunities to observe and discuss the traumas of development. I have reviewed many development plans, witnessed the success or failure of many programs, and observed the impact of projects upon economic and social growth. These experiences convince me that two other elements are vital.

Development Model

The first is a carefully researched and reviewed statement of long-range goals and programs to achieve them called a *development model*. Goals are needed for human conditions and living standards, as well as GNPs and growth rates. Such a model requires careful tailoring to the country's particular conditions—natural resources, economic resources, human resources, cultural characteristics, and human aspirations—and its governmental policies affecting ownership of industry, ownership of land, personal savings, personal investment, delivery of human services, taxation, and posture toward TNEs. Opportunities for economic cooperation with neighbors need consideration. Priorities are important for agricultural development, industrialization, environmental protection, and balancing of population and resources. The model should also deal with political objectives as they affect citizen participation.

The preparation of a development model necessitates consideration of the several economic and political alternatives open to each developing nation. Some may be well advised to pursue industrialization vigorously, with a view to competing with more developed nations. Many may be wiser to adopt labor intensive production programs which meet domestic needs but with less involvement in the world market. Some may elect a predominantly agricultural orientation; others may base their economies upon exploitation of mineral resources. No nation's development model will be complete without stressing the widening of opportunity for all citizens, including the poorest of the poor, to gain such basic human needs as food, shelter, health care, and literacy.

Political alternatives range from the tightly controlled socialist pattern of China to the open enterprise patterns of Western democracies. Most development models will likely focus upon patterns between these extremes. The desirable design is one that stimulates enthusiastic participation of the people and encourages a self-help approach. While strong governmental leadership is called for, it need not be autocratic. Although few developing nations are likely to adopt multiparty patterns of Western democracies, it is important that their governments develop models that foster personal participation and responsibility, enhance human rights and dignity, and move toward some form of meaningful franchise for their people.

However maximizing the use of private sectors, under appropriate governmental regulation, provides, in my opinion, the most favorable pattern for economic growth. To follow this pattern, developing nations need policies that encourage private ownership of land and housing, enhance personal savings and investment in domestic enterprises, stimulate managerial training, and utilize TNEs under adequate, but fair, controls. This conclusion results not only from a belief, perhaps a bias, in favor of free enterprise but also from study of conditions most likely to speed economic development by stimulating greater personal will to produce.

Such a development model is quite different from the usual five-year development plan. Five-year plans properly come later as a useful technique to outline near-term goals and specific programs for managing the development process. But a development model would define the kind of human, social, economic, and political development the country wants and can realistically provide. Substituted for the current "me too" development approach, the model would greatly improve the logic of development goals and increase the probability of achieving them.

Commitment   The other need is a widely shared commitment among citizens and leaders. The national wealth required for development can only be created as production exceeds consumption. Nations now enjoying affluence have gained it through hard work, sacrifice, and internal savings. This has been the pattern whether it occurred voluntarily in anticipation of personal gain or was forced by a totalitarian government. The affluence of the North American Midwest, my home base, results from the accumulation of wealth created by generations of hardworking pioneers and their descendants. Few nations will find a quick or easy road to development.

It is my personal observation that many developing countries have not established work ethics consistent with their aspirations for rapid development; incentives for hard work and personal saving are lacking. Leaders in these countries demand growth at a more rapid pace than has ever occurred historically and seek to establish fringe benefits which affluent countries achieved only after decades and generations of effort. While strong advocacy of increased transfer of financial, technological, and managerial aid from the affluent world is warranted, the nations with internal determination and self-reliance are most likely to achieve their development goals.

Multilateral Aid System

Multilateral aid is an important vehicle for the transfer of technology, management, and limited capital to developing countries, and the concept is increasingly acceptable to both donor and recipient nations. It avoids the political implications of bilateral aid because the assistance carries no national flag.

The multilateral aid system consists of the United Nations and certain of its family of agencies such as the Food and Agriculture Organization (FAO); International Labor Organization (ILO); United Nations Development Programme (UNDP); United Nations Educational, Scientific and Cultural Organization (UNESCO); United Nations Industrial Development Organization (UNIDO); United Nations Institute for Training and Research (UNITAR); and World Health Organization (WHO); together with regional economic commissions—the Economic Commission for Africa (ECA); Economic Commission for Europe (ECE); Economic Commission for Latin America (ECLA); Economic Commission for Western Asia (ECWA); and Economic and Social Commission for Asia and the Pacific (ESCAP)—plus many standing and ad hoc committees and commissions. The services of these agencies emphasize planning and focus more upon transfer of technology and management than upon capital. While extremely valuable assistance is provided now, change to improve coordination, control, and cooperation and to encourage enlarged funding is overdue. The present system, a hodgepodge of units each created to meet a specific need, defies basic concepts of organization and management. That it works as well as it does is a tribute to the dedication and persistence of many devoted persons who seek to benefit humanity through these agencies.

ECOSOC, charged with coordinating and controlling the many UN units of the multilateral aid system, has consistently fallen short of desired performance. The General Assembly and its Second Committee overlap and duplicate ECOSOC. The specialized agencies plus five standing committees, five regional economic commissions, six functional commissions, and a number of ad hoc committees report to ECOSOC. But UNDP and UNIDO report directly to the Assembly. The specialized agencies, each with its own membership, governing board, and income sources, often flaunt their autonomy. The General Assembly's Administrative Committee on Coordination (ACC) and Committee on Administration and Budgetary Questions (ACABQ) have endeavored to ride herd on these many diverse and sometimes conflicting components.

Fortunately, reorganization is under way, spurred by the study and report of a group of experts and two years of work by the Committee on the Restructuring of the Economic and Social Sectors of the UN System, appointed in 1975.[3] In 1976 the General Assembly's restructuring resolution instructed the Secretary-General to appoint a director-general for development and international economic cooperation, reaffirmed the General Assembly as the principal policy-making forum for development matters, and recommended a single annual meeting for pledging to all UN operational development activities. The resolution called for ECOSOC to concentrate on its Charter responsibilities, to formulate policy recommendations, to organize its work on a biannual basis, and to abolish as many of its subsidiary bodies as possible by assuming direct responsibility for their functions. Subsequently, a director-general has been appointed and certain research and operational functions of the Secretariat have been placed under him.

While these steps are encouraging, further reform is needed, aiming at doubling or tripling the services available to developing nations as rapidly as practicable. Sounder concepts of management, coherence, order, and discipline are needed in the following areas: the General Assembly, ECOSOC, the Secretariat, agencies, funding, and member state participation.

General Assembly   The Charter (Article 60) clearly vests responsibility for UN action on economic and social matters "in the General Assembly and,

3. The Ad Hoc Committee had before it a number of reports, including "Towards Greater Order, Coherence and Coordination in the United Nations System," report to UNITAR prepared by Martin Hill, 1974; "A New United Nations Structure for Global Economic Cooperation," report to the Secretary-General prepared by the Group of Experts on the Structure of the UN System (Group of 25), 1975; and reports of The Stanley Foundation's Sixth Conference on United Nations Procedures, 1975, Seventh Conference on United Nations Procedures, 1976, and Tenth United Nations of the Next Decade Conference entitled "Coordination of the Economic and Social Activities of the United Nations," 1975.

under the authority of the General Assembly, in the Economic and Social Council." Hence, the General Assembly is the final decision-maker, acting upon recommendations from ECOSOC and other subsidiary bodies.

Desirable reforms affecting General Assembly functions related to the multilateral aid system are largely procedural in nature. They include (1) assuring the revitalization and reorientation of ECOSOC; (2) implementing a thorough examination of the function and performance of all specialized agencies; (3) shifting such agencies as UNDP and UNIDO from direct reporting to the General Assembly to reporting to ECOSOC; (4) eliminating, to the maximum extent practicable, duplication between the work and debate of ECOSOC and the General Assembly and its Second Committee; and (5) continuing the use of special sessions from time to time to further economic and social development.

To perform the responsibility assigned by the Charter for comprehensive policy formation and coordination, ECOSOC needs revitalization and reorientation. Its role should be to establish broad policy, anticipate needs, develop and consider alternatives, reconcile differences, monitor progress, and make appropriate recommendations to the General Assembly. *ECOSOC*

ECOSOC has not fulfilled this role, partly because it has become overwhelmed by administrative matters pertaining to its subsidiary groups and agencies. Specific steps that would help to restore ECOSOC to its intended role include (1) significantly reducing the number of ECOSOC's standing, functional, and regional organs by merger or elimination (the total of such groups is now 25); (2) utilizing a "think tank" within the Secretariat for technical analysis and expertise helpful to policy decisions; (3) transferring to the Secretariat administrative functions related to ongoing programs of the agencies; (4) simplifying ECOSOC's agendas and procedures; and (5) resisting politicization on issues that belong in the General Assembly or Security Council.

These reforms can be instituted without Charter change. A further desirable change, requiring amendment of the Charter, would remove ECOSOC's responsibilities for human rights. This could be done by placing such matters in a Human Rights Council as proposed in chapter 10.

The Secretariat's capability in economic and social matters requires substantial upgrading. The new role recommended for *Secretariat*

ECOSOC will require more of the Secretariat. The recent creation of the post of director-general for development and economic cooperation, reporting directly to the Secretary-General, is an important beginning. Further suggestions include (1) strengthening the authority of the director-general commensurate with his responsibilities; (2) creating under him a unit to support ECOSOC in its expanded planning and policy-making functions; (3) creating under him a parallel unit concerned with coordination and oversight of the operational administration of the UN economic and social system; (4) establishing within the Secretariat a more adequate information and data system for member states, units of the UN system, and the proposed Center for Economic and Development Research; (5) upgrading the caliber of the Secretariat staff; and (6) providing to smaller member states, on request, assistance in utilizing effectively the UN economic and social multilateral aid system.

Agencies   The effectiveness of the multilateral aid system depends, to no small degree, upon the harmonization and coordination of the activities of the numerous UN agencies. As most of the specialized agencies are autonomous bodies created by member states, the United Nations does not have direct operational control. However, the constitutional relationships between the United Nations and the specialized agencies are subject to renegotiation under the provisions of Articles 57, 58, and 63 of the Charter.

The need to revamp relationships between agencies and the United Nations and among all agencies is widely recognized. The programs of agencies should be consistent with reforms in the total multilateral aid program and the development policies established by a revitalized ECOSOC. Procedures are required to maximize cooperation and minimize competition and conflict among them. Some agencies should be restructured, others combined.

To advance reform, the following steps could be taken:

1. Reexamining and, as desirable, recasting and enlarging the functions of the agencies
2. Renegotiating the relationships between the specialized agencies and the United Nations to bring all agencies into closer and similar relationships with ECOSOC and the General Assembly, possibly by means of an international conference of diplomats with plenipotentiary authority
3. Establishing more effective procedures for harmonizing and coordinating the programs, budgets, and activities of the agencies

4. Assuring periodic high level discussions of goals and accomplishments between the agencies and ECOSOC
5. Preparing to operate greatly enlarged development programs
6. Formally resisting agency politicization on issues that belong in the General Assembly or the Security Council

The present capacity of the multilateral aid system to accelerate *Funding* development is directly dependent upon voluntary contributions of member states. The fund-raising system is decentralized and competitive. None of the agencies is financed by the regular UN budget; each solicits funds from its own constituencies, usually ministries of member states. Aggregate financing for multilateral aid channels needs to be doubled or tripled promptly.

A hotly debated question concerns the responsibility of developed nations to provide aid. The Charter of Economic Rights and Duties of States placed upon "all states" the responsibility to cooperate in activities related to economic and social development of the developing nations. While financial assistance is clearly implied, there has been no rush of donor nations to increase their contributions. All have domestic demands on their resources and many are disillusioned with multilateral aid programs.

Reform of the system would reduce somewhat donor nations' concern for lack of coordination and inefficiency. But that alone will not double or triple funding. I propose a consolidated budget for all agencies, with centralized fund raising. Upon budget approval by ECOSOC and the General Assembly, a central office would generate and distribute funds based upon project needs to the agencies, thus allowing stronger UN control. Strong, persuasive efforts could increase national contributions, broaden them to cover all agencies, and avoid falloff due to disfavor with certain agencies—all premised on donor nations translating accelerated development into their long-term self-interest.

In the longer range, the key must be independent sources of revenue for the United Nations and its agencies to supplement the regular assessed budget and voluntary contributions of member states.

Both donor and developing nation-states confront several obsta- *Member* cles when dealing with the multilateral aid system. Ministries *States* within governments have differing priorities, information, and interests; internal reconciliation is often difficult and time-consuming. The connection between seemingly unrelated development plans may elude governments immersed in difficult and complex domestic tasks. The mass of data to be assimilated by national delegations to the United Nations and to its specialized agencies is overwhelming.

Each nation should be encouraged to examine its internal structure and procedures as they relate to UN economic and social activities. A high level post to oversee such activities would seem appropriate. Harmonizing national decisions regarding international organizations through inter-ministerial committees would help assure that the representatives of each nation had a single national position to speak from. Attention should be paid to the competence of delegates and to making assignments reasonably continuous. Most governments would benefit from a central information system to better utilize UN resources.

Such reforms, no matter how logical, cannot replace the political will of member states. The multilateral aid system will not fully accomplish its desired objectives until nations demonstrate a willingness to commit necessary resources and human talent to support the work of the United Nations.

Bilateral Aid System

The bilateral aid system is the second vehicle of public sector participation in economic and social development. While both bilateral and multilateral aid provide technical assistance and preinvestment services, bilateral aid usually includes loans or grants for financing projects. Thus bilateral aid is a major source of transfers of capital, technology, and management on a government-to-government basis, and its magnitude exceeds that of multilateral aid.

Although bilateral aid is subject to both warranted and irresponsible criticism, it is certain to continue in the foreseeable future. France, for example, is unlikely to use multilateral channels for her appreciable aid to former colonies. Canada, the Scandinavian countries, and others have long-standing direct relationships with certain developing nations. Nor can one imagine the United States soon directing all aid through the multilateral system.

The directness and simplicity of bilateral aid reduce red tape and speed implementation. Donor nations find it advantageous to tie aid to use of their nationals and materials through buy-American type provisions. The uses and results of bilateral funds often are easier to appraise.

Hence the issue is not one of multilateral versus bilateral aid. While multilateral aid is properly encouraged and enlarged, bilateral aid is welcome as an added transfer mechanism. The two systems are complementary, not conflicting.

The world community plays a minimal role and exerts little control over bilateral aid. But it can encourage the best aspects of bilateral aid and discourage objectionable ones. The United Nations should develop guidelines to assist both developing and donor nations in (1) facilitating coordination with multilateral aid, (2) assuring that bilaterally financed projects are consistent with the recipient's development model, (3) promoting favorable debt service terms correlated with the developing nations' financial capabilities, (4) discouraging excessive political emphasis, and (5) discouraging loan provisions unduly tying purchases to the donor country.

The United Nations, through its multilateral aid system, can be of great help to developing nations by assisting them in preparations for the proper administration and management of bilaterally financed projects.

Care should be taken that efforts to improve the multilateral aid system do not reduce the magnitude of bilateral aid without a compensating increase in multilateral aid. The developing nations need all possible assistance, whatever its source. Bilateral aid is related to the development climate in the same manner that multilateral aid is. An improved climate should stimulate more aid and, in turn, more aid should favorably affect the climate.

Development Banking System

The development banking system is the third public sector mechanism transferring resources to developing nations. Development banking plays a growing role that will become more important as donor nations increasingly turn to multilateral approaches. The system consists of worldwide and regional banking institutions created and managed by cooperative action of nation-states. The performance of the development banking system is one of the brightest lights in world community response to the development challenge.

The core of the system is the World Bank with its two affiliates, International Development Association (IDA) and International Finance Corporation (IFC). These institutions are supplemented by the Inter-American, African, and Asian regional development banks and subregional banks. While the IMF functions primarily in the monetary system, it also operates partly within the development banking system.

World Bank   The World Bank was established as the major postwar mechanism for multilateral transfer of capital to needy nations. Soon after its creation, the bank shifted emphasis from rebuilding war-torn nations to financing productive projects to help developing country members achieve development goals. So-called hard loans made only when funding is unavailable from other sources have grace periods of several years, maturities up to 25 years, and interest rates (7.45 to 8.20 percent during fiscal 1978)[4] reflecting cost of money to the bank. Interest rates are adjusted quarterly to reflect weighted cost of funds borrowed by the bank during the preceding 12 months.

The World Bank carries on a wide program of technical assistance benefiting its members, including project assistance, training of governmental officials, coordinating bilateral and multilateral aid, cooperating on an inter-agency basis, cosponsoring the Consultative Group on International Agricultural Research, and studying and researching the economics of development processes. The bank also sponsors the recently organized International Centre for Settlement of Investment Disputes, a convention presently signed by 71 nations.

Members of the World Bank, who are required to be members of IMF, hold shares and vote in proportion to their capital subscriptions. The powers of the bank are vested in a board of governors, one appointed by each member, meeting annually and dealing with such matters as membership, allocation of net income, and changes in capital stock. Most powers are delegated to 20 full-time executive directors, five appointed by the members having the largest number of shares, the others elected every two years by the governors of the other members. Votes of the executive directors are weighted by the sum of the voting power, or shares, of the country or countries they represent. The directors choose the president who is responsible for the conduct of bank business; only the president can propose loans. Some of the bank's capital comes from member subscriptions paid partly in gold or US dollars—freely usable by the bank—and partly in the member's own currency—available for lending only with the

4. Data on the World Bank and International Development Association, unless otherwise noted, are compiled from the World Bank *Annual Report 1978*, Washington, D.C.

member's consent. At the end of fiscal 1978, capital subscriptions totaled $33.045 billion (US), of which only 10 percent had been paid in. The balance is subject to call when required by the bank to meet its obligations. The bank also sells, on the international money market, its own bonds and notes from borrowing members. During five fiscal years (1974–1978) the bank borrowed $17.531 billion.

During fiscal 1976 the World Bank implemented a new financing facility called the Third Window. It provides loans on terms intermediate between the normal hard loans of the bank and the fully concessionary loans of IDA (see below). Voluntary contributions of 10 members (not including the United States) and Switzerland provided a subsidy fund to reimburse the bank in an amount equal to 4 percent of the outstanding principal of Third Window loans. Borrowers paid the difference between the bank's standard interest rate and the 4 percent paid by the subsidy fund. Third Window loans were normally restricted to countries with per capita incomes under $375. Subsidy receipts were only $125 million in the first year; Third Window loans aggregated $478 million.

IDA was established in 1960 to promote economic development through concessionary loans on terms more favorable than those of the World Bank. Such soft loans—noninterest bearing but with a 0.75 percent service charge and up to 50-year maturities—are used for many infrastructure capital requirements. Members, who must also belong to the World Bank, are represented by the governors and executive directors who represent them in the bank. IDA shares the president and staff of the bank. IDA's capital is partially obtained from members' subscriptions. The more economically advanced members pay their full subscriptions in convertible currencies, all available for lending. Less developed members pay one-tenth of their subscription in convertible currency freely available for lending, and the remainder in their own currencies available for lending only with the member's consent. Most of IDA's funds, however, come from periodic contributions called replenishments, paid in by the more affluent members. The fifth, and latest, replenishment commitment aggregates $7,732 billion, payable in the 1978–1980 fiscal periods from 26 donor countries. IDA's funds are augmented by net income transfers from the bank and borrowings from countries such as nonmember Switzerland. Money repaid by borrowers, plus margins of IDA revenues over operating costs, are available for new loans. At the end of fiscal 1978, IDA's usable resources (including replenishments) totaled $18,062 billion.

IFC was established in 1956 to invest together with private investors in productive private enterprises located in developing countries. Although closely affiliated with the World Bank, IFC is a separate legal entity with separate capital largely borrowed from the World Bank. Membership is open only to members of the bank. The members each appoint a governor to the board of governors; 20 executive directors are elected and function in a pattern similar to that of the World Bank. The president of the bank is currently the president of IFC. At the end of fiscal 1977, IFC had capital and surplus of $195.7 million and owed the bank $404.6 million.[5]

The contribution of the World Bank Group in transfer of capital to the developing world is substantial as shown in table 5.

Table 5

INVESTMENT COMMITMENTS DURING FISCAL 1978

Unit	Number of Commitments	Amount ($ billion)
World Bank	137	6.098
IDA	99	2.313
IFC	34	0.259
Total	270	8.670

Sources: International Finance Corporation, *1977 Annual Report*, Washington, D.C.; World Bank, *Annual Report 1978*, Washington, D.C.

As of June 1978, 132 nations were members of the World Bank, 120 of IDA, and 106 of IFC. Hence the World Bank Group is broadly representative of the world community, except that neither the Soviet Union nor the Warsaw Pact countries other than Romania (since 1972) are members. Although the Soviet Union participated at Bretton Woods, it has since avoided any connection with these banks. Poland, an original member, withdrew—reputedly under Soviet pressure; Czechoslovakia, also an original member, was dropped for nonpayment of balance due on its subscription.

One of the paradoxical situations at the United Nations is the Soviet Union's constant support of developing world proposals for a new international economic order, while it remains aloof from the

5. Data on IFC are compiled from the International Finance Corporation *1977 Annual Report*, Washington, D.C.

World Bank, IDA, IFC, and IMF, the key multilateral mechanisms for transferring capital to the developing world and stabilizing the monetary system. It is no wonder the other developed nations, which provide the bulk of the financial resources for these institutions, resent the Soviet attitude and find it hard to understand the willingness of some developing nations to seek and encourage Soviet support.

The Inter-American Development Bank (established in 1959) has 41 members, including 26 from the Western Hemisphere; two other non-Western hemisphere states have signified intention to join. The African Development Bank (established in 1964) has 48 members, all from Africa. The Asian Development Bank (established in 1966) has 43 members, including 14 nonregional members. While there are variations, each bank has a board of governors—one per member nation—and a board of directors, elected by the governors but with some restrictions regarding representation of certain countries and nonregional members. These banks promote economic and social development through development loans. Capital is obtained from member subscriptions, and the banks borrow additional funds against callable capital subscriptions. The magnitude of operations through 1977 is shown in table 6. *Regional Banks*

Several subregional banks have been organized to make contributions to economic development. These include the Central American Bank for Economic Integration, the West Africa International Bank,

Table 6
REGIONAL BANK OPERATIONS

Bank	Total Subscriptions ($ million)	Cumulative Loan Commitments Through 1977	
		Number	Amount ($ million)
Inter-American	$16,102	1,046	$11,945
African	859	162	562
Asian	6,961	642	4,246

Sources: Inter-American Development Bank, *Annual Report 1977*, Washington, D.C., 1978; African Development Bank, *Annual Report 1977*, Abidjan, Ivory Coast, 1978; Asian Development Bank, *Annual Report 1977*, Manila, Philippines, 1978.

the Arab Bank for Economic Development in Africa, the Islamic Bank for Development, and the Caribbean Development Bank.

The International Monetary Fund's primary role in development banking has been one of assisting troubled nations in putting their financial houses in order and rescheduling burdensome debt service. Other IMF activities, as outlined in chapter 6, include issuing special drawing rights (SDR), managing special international funds for loans to nations classified as those most seriously affected (MSA) by recent world economic conditions, and recycling petro money through its oil facility.

While the institutions comprising the development banking system are operationally independent, they maintain close connections with one another, the United Nations, and many of its specialized agencies. The president of the World Bank is a member of the UN Administrative Committee on Coordination. The World Bank and IMF are closely linked through overlapping boards of governors and jointly hold annual meetings.

Despite fine performance, the development banking system is not without its detractors among developing nations. First and foremost, funds available for loans are inadequate; second, interest rates are too high; third, maturities are too short; and, fourth, the influence of developed nations upon policy is too great.

Increased Funds   Because capital is a basic development element, no one seriously disagrees that more is needed. The 1974 report of the World Bank forecasts that the need for additional long-term capital inflows will rise from $10.6 billion in 1976 to $27.5 billion in 1980. Of these incremental amounts, about $3.9 billion in 1976, rising to $11.2 billion in 1980, will have to be on highly concessionary terms (long maturities and low interest). According to the World Bank's estimates, the higher income developing countries could afford to borrow most of the additional external capital on conventional terms. The middle income countries need a large concessionary element in their borrowing. The lower income countries must be financed almost entirely on concessionary terms.

While bilateral loans may constitute part of this increased inflow, most of it will need to be multilateral through the development banking system. How can more capital be brought into the development banking system? Currently, nation-states are the primary sources of capital through membership subscriptions and replenishment or other additional contributions. The private money market is another source, but only the World Bank and the Inter-American Bank have made much use of it. The banks also recycle the amortization payment received on outstanding loans less operating expenses.

Avenues to enlarge development loan funds include (1) increasing the size of member subscriptions, particularly for nations gaining greater economic strength; (2) raising the current 10 percent requirement of paid-in subscriptions; (3) encouraging more affluent nations to make greater contributions to the IDA replenishments; and (4) selling more securities to investors in the private money market. Another possibility is to influence the Soviet Union and Warsaw Pact nations to join the development banking institutions.

Some combination of these avenues must be pursued actively if the development banking system is to contribute better to achieving the 0.7 percent of GNP target of the United Nations for official development assistance.

Borrowers commonly express the desire for lower interest rates on development financing. While stabilization and reduction of interest rates are desirable, the development banking system can do little about this; it cannot control money costs on the world market. In fact, interest rates have increased substantially over the years. The banks' borrowing costs in fiscal 1978 averaged 6.95 percent. Hence the 1978 World Bank's rates on nonconcessionary loans were 7.45 to 8.20 percent. *Terms*

Interest rates on concessionary or soft loans are another matter. They depend upon the system's capability to subsidize the difference between the applied rate and the cost of money. Current IDA loans, carrying only a 0.75 percent service charge, are largely granted from funds donated by developed nations under replenishment agreements or funds transferred from net revenues of the World Bank.

If concessionary loans were enlarged by borrowing on the world money market, subsidization costs would be high. Had IDA's 1976 credit commitments of $1.655 billion been financed from proceeds of the bank's 8 percent bonds, the annual subsidy would have been $120 million. Third Window loans of an intermediate concessionary nature require annual subsidy at the rate of 4 percent or $40 million to support $1 billion of loans.

In the near-term, this requires that the more affluent nations be fully convinced of the importance of concessionary loans to the Low and Lower-Middle Income developing nations, retain confidence in the management of the development banking institutions, and make larger replenishments. In the longer range, however, successful management of the needs for concessionary loans undoubtedly depends upon independent sources of revenue for the United Nations.

Repayment schedules are a concern of both borrower and lender. Debt service requirements are affected by maturities and interest rates. Maturities of hard loans made by the development banking system range up to 25 years and of soft loans to 50 years. Most loans have grace periods at the beginning (4 or 5 years on hard loans and 10 years on concessionary loans) when no principal payments are required.

Nevertheless, debt service requirements are increasing more rapidly than growth of GNP in all but a few well-favored developing nations. Aggregate official and private external debt of 96 developing countries was $160.5 billion in 1976, nearly triple that of 1970. Debt service requirements in a number of countries have become so burdensome that maturities have been rescheduled, usually with IMF assistance. The causes of excessive debt service costs include overcommitment on intermediate term debt, high interest rates, worsening of borrower's economy (often because of lower commodity and raw material prices on exports), unwise selection of projects and programs, and unrealistic estimates of capacity to repay.

Avoidance of excessive debt service depends largely upon the manner in which developing nations manage their development process. Sounder development models, less fluctuation of commodity and raw material prices, greater availability of concessionary loans, and sounder management of financial affairs would be beneficial.

Although such steps may help, IMF will undoubtedly continue to be called upon to aid developing nations in sorting out financing, to reschedule maturities, to assure proper use of SDRs, and to provide other standby help. In the long run, some countries will, undoubtedly, default on debt payments, clouding the attractiveness of loans to developing nations.

Management: Procedures and Voting   On the whole, the development banking system is well managed. The World Bank institutions and IMF have made good use of available resources and have constantly improved operating procedures and mechanisms. The World Bank Group has a sound approach to the development problems falling within its scope of activity. Its studies are penetrating and the technical assistance it renders to borrowers is useful.

There is no need for new global institutions. There is, however, continuing need to improve procedures and strengthen coordination within the development banking system and with other systems of the international economic order. Both the World Bank Group and the regional banks should become involved with the proposed Center for Economic and Development Research.

Is there a need to alter drastically the voting system of the World Bank? As with IMF, the weighted voting structure permits the executive directors who represent the countries contributing the majority of the capital to control decisions. As with IMF, many developing nations advocate the one-nation/one-vote system.

In the World Bank itself, some modification of weighted voting will inevitably occur as nations change their contributions; the voting power of OPEC nations has been increased recently. The arguments against drastic change of the voting system in IMF, discussed in the preceding chapter, are equally applicable to the World Bank. Near-term enlargement of loan funds depends upon contributing countries maintaining confidence in the management and the decision-making processes of the World Bank. The present voting pattern favoring suppliers of funds has been accepted by the developed nations—now the primary sources of funds—and apparently by OPEC nations. So long as the World Bank's capital comes largely from affluent nations, major changes in voting structures are unlikely.

Viewed against the needs of the next decade, the US posture on economic and social development is now grossly inadequate. *United States Posture*

The United States played a positive role at Bretton Woods and in the creation of the World Bank and IMF. It was both forward-looking and generous when it fostered government-to-government bilateral aid, first the Marshall Plan and then worldwide assistance through what is now AID. Without these stimuli, the world community might not have accepted any important degree of responsibility for economic and social development: certainly the magnitude of assistance from the industrialized world would have been less.

The United States has supported the UN multilateral aid system. Our contributions to the United Nations Development Programme (UNDP) and to other specialized agencies have been substantial. Occasionally, though, we have damaged our image by injecting cold war reactions into our funding.

In recent years the United States, increasingly disillusioned with economic assistance, has reduced substantially bilateral and multilateral aid as a percentage of GNP. We still err by evaluating the usefulness of aid in terms of friends—compatible governments or allies—not in terms of improvement of economic and social status of developing nations. We have great difficulty in separating economic aid from military aid and support.

The United States has generally recognized the need for change, but our leadership has been less than dynamic. Our positions regarding aid are often handicapped by undue concern for near-term self-interest to the detriment of the longer range well-being of our nation and the world.

Despite such US proposals as those made to the Seventh Special Session of the UN General Assembly in 1975 and our ongoing deliberations with industrial and developing nations regarding oil and commodity pricing, the United States has shown little willingness to deal aggressively with the critical world issue of economic development.

8 RESOURCE/POPULATION BALANCE

Two widely held beliefs have been challenged by technological change: One is that the earth's resources are vast, bountiful, and fully sufficient to meet all future needs or desires of the human race. The second is that the rate of population growth adjusts with increasing affluence and, meanwhile, fecundity benefits the family and the nation. During recent centuries, these two historic beliefs, riding the wave of technological change and exploited by human drive and imagination, have fostered uncontrolled growth. The issue facing us now is how to manage the finite resources of the earth and stabilize population growth to achieve and sustain a quality of life fully compatible with human dignity.

Must growth of population and consumption of critical resources be constrained? Must life-style and economic strategies be altered? The search for answers vividly reveals the total interweaving of the world's nations and peoples. Resource/population balance promises to dwarf all other critical issues in future centuries, if not within the next decade or two.

Nearly two centuries ago, Thomas Robert Malthus, an English *The Problem* clergyman-economist, advanced the theory that population growth would disastrously outstrip increases in the means of human subsistence. His theory was ridiculed for many generations. Population did increase in the developed nations, but so did agricultural production and nutritional quality. While in the colonies and the poorer nations, disease and death kept population relatively balanced with subsistence-level agricultural production. The Malthusian theory was negated by advancing technology.

From the beginning of history until 1830, the earth's population rose to only a billion. But by 1930 it had doubled to two billion, largely because of growth in the more developed areas. By 1976 the world's population shot up from two billion to four billion.

This rapid growth in four and a half decades, in contrast to prior periods, occurred largely in the poorer countries. Mortality rates, particularly of infants and children, were greatly reduced through the introduction of modern health care and public health measures. Longevity increased significantly, as killer diseases (smallpox, malaria, cholera, typhoid fever, and others) were stamped out or contained. As birth rates remained high, population rose and the proportion of people under 25 years of age climbed dramatically.

Growing at 2 percent per year (the rate of the last decade), today's world population will compound to some 6.5 billion people by the year 2000. Should a 2 percent per year growth rate continue for a century, population would increase to just under 29 billion people. Demographers forecast population stabilization late in the twenty-first century at levels ranging from 10 to 16 billion. Against such projections, Malthusian concepts seem less ludicrous.

Increased population automatically demands proportionally larger supplies of food and other resources. In addition, the revolution of rising expectations leads to greater consumption; the more affluent nations continue to raise their standards of living. These trends combine to propel the demand for resources upward at an amazing rate. Comparison of current demands projected ahead a few decades with current production and known reserves pinpoints petroleum, feed grains, and food fish as some of the trouble spots.

The world's production of petroleum in 1973, totaling 21,100 million barrels as compared to then known reserves of 542,200 million barrels, indicates a 27-year supply, assuming consumption at 1973 levels.[1] Consumption of petroleum, however, increased at an annual rate of 7.6 percent from 1960 to 1973. Even with a lesser rate of consumption increase and discovery of additional reserves, exhaustion of petroleum supplies in the near future is predictable.

The world's annual consumption of grains by humans and animals was 1,214 million metric tons in 1972–1973. But global grain production in the same period was 1,176 million metric tons, resulting in a 38-million metric ton depletion of world grain reserves.[2] Consumption rates would, of course, rise significantly if the inadequately fed 60 percent of the population in the developing world were supplied minimal nutritional requirements.

1. US, Department of Interior, *Energy Perspectives*, Washington, D.C., 1975, pp. 8–14.
2. Food and Agriculture Organization, *The State of Food and Agriculture 1975*, Washington, D.C., 1976, pp. 72–73.

By 2000, assuming a world population of 6.5 billion and the currently prevailing global food-consumption level of nearly a half ton of grain per person each year, we can project the need for roughly 2.5 times the current grain output.[3] The outlook is distressing, even with optimistic forecasts of increased areas of tillable land and higher yielding grains. Higher yield is currently directly dependent upon fertilizers manufactured from petroleum, which is already recognized as a finite resource.

The catch of fish from our oceans, a major source of protein, has not risen recently despite intensified activities by modernized fleets: 70.2 million metric tons in 1970 versus 66.1 million metric tons in 1973 and 69.8 million metric tons in 1974.[4] The seas are being overfished, and some species are near extinction. Vigorous conservation is already needed to maintain current catches. The opportunity for enlarged protein supply for more hungry stomachs from this source is not bright.

While these and similar analyses convince experts of the limitations of the earth's supply of certain critical resources, it has taken recent events to dramatize the situation. The 1973 energy crisis forced many national leaders to acknowledge reluctantly that the earth's supply of petroleum cannot long be counted upon as a major source of energy.

The Club of Rome's controversial book *The Limits to Growth*, published in 1972, received worldwide attention and stimulated awareness of resource limitations. Its computerized analyses of current trends of population growth, resource consumption, and environmental pollution projected global tragedy in the twenty-first century. Whatever validity its projections may have, the book precipitated extensive and heated debate. Subsequent Club of Rome reports retreat from the doomsday predictions of *The Limits to Growth* but continue to stress the seriousness of the economic, resource, population, and environmental problems.

The fabulous exploits of courageous space pioneers have focused visual attention upon the finiteness of the earth's resources. Mother Earth, as seen through their TV cameras, is a spaceship orbiting the sun with no near celestial neighbor. Our globe is a closed system isolated from external input other than solar energy. We, and all the

3. Lester R. Brown, *Our Daily Bread*, Head Line ser. no. 225 (New York: Foreign Policy Association, April 1975).

4. United Nations, *Statistical Yearbook 1975*, New York, 1976, p. 160.

generations to follow, are utterly dependent upon the resources of this earth.

Growth
Syndrome   The near worship of growth clouds recognition of the urgency of controlling the balance of resources and population. The concept that growth measures progress is widespread. All is well if this year's GNP, budget, income, profit, production, membership, population, or what have you exceeds last year's. Nowhere has this growth syndrome had greater emphasis than in the United States. But much of the world, now including many developing nations, seeks to emulate the US pattern. Even modest rates of annual growth, compounded over a period of years, create incredible increases as shown by my mathematical analysis in table 1.

Table 1

IMPACT OF GROWTH
ON WORLD POPULATION AND RESOURCE DEMAND

Item	Annual Growth (%)	1976	Growth Ratios (to Date) 1980	1990	2000
Population	2.0	1.00	1.08	1.32	1.61
Resource demand per capita	3.0	1.00	1.13	1.51	2.03
Global resource demand	5.0	1.00	1.22	1.98	3.23

Whether exponential growth rates are applied to population, resource demand, or other indicators, the magnitude of expansion is staggering. At an optimistic 2 percent rate, world population would increase 61 percent by 2000, from 4.0 billion to 6.5 billion. Per capita resource demand, at a modest 3 percent rate, would double by 2000, and global resource demand would increase 3.2-fold.

The power of the growth syndrome may be emphasized by another approach. What would be the demand for resources should the whole world achieve the economic levels of the United States? It is generally assumed that the United States with but 6 percent of the world's population now consumes about 40 percent of the resources used on the earth. Most of these resources are produced or extracted within the United States. The remaining resources (petroleum, minerals, coffee, etc.) provide markets and income to other countries, including many developing nations.

If the current world population were suddenly to consume resources at half the current US rate, the global demand for resources would be increased by a factor of 3.5. For equal affluence, the increase would be 6.7-fold. If the population of the world increases to 6.5 billion by 2000, and if all people reach the present US levels of affluence, global resource demands will multiply by 11.

Those politicians or scientists who deprecate these warnings as doomsday prophecies would do well to pause, reflect, and make certain they fully comprehend the powerful dynamics of exponential growth in a finite world. Increasing population and increasing per capita consumption are on a collision course with resource supply.

As the resource crunch tightens, the world community will be forced to face several critical humanitarian, economic, political, and moral problems.

Physical Consequences and Moral Questions

Famine can be expected to occur more often. True to the Malthusian theory, a sizable part of the world's population already suffers from hunger or malnutrition. The Food and Agriculture Organization calculates that as many as 1.5 billion people are inadequately fed, that 0.5 billion are severely malnourished, and that the total number of malnourished will increase 50 percent by 1985 even without major droughts or crop failures.[5] Tragedy is occurring now in limited geographical areas. Rain-starved land cannot feed Sahelian people, and teeming hordes have exhausted the food supply in Bangladesh. Despite temporary improvements in both areas thanks to weather conditions, utter degradation and death remain real threats to these people. Similar situations in other areas are likely wherever the needs of burgeoning populations outstrip food production.

Economic pressures are an inevitable result of resource/population unbalances; sellers' markets occur when the demand for scarce foods, commodities, or products exceeds the supply. Neither private enterprises nor nation-states will overlook the opportunity to demand higher prices, as the OPEC nations clearly demonstrated in 1973. It will cost more to increase the production of scarce commodities and raw materials. The cultivation of yet untilled marginal land will require more fertilizer and irrigation. Costly marine farming will be necessary to supplement once abundant catches on the open seas. Mines will be opened at less accessible locations and at greater

5. Population Crisis Committee, *Population*, briefing paper no. 1, Washington, D.C., 1976.

depths, producing lower quality ores. Because of high research and development costs, substitute products will be more expensive. Recycling, while conserving materials, will not be inexpensive. Though a few favored nations may profit enough from higher prices for resource exports to offset increased costs on imports, most nations will suffer under price squeezes: the heaviest impact will fall on the poor.

Higher prices of gasoline and diesel fuel have already affected life-style in countries dependent upon imported petroleum. Reduced highway speeds, less pleasure driving, and a partial trend to smaller automobiles have resulted in the United States. Shortages and higher costs will combine to force greater use of protein grains as food rather than as animal feed. Such pressures will produce changes in life-style in the more affluent countries. Tragically, many Low and Middle Income countries are highly vulnerable to further degradation of basic living conditions.

Two types of political problems are predictable. Instability of national governments will increase as leaders fail to assure acceptable resource/population balances within their countries. Faltering development progress, mounting unemployment, and growing food shortages will stimulate discontent and rebellion. The resulting potential for civil war threatens international peace and security.

Shifts in national power are another certain political consequence; witness the sudden rise of influence of the oil-rich nations. The power position of nations possessing or producing critical commodities and raw materials will be significantly enhanced. Zaire with uranium deposits, Iran and Saudi Arabia with petroleum, and the United States with food-producing capability will gain near-term leverage and improve their bargaining positions. So, too, will nations possessing the technology and capital to develop substitute materials. These elements of national power may become far more important than nuclear weapons and army divisions.

Complex moral questions will certainly emerge as the imbalance of resources and population becomes more severe. At what point does the common well-being of the planet take precedence over the national right of action or inaction? With population growth, for instance, how long should the world community tolerate continued population growth in poverty-stricken, resource-poor nations? Should the world community respond to repeated relief calls from within nations among the most seriously affected (MSAs) which are possibly unwilling or unable to stabilize their population and intensify programs for increasing food supply? Who owns the natural resources—property owners, nations, or the people of the world? What responsibility have nations regarding the use of these resources? Are they only to assure domestic affluence? Should other nations be deprived of access?

Such moral questions generate political issues. Consumer nations denied access to needed resource supplies will undoubtedly counter by decreasing transfers of capital, technology, and management to the developing world. Controversy over access to resources will further divide the world community, retard international efforts to manage other critical world issues, and, in the extreme, may lead to armed conflict.

Like equilibrium in the environment a few years ago, resource/population balance has not yet been adequately recognized as a global problem. The world community has, however, through the United Nations, given attention to resource development, population problems, and emergency relief. Awareness is emerging. *Accomplishments*

For nearly three decades, development programs administered through the multilateral and bilateral aid and development banking systems have encouraged increased agricultural production and raw material exploitation. The reports of the Food and Agriculture Organization (FAO), the United Nations Development Programme (UNDP), the World Bank, and other UN agencies chronicle many outstanding successes. Unfortunately, accomplishments to date are dwarfed by current and future needs.

Food scarcity was further emphasized by the UN sponsored World Food Conference (Rome, 1974). Delegates from 130 nations debated, angrily at times, initiatives to expand food production and enlarge food reserves. The conference agreed to set up an International Fund for Agricultural Development (IFAD) with a proposed $1.0 billion target to finance increased food production primarily in developing countries. IFAD is in operation: by December 1976 OPEC nations had pledged $435.5 million and industrial nations $567 million, including the United States pledge of $200 million.

The conference endorsed FAO's International Undertaking on World Food Security and agreed to establish, under FAO, a Global Information and Early Warning System on Food and Agriculture. The UN General Assembly subsequently endorsed the work of the conference and established a 36-member ministerial level World Food Council (WFC) located in Rome and serviced by FAO. The

WFC reports through the Economic and Social Council (ECOSOC) to the General Assembly. The WFC and its small staff are charged with reviewing major policy issues and coordinating action among relevant United Nations and other international bodies.

Population stabilization received formal recognition when the United Nations Fund for Population Activities (UNFPA) was authorized in 1967. Now governed by the United Nations Development Programme (UNDP) and reporting through ECOSOC to the General Assembly, UNFPA's aims and objectives are (1) building capacity to respond to global needs, (2) promoting awareness of population problems, (3) extending assistance to developing countries, and (4) playing the leading role on population matters within the United Nations. Voluntary contributions ($90 million from 78 governments in 1976) fund UNFPA's projects, mostly administered by other UN agencies.

The World Population Conference (Bucharest, 1974) organized under UNFPA's auspices and attended by 135 nations broke new ground. After stormy debate, the conference adopted by consensus a lengthy World Plan of Action. This plan firmly recognizes the right of individuals to decide the number and spacing of children, calls upon governments to provide information and the means to enable them to accomplish this, and reaffirms the principle of national responsibility for demographic matters. The plan suggests the need to reduce the world's annual rate of population growth to 1.75 percent by 1985.

The plan is full of expected compromises and trade-offs reflecting varied cultural, religious, and political backgrounds of participating nations. Nevertheless, the conference succeeded in focusing attention upon population and thus encouraged the continuing efforts of UNFPA to aid those nations prepared to activate family planning and population stabilization programs. Not unexpectedly, one major theme emerging from the Bucharest conference was the interrelationship of population growth and development embellished by customary Third World criticism of the developed nations.

The General Assembly in 1971 formalized a world community role dealing with emergency short-term resource scarcities, principally food, when it created the Office of the United Nations Disaster Relief Coordinator. With a limited budget and a small staff, the coordinator's responsibility is to prepare for emergencies; mobilize, direct, and coordinate relief activities of the UN system; and facilitate prevention of natural disasters.

These several UN efforts are but stepping stones to the greater action needed to manage resource/population balance in the common interests of the world community.

Management of the resource/population issue should be directed toward achieving three goals. The first, of course, is to assure the survival of human beings. While the survival of the human race may not be in jeopardy in the foreseeable future, the lives of hundreds of millions of people in resource-poor areas are threatened.

Seeking a Solution

A second closely related goal is to achieve and maintain a tolerable quality of life for the future inhabitants of the earth. Animal-like existence in an overcrowded world would hardly be considered successful management of the problem.

The third important goal is to reduce the probability of serious international controversy and armed conflict over resources.

Achievement of these goals requires tolerable global balance between supply and demand of critical resources, as well as regional and national balance partially accomplished through trade. Mathematically, demand for resources may be stated as $D = P \times C$, where D is demand, P is population, and C is per capita consumption. Currently, demand is expanding exponentially because of the dynamics of population growth, the universal human desire for better living conditions, and the increasing military and civilian demands of a larger number of national governments.

The point of departure must be recognition of our total dependence, now and in the future, upon the discovered and yet-to-be-discovered resources of this globe, plus solar energy. Any remaining hopes or contentions that resources are infinite must be refuted. Because few yet recognize—or admit to recognizing—this fact, generating a motivating awareness and sense of responsibility is a further near-term objective of managing the resource/population issue.

Meeting future demands for critical resources calls for action to enlarge supplies and substitute, where possible, renewable for non-renewable materials. Limiting future growth of demand for critical resources involves stabilizing population and constraining per capita consumption through conservation and substitution.

Excluding consideration of human concerns for the moment, problems of this type are normally resolved by increasing supply, limiting demand, or some combination of these two actions. Historically, adjustment has been allowed to occur through the operation of the free market. Barring external influences and governmental restrictions, shortages cause prices to rise, and higher prices serve as incentives to increase production. Depending upon the price-elasticity of the product or material, higher prices may discourage consumption, thus lessening demand and helping to ease the situation.

While such factors will certainly come into play to balance resources and population, the situation is complicated by the finiteness of the earth's resources and the fertility of its people.

Toward More Abundant Resources   Resource enhancement is primarily a task for modern science, technology, agriculture, and industry. The need for continued innovation will become increasingly compelling as resource shortages appear.

Exploration, using research satellites and other advanced technology, is needed to inventory more accurately the world supply of extractive resources. Improved processes must be developed to reach deposits not economically or technically accessible with current methods and to permit the use of lower grade ores. Recycling or reusing critical materials and developing substitutes can extend the supply.

Increasing the productive capacity of current agricultural and timber lands and bringing marginal lands under cultivation should prove possible, using improved hybrids, better methods, and stronger incentives. Incentives in the form of personal economic gain are important factors in the United States and Japan, for instance, where production exceeds comparable production in the USSR. Are not incentives the reason USSR per-acre production from private plots is so much greater than that of state or collective farms? Too many nations ignore or even deride private economic motivation.

Water resources likewise deserve attention to assure efficient development and reuse. In addition, the food productive capacities of lakes, rivers, and seas could be expanded through conservation and antipollution measures and by marine farming.

To meet expanding energy requirements, we must tap the inexhaustible energy of the sun, the heat within the earth's core, the winds, and other natural forces, and the use of bio-mass. Developing the technology for fusion and other so-called exotic energy sources is warranted.

Without question, effective management of resource supply calls for continuing research.

Although stabilization of the world's population is essential, the appropriate level is debatable. The success of technology, conservation, management of resource supply, and the quality of life that future generations are willing to accept are controlling factors. Estimates vary widely. One knowledgeable scientist friend of mine has predicted that the earth could comfortably support a population of 30 billion people. His confidence in technology knows no limits: high density living and substitutes for natural foods would meet human needs. Such thinking seems hazardous, given the uncertainties of future resource supply and the nonphysical factors affecting quality of life. Would future generations willingly live like animals in crowded experimental laboratories?

If we believe future generations should have the right to live in decency and dignity, the only sensible stabilization objective is achievement of zero population growth (ZPG) at the earliest possible date. Any less stringent goal precipitates unacceptable risks and indicates an unwillingness on the part of the present generation to accept responsibility for providing a livable world for those who will follow.

World population will expand greatly even if birth rates are promptly reduced to slightly above two children per pair of adults—the ultimate level ZPG requires. Even if ZPG were achieved instantly, population would continue to grow for a number of years as today's youth reach childbearing age; demographers estimate that population would not stabilize until well into the twenty-first century. The prospects of quickly attaining ZPG are not bright, particularly in the poorer, less literate countries, unless they adopt stern measures like those of China. Only in a few highly developed nations is it a near-term probability. Hence a world population of 10 billion or above is predictable, barring widespread famine, plague, nuclear war, or other catastrophe.

Evolutionary processes are unlikely to achieve population stabilization within permissible time limits. The temptation to rely upon economic development on the positive side or upon war and famine (both morally unacceptable) on the negative side to limit the world's population must be rejected. While family size tends to decrease with greater affluence, population growth of the developed countries—including Japan, the Soviet Union, and the United States—demonstrates the slowness of this process. Nations approaching ZPG have instituted extensive education on family planning, easy access to contraceptives, and/or legalized abortion.

Reduction of birth rates is the most humane approach to population stabilization. Rapid lowering of birth rates is desirable because death rates, particularly in developing countries, will continue to decline for several generations thanks to improved nutrition and health care. But family planning programs involve delicate and intimate personal decisions and run head on into cultural obstacles, prejudices, ignorance, and religious bans. The social status accruing to large families must be overcome. Dependence upon large numbers of children for economic support and security must be made unnecessary by other economic measures.

Family planning implementation worldwide is a most formidable and difficult task. To date, few developing countries have made significant progress. India, long reputed to have an outstanding population stabilization program, is admitting failure and searching for other alternatives, including promotion of voluntary sterilization. In 1976 four Indian states considered compulsory sterilization to replace the present programs of voluntary sterilization for a fee. The Minister of Health and Family Planning told Parliament that to limit family size, India may need to resort to a national sterilization mandate. Indira Ghandi's 1977 election defeat was partially attributed to public resentment against forced sterilization. Japan's success in reducing birth rates is partially due to widespread use and acceptance of abortion.

While the world community has a part to play in promoting population stabilization, only nation-states now possess the authority and bear the responsibility for accomplishing it. Progress will occur only as national leaders become convinced of the need and committed to implementing effective programs of education and persuasion backed, if need be, by incentives, disincentives, and perhaps compulsion. Meanwhile, the population explosion is a time bomb ticking away toward disaster.

Limiting Consumption   Restricting per capita usage of critical resources to help balance demand to supply presents difficult challenges. Neither the haves nor the have-nots will readily abandon the determination to acquire and consume more worldly goods. Citizens of affluent nations continue their pursuit of more gadgets and machines, better homes, finer clothes, and richer diets. At the other end of the economic scale, hundreds of millions of hungry people clamor for enough of the basics of life to allow them to live decently and healthfully. Between these extremes, other multitudes can be counted upon to strive for economic progress. Based upon today's attitudes, all peoples will be pressing to increase per capita consumption until forced to do otherwise. This pattern will continue with little modification until change is compelled by actual widespread shortages, prohibitive prices, or governmental restrictions. People must become convinced that limitation of consumption is economically wise for current generations and morally essential to the well-being of future generations.

The wise course is for nations to anticipate the future and begin now to limit the per capita consumption of critical resources. Alternatives fall within the four categories of conservation, improved methods, modification of life-style, and curbing military waste. Some effort along these lines has begun, though not on a sufficient scale. While the potential reductions and the responsibility for making them are greatest in the countries of highest development, opportunities for resource economy are open to all nations, whatever their stage of development. Developing nations can contribute without scuttling their legitimate development programs.

Conservation in the broadest sense is the place to start. Eliminating waste, improving efficiency of resource use, and conserving both renewable and nonrenewable resources make sense from all perspectives—economic, development, and resource supply. Opportunities are legion, including (1) reducing loss and damage in the harvesting, storing, shipping, and processing of food stuffs; (2) salvaging, recycling, and reusing critical materials; (3) adopting lower vehicular speeds and using car pools and smaller cars; (4) lowering room temperatures in heating seasons and raising them in cooling seasons; (5) economizing energy usage in industry, commerce, and the home; and (6) modernizing and expanding the use of mass transportation.

Improvement of designs and methods is a second promising approach to economizing critical materials. This responsibility now falls heaviest upon the industrial nations, but to a lesser degree upon every nation. Opportunities include (1) manufacturing smaller and more efficient vehicles; (2) accelerating development and use of mass transportation; (3) reducing the built-in obsolescence in all types of consumer products; (4) designing new buildings and modernizing old ones to lower energy requirements; and (5) improving production processes to reduce energy requirements and minimize waste and spoilage.

Thirdly, alteration of life-styles will undoubtedly prove necessary with respect to some resources. Obviously, both the opportunities and responsibilities vary with each country's stage of economic development; they are greater in the more affluent countries. Some of the potentials are indicated by the following questions directed specifically to the United States. How much is our quality of life improved by constantly increasing consumption of capital goods? Would our quality of life be appreciably deteriorated by aggressive programs to conserve critical materials and reduce waste? Would we not be healthier were we to adopt nutritional patterns decreasing use of grain-fed meats and thus freeing increased quantities of grains for export? Must our pets consume large quantities of food when people are starving in other parts of the world? Does not our present pattern of extreme mobility create unnecessary consumption?

The more affluent countries may soon find it necessary to deal with such questions. High prices may force return to a more simple, but perhaps better quality, life-style. More than economic and scarcity pressures are likely to be needed, however—for example, carefully fashioned tax incentives and disincentives.

Meanwhile, developing nations seeking transfers of capital, technology, and management from the industrialized nations must look carefully at the quality of life they seek. Sound and sensible development models need not necessarily imitate the affluent.

Reducing military waste offers a fourth potential for significant resource savings. Even in peacetime, military establishments are prodigious and irresponsible consumers of critical resources, particularly rare metals and energy. Competitive development of new weapon systems and equipment leads to constant obsolescence and discard. Wartime resource demands become enormous. Progress in this area would not only conserve critical resources but would release substantial human resources for application to the solution of critical world issues and the meeting of domestic and global needs.

Management   Two aspects of resource/population balance deserve reemphasis. First, because of the powerful dynamics of growth, time is short. Second, national sovereignty is strongly challenged; scarcely any nation is capable of weathering the stormy resource/population controversy alone. Progress from near-term strategies to the longer range view will depend upon how seriously national leaders treat the problem.

In the near-term, world community efforts should be focused upon (1) continuing current UN activities, (2) stimulating research,

(3) developing a greater sense of world community responsibility, and (4) developing better management mechanisms.

Three related UN programs require prompt attention:

FAMILY PLANNING The UN Fund for Population Activities (UNFPA) needs to be greatly expanded and more adequately financed to carry on vigorous educational programs and extend more assistance to national family planning programs.

FOOD SUPPLY The recently established World Food Council needs greater financing and stronger leadership to better discharge its functions concerning adequate food supply and the maintenance of suitable reserves by producers and governments.

DISASTERS The office of UN Disaster Relief Coordinator needs to be made more effective.

Research to better establish the parameters of the resource/population balance issue deserves high priority. Ongoing official panels of eminent persons—doctors, demographers, scientists, agriculturalists, industrialists, economists, politicians, and others—should be promptly authorized by the General Assembly and appointed by the Secretary-General. They should be charged periodically with looking ahead 10, 20, and 30 years to forecast the impact of mounting population and resource shortages upon the life support systems of the earth: futurism is essential.

Nongovernmental organizations could be stimulated to intensify their study and research of resource/population matters. Every nation-state, too, needs encouragement to undertake futuristically oriented study and research.

A permanent international research body might be activated soon to serve as a clearinghouse for the research of UN agencies, nation-states, and NGOs. This function could well be undertaken by the Center for Economic and Development Research already proposed, since management of resource/population balance is intimately related to development and economic order. Should this prove unworkable, a similarly structured separate body could be established.

Events of the next decade will give the problems and hazards associated with resource/population balance greater visibility. We can expect price increases and scarcities, particularly of food, to reveal more clearly the finiteness of the world's resources. Controversies over access to resources and serious local, regional, or even global food/population imbalances will develop awareness of the problems and promote a global sense of responsibility.

There is need, however, to supplement such natural developments with human activities, for example, wide publicity stressing the seriousness of the matter and linking together food and other resources with population. The United Nations should, at an appropriate time, call a world conference dealing with resource/population balance. It might be styled a World Conference for Survival. Building upon available research findings, including reports of the panel of experts suggested above, the conference could emphasize the seriousness of the resource/population issue and propose programs of actions and machinery to deal with it.

Implementation of these early management steps is not likely to prove adequate. At some point, the world community will find it necessary to place common global interests above the currently perceived near-term interests of some nation-states. When this need becomes pressing, extranational or supranational authority will be required to (1) establish economic sanctions for application against nations that fail to achieve population stabilization and to conserve critical resources; (2) establish guidelines and procedures stimulating the development of resources and governing access to them; (3) create suitable tribunals, related to the International Court of Justice, to resolve the inevitable controversies arising among nations over resources.

So convinced am I of the seriousness of the resource/population issue that I believe it will all too soon dominate the affairs of nations, provided, of course, that nuclear warfare is avoided. The economic and social pressures arising from imbalances of resources and population will force change upon the world scene—change now considered anathema to sovereign states. The question is not *if*, but *when*, this will occur.

United States
Posture
     The posture of the United States on this critical world issue is basically not much different from that of most nation-states. The resource problem is not viewed especially seriously. The public has yet to accept the full reality of the energy crises. This attitude results, in part, from undue concentration upon current crises and near-term issues. Government officials are too busy dampening diplomatic fires and dealing with domestic problems to give adequate attention to the longer term questions.

In fairness to US leaders, they have indicated greater concern about the hazards of population growth than have the leaders of most nations. Our population growth rate is declining steadily. We are encouraging conservation and protection of the environment. Moreover, the current energy crisis finally is compelling attention to the supply and the conservation of one critical resource—petroleum. Yet, the US reaction remains nationalistic. We look to self-sufficiency, not global management of growing interdependence.

9 BIOSPHERE

Only within the last decade has the world community been reluctantly shocked into realization that the need for protection and enhancement of the environment is critical. Evidence is everywhere. Thor Heyerdahl encountered oil and flotsam as the Kon Tiki floated across the Atlantic Ocean; atomic radiation has been only partially checked by the 1963 Test Ban Treaty; Jacques Yves Cousteau has warned of the imminent dangers to marine life from chemicals, sewage, and wastes; recurring showers of airborne particles and gases cross national boundaries; transnational rivers, lakes, and seas are near death; and eminent scientists predict deleterious effects from pollutants on the earth's climate and life support capability. Astronauts' cameras have highlighted the earth as an isolated planetary village. People throughout the world have become alarmed.

What a change! From time immemorial the human race has placidly taken for granted the bounty of the earth's biosphere, including the oceans. For centuries mankind's use or abuse of the biosphere has had seemingly little impact upon its natural beauty or its rich resources. People assumed a healthy and pleasant physical environment as normal; nations presumed the oceans as theirs to use and exploit—a common heritage.

But modern civilization with its exploding populations, burgeoning cities, intensive agriculture, and booming industry has drastically reduced the harmony between the human race and the environment. Clearly, the problems of the biosphere have become a critical world issue.[1]

Until a decade or so ago, pollution of land, water, and air remained a local or, at most, a state or national problem. For a century

1. While outer space is also a common heritage, I am not treating it as a separate issue. Military aspects of outer space, including the banning of nuclear tests and antisatellite weapons and systems, are a part of the issue of peace and security.

or more, communities have abated as best they could the unhealthy and unsightly pollutives. London and Los Angeles have struggled with their smog, the United States and the Soviet Union with their Lake Eries and Lake Baikals, and Japan with its combination of hazardous air and sea pollution in the Tokyo-Yokohama area. Nations and their political subdivisions, by initiating research and establishing standards, have sought to control the rampant onslaught of pollution.

Only recently has management of ocean space, on the other hand, been recognized as a global problem, as the seas become polluted by the harmful by-products of modern industry, agriculture, and transportation. Competition for the resources of the seas and the seabeds have caused nations to stake out claims for ocean space. The historic doctrines of freedom of the seas and common heritage of ocean resources are no longer adequate for the problems created by technological, economic, and political change.

Several serious threats to the biosphere must be thwarted. *Hazards* Hazards immediately endangering human life and health include dangerous concentrations of noxious gases and precipitates; human, agricultural, and industrial wastes; and mercury, lead, DDT, and other toxic contaminants. These pollutants, released within one nation, often invade others and contaminate the atmosphere and the oceans. These substantial hazards are overshadowed by the ultimate pollutive threat of inadvertent, accidental, or deliberate release of lethal nuclear radiation from power plants, processing facilities, stored wastes, or weapons.

The life support capability of the biosphere is increasingly threatened. Misuse and mismanagement of land areas reduce their productive capacity. Soil erosion robs rich farmland, dumps harmful sediments into the seas and oceans, and wastes fresh water. Contamination hampers the food productivity of rivers, lakes, and oceans.

The possibility of upsetting the delicate chemical and thermal balances of the biosphere is less certain but more frightening. Disaster could follow disturbance of the atmospheric ozone layer which governs the earth's temperature. Rising temperatures from this source or from mounting quantities of heat emitted into the atmosphere because of the increasing consumption of energy could melt ice caps, raise ocean levels, alter weather cycles, and affect agriculture. Receding temperatures, on the other hand, could extend ice caps, shorten growing seasons, and reduce food supplies. The photosynthesis process whereby marine organisms and green plants produce the earth's vital supply of oxygen may be vulnerable to biospheric pollution. While scientists do not agree upon either the nature, certainty, or magnitude of such hazards, their potential threat is sufficient to justify extreme caution.

Quality of life is also at risk from environmental hazards. Potential diminution of resources—agricultural lands, timberlands, water supply, and marine life—through biosphere deterioration makes the achievement of suitable resource/population balance more uncertain and lowers the sustainable quality of life. Among potential losses are aesthetic, as well as physical, elements. As contact with nature becomes more difficult, as endangered species fail to receive protection, and as landmarks are ruthlessly destroyed, future generations lose a valuable heritage. And in man-made realms, disregard for aesthetic and natural elements in the planning of urban, suburban, and rural development increases ugliness and tensions.

Potential conflict between nations is a final environmental hazard. Competition will be increasingly keen for access to water, tillable land, and the living and mineral resources of the oceans. Serious threats, or actual use, of armed force may arise from failure to establish acceptable law for the seas with mechanisms to resolve controversy or from failure to establish, administer, and enforce controls over transnational pollution.

The Immediate Environment: Land, Air, Water

Where We Stand   The world community has accomplished a great deal in the relatively short time since proposals were first made to consider environment a critical world issue. Growing awareness of the problem is perhaps most significant. Facing real domestic threats has fostered broader environmental concern on the part of industrialized nations. Awareness has grown less dramatically, however, in the developing nations where only a few years ago a common response was that they had no serious environmental problems.

This attitude was clearly demonstrated at The Stanley Foundation's Sixth Conference on the United Nations of the Next Decade in Sinaia, Romania, June 1970, titled "Environmental Management in the Seventies." Participants from the less developed countries were critical of industrialized nations. Some argued that industrialized nations having heavily damaged the global environment, ought now to protect and repair it and bear the costs of doing so. Others dismissed pollution abatement proposals as nothing more than another move by the developed world to handicap the developing world's industrial growth.

The United Nations Conference on the Human Environment held in Stockholm in 1972 assembled 113 national delegations plus thousands of observers. Under the leadership of Maurice Strong of Canada, the preparatory committee's groundwork for the conference had been outstanding. Delegates came prepared to deal with the problems before them. The crowded two-week conference clearly established environmental protection as a critical world issue and set the stage for the United Nations Environmental Programme. Its success emphasizes the value of adequate preparation and the impact of dedicated, able, personal leadership; the mediocre results of some UN conferences, on the other hand, demonstrate the frequent absence of these two ingredients.

The Stockholm conference, including preparatory efforts, did much to encourage national leaders to recognize their real stake in the environment. Conference topics included problems of particular concern to the developing nations—human settlements, natural resources, wildlife, and others—as well as those more commonly associated with industrial nations. Developing as well as developed nations listed poverty, disease, and slums as elements of environmental concern. Many developing nations overcame their hesitation on environmental matters and joined wholeheartedly in the work of the Stockholm conference.

The conference drew the world's attention by adopting a precedent-setting document of principles. Its Declaration on the Human Environment includes the following statement:

> The protection and improvement of the human environment is a major issue which affects the well-being of peoples and economic development throughout the world; it is the urgent desire of the peoples of the whole world and the duty of all Governments.

The conference also produced an action plan of more than 100 items, including some for implementation by individual nations, by nations collectively, and by the United Nations and its various agencies.

The United Nations Environment Programme (UNEP) was established in 1972 by the 27th General Assembly upon the recommendation of the Stockholm conference. The agency, located in Nairobi,

Kenya, built up a staff of 300, including 100 professionals. It is financed by national pledges—over $107 million for 1973–1976. The United States pledged $40 million, and the remainder will be contributed by 68 other nations. Four-year expenditures (1973–1976) aggregate $69 million. Future funding is uncertain.

UNEP operates as a catalytic agent identifying prime environmental problems; inspiring nations, UN agencies, and regional organizations to undertake research or corrective programs; and providing initial funding and technical assistance. Through 1976 it had instigated 444 projects, using seed money to generate many times that amount in national or agency expenditures. The UNEP 58-member Governing Council has restructured the Stockholm action plan to deal with six priority areas: (1) human settlements and health; (2) land, water, and desertification; (3) trade, economics, and technology; (4) oceans; (5) wildlife and genetic resources; and (6) energy. UNEP also created a special adjunct to deal with human settlements leading to the World Conference on Human Settlements held in British Columbia in 1976. UNEP also arranged the 1977 UN Conference on Desertification.

Most nation-states are already dealing with some facets of environmental matters. Even the least developed find it necessary to cope with urban blight, water resources, sanitation, natural resources, and other elements affecting health. Industrial nations have found it necessary to force compliance with quality and emission standards for many pollutants, initiate programs to clean up rivers and lakes, protect scenic and historic areas from the onslaught of developers, and otherwise protect and enhance the environment.

Regional projects, approached best by joint action, are under way. The Soviet Union, East Germany, West Germany, Finland, Sweden, Norway, and Denmark have initiated discussions with a view toward establishing a Baltic Sea program. The preliminary Mediterranean conference of 18 nations—including such antagonists as the Arab countries and Israel, and Greece and Turkey—held at Barcelona in February 1976 established agreement for a joint program rehabilitating the badly polluted Mediterranean. Another regional effort is the first European Ministerial Conference on the Environment sponsored by the Council of Europe. Thus the wheels are turning slowly.

Abatement and Compliance   The objectives of world community management of the environment are simply stated. Systems need to be established and operated to abate pollution detrimental to the biosphere, prevent encroachment of one nation's pollutants upon others, and stimulate enhancement of the environment. The eventual goal is a steady state condition wherein the regenerative forces of nature, aided by man-made treatment facilities, are able to process pollutants and maintain an acceptable environment.

Only global effort can effectively and justly approach those environmental matters affecting the earth's biosphere as a whole, for example, the flow of harmful pollutants across national boundaries. This responsibility suggests three interrelated needs: research, standards, and enforcement.

Many pollutants harmful to human and animal life cycles have been detected; others are yet to be identified. Thus extensive research is needed to anticipate hazardous situations and to develop remedial alternatives, particularly regarding upsets of the biospheric balance. So rapid is the pace of technological change that its impact upon the environment is little understood. The few scientists willing to offer opinions about the complicated effects of pollution upon the biosphere are in substantial disagreement. Whose judgment is to prevail—the sponsors of the Concorde, for instance, or the scientists who urge caution lest the ozone layer be damaged? What restrictions upon ocean pollution are vital to avoiding damage to the photosynthesis process that maintains the biosphere's chemical balance? Because these matters are on the frontiers of current knowledge, a cautious course tilted toward safety without panic is called for.

Delineation of the world community's role in achieving environmental objectives and assuring compliance, however, is difficult. With few exceptions, the preventive or remedial actions must occur where pollution originates—mostly within nations.

World Community Role

Nevertheless, establishment of standards regarding environmental quality and pollutive emissions is a first appropriate function to be performed at the global level.

Both quality and emission standards are needed for environmental protection. Quality standards establish maximum allowable concentrations of specified pollutants, from whatever source, at specific locations; emission standards establish maximum discharges of specified pollutants from specific sources (i.e., power plants, manufacturing plants, etc.); discharge of certain pollutants may be banned completely. Quality standards are easier to establish but more difficult to enforce because the source may not be easily identified.

Certainly the world community must determine the permissive limits of pollution entering international waters and air space. These decisions dare not be left solely to chemical manufacturers, shippers, industrialists, or city officials who now use the biosphere as a cheap repository for wastes.

Secondly, global standards are needed to limit movement of pollution across national boundaries, limit certain pollutants, and ban others known or presumed to be hazardous. Even though discharges into the oceans may not threaten the balance of marine life, they may constitute hazards or nuisances to neighboring countries and to those bordering common water bodies. But the world community need not intrude upon nation-states when they are dealing with pollutants not exported to other countries or wasted into the oceans or the atmosphere. Nations may likewise decide on the disposal of solid wastes on national soil; they may deal with urbanization, preservation of natural resources, and the aesthetics of natural and man-made environment within their territory.

An ultimate major role for the world community is to achieve compliance with these established standards, partly through direct administration and enforcement of agreed regulations applicable to vessels and planes using air and ocean space, partly through the exercise of surveillance to determine violations—the earth watch approach—partly, also, through the provision of appropriate mechanisms for adjudication of controversies over environmental matters, and, if need be, for the application of sanctions or other enforcement measures.

As regards the preservation of endangered species, natural wonders, historic buildings, and structures of lasting value, nation-states should act with world community encouragement and assistance.

Management   Because UNEP has made a good start, it is a proper focus of near-term reform: UNEP should be strengthened and enlarged. It needs greater and more secure funding to continue its current activities and to fully implement an adequate earth watch (satellite observations and reports from a variety of sources).

Periodic worldwide environmental conferences similar to the one held at Stockholm are desirable to broaden awareness and understanding of environmental problems, publicize achievements, and set new objectives and priorities. These could be structured as separate conferences, rather than General Assembly special sessions, to afford greater access and participation by NGOs. Already the 1977 UN Water Conference dealt with one facet of environmental management and the 1977 UN Conference on Desertification with another.

Considerable research dealing with environmental matters is now carried on by UN agencies, national governments, universities, and NGOs. Nevertheless, as stated earlier, the effort should be enlarged and better coordinated. This need could be met by an international research organization perhaps called a World Environmental Research Institute (WERI). This institution should enlist the best minds of the world's scientific community and foster the participation and support of NGOs as well as nation-states and UN agencies. The United Nations, either directly or through UNEP, could charter and endorse the institute and encourage voluntary contributions from governments and the private sector.

The role of WERI would include advising and counseling UNEP and other UN bodies. To assure credibility, the institute would have to be tolerably insulated from political influence and have a highly qualified governing body and staff. It must have access to adequate laboratory and computer facilities.

A strengthened and enlarged UNEP, plus the proposed WERI, would be inadequate, however, for two longer range functions that must be managed on the global level: establishing pollution standards and enforcing them. It would be naive to expect favorable response from all nations to the research institute's findings or UNEP's proddings. Many will not, of their own volition, adequately and promptly limit pollutive emissions or take other essential steps. At some point—and the sooner the better—the world community needs procedures and institutions to set and enforce environmental standards.

Documented environmental law will undoubtedly prove necessary as a foundation for enforceable standards. The approach might well parallel that used in developing the law of the seas. First an ad hoc and then a continuing committee could be empowered by the General Assembly to prepare for a UN Conference on the Law of the Environment. UNEP, already studying environmental law, would work closely with the committees, perhaps serving as the secretariat for the committees and, subsequently, for the conference.

The conference, in contrast with that at Stockholm, would deal with the *legal* structure for environmental protection and enhancement rather than need and urgency. On its agenda, and included in subsequent international treaties, would be items concerning the environmental problems and methods of solution I have discussed so far. In addition, the treaty might specify types of sanctions to be employed against nations refusing or failing after due process to cease violations. Finally, the treaty would establish the mechanisms and institutions—preferably by delegation of greater authority to UNEP—to manage the global aspects of environmental protection and enhancement.

The world community simply cannot manage environmental problems and protect the biosphere's life support system for future generations with timid resolutions. Bold steps, such as those proposed, may be resisted initially by many nation-states. Logic, reinforced by mounting uncontrolled pollution, may overcome such resistance before too many points of irreversibility are passed.

Ocean Space

Accomplish-
ments   The urgency to establish laws governing the seas became evident in 1945 when the United States touched off a scramble to stake out seabed claims beyond territorial waters as President Truman proclaimed sovereignty over seabed resources—meaning petroleum—of the US continental shelf. This unilateral action stimulated the convening of the 1949 UN Conference on the Law of the Seas. Although the conference ended in deadlock, it signified world community recognition that management of ocean space was a global problem.

Within a few years, preparations began for another conference, the 1958 UN Conference on the Law of the Seas, which produced the Geneva Convention on the Continental Shelf, a less than satisfactory treaty. The treaty, among other things, gave coastal states rights to the natural resources—again meaning petroleum—of the continental shelf adjacent to their coasts "to a depth of 200 meters or beyond that limit to where the depth of the super adjacent waters admits to the exploitation of the natural resources of said areas." In other words, coastal states were able to claim what they could reach.

Efforts to rationalize ocean management remained dormant until 1967. Then, spurred by Malta's Ambassador Arvid Pardo's dramatic presentation to the General Assembly, the United Nations began to act. After an ad hoc committee looked into the peaceful uses of the oceans, a continuing UN Seabed Committee was authorized to begin preparations for a new Conference on the Law of the Seas. And in 1970 the General Assembly adopted a declaration of principles governing the seabed beyond the limits of national jurisdiction. The Seabed Arms Control Treaty prohibiting the placement of nuclear or other weapons of mass destruction upon the seabed and ocean floor entered into force in May 1972.

After extensive preparatory work, including research by NGOs, the Third UN Conference on the Law of the Seas convened in Caracas, Venezuela, in 1974 and, subsequently, has reconvened in Geneva or New York for several sessions.[2] A draft of a proposed convention—called an Informal Composite Negotiating Text—is well advanced, and according to some observers, agreement has been reached on perhaps 95 percent of its articles. Despite uncertainties over treaty provisions regarding the financial aspects of mining deep-sea nodules and the structure and voting arrangements of a proposed International Seabed Authority, it is hoped that a treaty may be ready for adoption soon.

Meanwhile, coastal states one after another have extended national sovereignty far beyond territorial waters. Many are claiming jurisdiction up to 200 miles from the coast and, in some cases, to the continental shelf beyond this distance. The United States did so in 1977 after several years of waiting for a treaty from the Conference on the Law of the Seas. Legislation unilaterally authorizing and governing mining of deep-sea nodules is pending in the US Congress. Through these actions the common heritage that Ambassador Pardo sought to protect for the common use of humanity has been greatly reduced in area.

Physical Management of Ocean Space

Because the ocean space is at once a biosystem, an economic resource, and a political entity, three sets of objectives are needed.

The physical objectives are relatively noncontroversial. A first priority is protecting the ocean's ecological system and restoring areas where serious damage occurs. Oceans must be kept clean. This function, vital to the longer range life-support capability of the biosphere, is the ocean facet of global environmental protection and enhancement. A second priority is the optimum exploitation of the living resources of the seas consistent with wise conservation measures. Seafood will become increasingly vital to resource/population balance. Conservation and regulatory measures are, therefore, needed now to enlarge living marine resources, limit catches, and facilitate marine farming. The third priority is to control exploitation of mineral resources of the seabeds so that neither the ecology of the seas nor the production of living resources is harmed sig-

2. As this book goes to press, the Eighth Session is convening in New York.

nificantly. The fourth is to regulate other uses of ocean space—including transoceanic cables, pipelines, oil drilling platforms, offshore airports, and marine ports—to protect its ecology and productivity.

Economic
Management

Objectives related to the economic aspects of ocean space are more complex and highly controversial. The question of who is to benefit from exploitation of ocean space resources is a major stumbling block to agreement in the current Conference on the Law of the Seas. Developed nations with major fishing fleets and the technology to mine the minerals of the deep sea or produce petroleum from seabed wells want to protect their advanced positions. Developing nations demand participation in the production, technology, personnel training, economic sharing, and decision-making. Producers of land-based copper, cobalt, nickel, and manganese fear that deep-sea mining would damage their economies by altering prices. Land-locked nations want guaranteed access to the seas and part of the take.

What reasonable economic objectives may be proposed in the face of these conflicting contentions? The soundest approach is the fundamental principle that ocean space beyond territorial waters (preferably 12 miles) belongs to the world community. Thus ocean space and the exploitation of its resources should be open to all under appropriate regulations and effective controls established by treaty and administered by a world organization. This concept ought to apply broadly while recognizing the reasonable rights and corresponding responsibilities accorded coastal states in adjacent "economic zones" (perhaps 200 miles offshore). The creation of economic zones now appears certain as a necessary compromise and will give the adjacent coastal states first priority to exploitation of resources in the zones. Procedures are needed, however, to assure that resources of economic zones are fully and efficiently developed.

Consistent with the philosophy of the common heritage, users of ocean space, including economic zones, ought to pay fair fees accruing to the benefit of the world community. Potential revenue sources include licensing fees, royalties, or profits from the exploitation of mineral or living resources; registration fees for vessels plying the seas and planes flying the international airways; and surcharges applied to communication services using ocean space or the skies above it.

The first allocation of revenues from these sources should finance the institutions charged with managing ocean space. The remainder of funds could be used to benefit the world community, landlocked as well as coastal states, developed as well as developing nations. Here is the grand opportunity to develop independent funding for recognized global needs. A strong case can be made that allocating directly to the United Nations some portion of revenues from the use and exploitation of ocean space will aid in lessening its dependence upon national contributions.

The controlling political objective in the area of ocean space management should be its preservation as a common heritage. Nation-state efforts to carve up the oceans and stake out claims to the seabed are unsound for two reasons, one pragmatic and the other philosophical. Pragmatically, piecemeal management of ocean space would be ineffective; its biosystems and ecosystems cannot be sub-divided. The same is true of the regulation of resource exploitation. Fragmented management of ocean space is destined to become a shambles and to foster controversy. *Political Management*

Retaining the common heritage principle is also sound philosophically. Ocean space and outer space are now the remaining areas beyond the jurisdiction of nation-states. Abandonment or appreciable reduction of this common heritage would be a backward step, further emphasizing national sovereignty at the very moment when global interdependence demands restricted national authority.

A second political objective concerns such uses of the oceans as navigation, overflight, and construction of any facilities beyond territorial waters. Regulation is required to avoid physical or environmental damage and promote safety. But the historic freedom of the seas ought to be maintained.

A final political objective is the minimization of opportunities for controversy. Particular attention in a treaty on ocean space will have to be placed on regulations and procedures within economic zones, mechanisms for the settlement of disputes, and enforcement measures.

The convention now under consideration by the Conference on the Law of the Seas will establish the basis for near-term management of ocean space; a basis less satisfactory than many desire but better than others fear. The probable provisions of the treaty, as revealed in current working drafts, fall far short of meeting the objectives I have suggested. But since coastal states claimed economic zones and blocked every move to restore the continental shelves as part of the *Law of the Seas Convention* common heritage, the final treaty may be as much as can be expected.

One section of the draft convention deals specifically with the seabeds, defined as the area beyond the economic zones. An International Seabed Authority is proposed to manage the research, exploration, and exploitation of mineral resources of the seabed. Its complex structure would include an Assembly; a Council; three commissions (Economic Planning, Technical, and Rules and Regulations); a Tribunal; and an Enterprise. The several organs of the Seabed Authority provide substantial checks and balances, but may prove unwieldy. The proposed function of the Seabed Authority is to produce seabed minerals either through contracts with private or national enterprises or through the operations of the Enterprise. Net proceeds, whether in cash or minerals, are intended to benefit member nations, particularly developing countries. The Tribunal would have mandatory jurisdiction over disputes regarding the Seabed Authority arising between states or their nationals. Currently, the Conference on the Law of the Seas is stalled on the provisions of the chapter dealing with the Seabed Authority.

The proposed convention deals separately with the rest of ocean space (the area not under the jurisdiction of the Seabed Authority), that is, the seabeds within economic zones and the high seas exclusive of the seabeds. Within the economic zones and upon the high seas, nation-states would remain supreme, subject only to the limitations of the convention. Coastal states would manage the living resources in the economic zones and the petroleum resources within economic zones and on continental shelves. The world community might benefit slightly from some small commission on petroleum resources developed beyond the 200-mile economic zone. Nations other than the adjacent coastal states would presumably have secondary access to living and mineral resources within economic zones that are not fully developed by the coastal states.

The proposed convention establishes regulations regarding navigation and environmental protection, but administration is left to the nation-states. No central organization is created to assure appropriate management.

Finally, the proposed convention establishes mandatory provisions for settlement of disputes, other than those arising in connection with the Seabed Authority. If disputes are not resolved by conciliation, the parties may choose one of four procedures for settlement: the Law of the Seas Tribunal, the International Court of

Justice, an arbitral tribunal, or special procedures provided in the treaty.

As the convention is proposed, it has two serious weaknesses. First, nation-states remain supreme in the management process except for the area under the jurisdiction of the Seabed Authority. Second, the convention legitimizes the takeover by coastal states of a major portion of the resources long considered part of a common heritage.

If the proposed Convention on the Law of the Seas comes into force, the world community is likely to relax, assuming the management of ocean space problems is fully under control. Unfortunately, this may not be so.

Toward Improved Ocean Management

Besides converting the outline of the Seabed Authority into a going concern, other matters which require attention include establishing global standards, particularly with respect to environmental protection; developing multilateral agreements regarding the conservation and exploitation of living resources; and minimizing controversies over secondary exploitation of resources within the economic zones.

The need to coordinate the varied activities of UN and other organizations concerned with facets of ocean space management will continue. The Food and Agriculture Organization (FAO) is concerned with food fish production. There is an International Whaling Commission (IWC), consisting of the United States, the Soviet Union, Japan, and Norway. The Intergovernmental Maritime Consultative Organization (IMCO) deals with technical shipping and navigational matters; its Marine Environmental Protection Committee establishes regulations regarding protection against oil spillage and dumping. The World Meteorological Organization (WMO) is concerned with atmospheric effects of the interaction of air and sea. UNESCO's International Ocean Commission (IOC) fosters ocean exploration and research. UNEP deals with environmental matters. The proposed convention appears an inadequate vehicle to achieve fully the necessary coordination of these activities.

Management of resources within economic zones by the coastal states is unlikely to prove adequate. Management of living resources in the high seas through multilateral agreements can prove very difficult. The result is likely to be inadequate conservation and development programs and less than optimal production of badly needed protein. By according secondary priorities for development of living and petroleum resources within economic zones, the convention invites delay and controversy. Coastal states reluctant to allow others to develop living resources will delay in handling applications, impose unreasonable conditions, and encourage appeals to tribunals likely overwhelmed with petitions for relief. Controversy will arise over petroleum production from the continental shelves when coastal states, perhaps reserving oil for the future, procrastinate in offshore drilling and make it difficult for others to exploit undeveloped resources. Divided management of environmental protection within the economic zone is bound to be uneven.

As demands for revenue to finance economic and social development and other global needs mount, a realization may grow that the world community, as a whole, fails to receive just rents for the use of the bounties of the common heritage within economic zones.

As an international organization capable of handling the management of ocean space, I propose an Ocean Management Authority (OMA) with adequate authority, even within economic zones, charged with many of the functions related to ocean space now handled by other world organizations. A second possibility would be to delegate authority over environmental matters in the whole of ocean space to UNEP. Thirdly, neighboring coastal states having similar situations with respect to living resources and environmental protection might form regional managing units for their common concerns.

Emerging Patterns in the Management of World Issues

Discussion of the management of ocean space should not be concluded without calling attention to certain new patterns regarding the management of critical world issues likely to emerge from the Third United Nations Conference on the Law of the Seas. Three such patterns seem worthy of emulation if the final draft of the Convention on the Law of the Seas follows the expected course.

The first relates to decision-making. Broadly shared dissatisfaction with the UN decision-making process is the principal reason the Law of the Seas Conference has proposed a new Seabed Authority. As a precondition of broad ratification of the proposed convention, compromise agreement upon a credible decision-making pattern must be reached by the various groups of nations. Interests represented include nations providing the technology and financing for exploitation of seabed minerals, land-based producers of the same minerals, consumers, landlocked nations, and nations concerned with the interests of the world community. Negotiations may develop some combination of allotment of membership in the decision-making body by interest groups, weighted voting, or the requirement of larger majorities on certain key issues.

The second emerging pattern concerns improved processes for resolving conflicts which may find other applications among nation-states and their nationals. Ratification of the Law of the Seas convention would commit nation-states not only to peaceful resolution of controversy but also to acceptance of compulsory jurisdiction. Conflicts arising in connection with the seabeds would be taken to the Tribunal of the Seabed Authority by either party. Controversies arising over environmental or navigational issues or economic matters within the economic zones would require the parties to choose one of four methods of settlement. In any case, decisions would be final and members would be committed to enforce them upon their nationals. These processes, should the convention come into force, constitute a significant forward step toward the rule of law.

The Convention on the Law of the Seas makes a third contribution by establishing the principle of creating revenue for global use independent of assessments or voluntary contributions paid by nation-states. According to the convention, funds generated by the Seabed Authority through the exploitation of seabed mineral resources would be available, first, to cover its operating costs and, next, for distribution presumably to finance economic and social development. Even though these funds be only token amounts, this pattern sets an important precedent for future financing of global needs.

The United States has in recent years provided strong leadership in biospheric matters. Our awareness of the problems in these areas has been sharpened by our domestic environmental concerns and by our economic interest in the optimization of both living and mineral resources of ocean space. Our advanced technology pertaining to pollution abatement, offshore oil exploration, and seabed mining contributes to our understanding of the urgency of dealing with environmental and ocean space matters. *United States Posture*

The United States gave moral and technical support to the preparations for and the conduct of the Stockholm Conference on the Human Environment. Subsequently, we have made major commitments to the financing of UNEP.

The United States has also given strong support to the Third UN Conference on the Law of the Seas. Our action extending national jurisdiction to 200 miles was taken somewhat reluctantly, long after many other nations had made such claims. Proposed legislation regarding unilateral mining of deep-sea nodules by US nationals has been delayed pending the outcome of the Conference on the Law of the Seas. Within the conference we have taken a strong position in opposition to that of Third World nations regarding the Seabed Authority. We have insisted upon workable procedures permitting early nodule mining by private enterprise.

Our leadership in environmental and ocean space matters can be faulted only for reluctance to urge stronger world organization to deal with these problems. We have found it too easy to go along with other states in the extension of national control over economic zones, with consequent deprivation of world community interest in the common heritage.

10 HUMAN RIGHTS

There are sound reasons to discuss human rights only after considering the other critical world issues. Enlarging human rights and fundamental freedoms for more people on this earth depends in part upon successful management of other global problems by the world community. Moreover, the status of human rights throughout the world is a yardstick for how well other critical issues are managed. The extent to which people enjoy human rights and fundamental freedoms is related directly to the policies and actions of national governments which, in the eyes of most of the world, exist to serve the needs of their constituents. Governments rise or fall, albeit slowly at times, according to the way they meet vital human needs and enable their citizens to live with dignity. Ideologies and philosophies gain or lose adherents according to how they relate to actual or perceived human needs. Economic systems remain viable only so long as people believe they are well served. Many believe that religions remain relevant only as they respond to human concerns. Human rights and fundamental freedoms are the cornerstone of civilization, the alpha and omega of humanity's quest for a better existence.

Many concepts of human rights are more philosophic than pragmatic, more general than specific. From Aristotle, St. Augustine, and Mencius to present-day philosophers and religious leaders, rights and freedoms have been the subject of extensive thought. It can be helpful to recall the three main types.

What Are Rights and Freedoms?

Fundamental, at least in Western eyes, are the political and civil rights that evolve in open societies. Freedoms of worship, speech, assembly, and movement, plus rights of privacy, dignity, property ownership, and the right to be different fall within this group.

A second type relates to economic and social matters such as employment, food, shelter, health care, and education. These rights quite naturally have great appeal to developing nations, and con-

troversy rages over their attainment. Should governments be obligated to care for all? Or is it their duty to provide for those who
cannot provide for themselves and to assure the rest the opportunity
for education, employment, work, earning, and saving?

A third category of rights has emerged with the growing destructive power of modern weapons, the increasing impact of war upon
civilians far from battle lines, and the persistence of violence. Freedom from the fear, insecurity, and trauma of war, terrorism, and
barbarism is increasingly viewed as a basic human right.

National constitutions generally recognize the freedom, security,
and welfare of their citizens as the justification for existence of
governments. Many constitutions—often patterned after the US
Constitution—contain language equivalent to "we, the people";
"inalienable rights"; or "life, liberty, and the pursuit of happiness."
Thus the worth of the individual is an acceptable rationale for
national governments, even those that trample upon human rights.

The doctrine of human rights and fundamental freedoms is neatly
capsulized in the Golden Rule. This simple, but powerful, statement of human relations has its equivalent in many cultures.
Taoism, Confucianism, Buddhism, Islam, Judaism, as well as
Christianity, all state that one should not hurt others, but instead
treat them with the same love and respect desired for oneself. Were
the Golden Rule to prevail in human conduct, enhancement of
human rights would not be an issue.

The
Development
of Rights to
1948

The struggle to enlarge the freedoms and rights of people began
long ago. The deprived, the enslaved, and the persecuted have clam-
ored and schemed to gain some measure of justice and dignity, if
not of equality. Minorities—whether of race, sex, color, language,
creed, culture, or economic and social standing—suffering injustices
imposed by governing establishments have sought, and often fought
for, fair and humane treatment. Although demagogues have used
and abused human rights issues to further their political fortunes,
enlightened leaders have acclaimed the importance of human rights,
and many have made sincere efforts to expand them.

While progress has been frustratingly slow, as viewed by
present-day enthusiasts, numerous gains have been made. Mile-
stones have been passed along this rugged path: Athenian democracy
and Roman law established certain rights for some, but not all,
constituents; the Magna Charta of 1215 restricted the sovereign
power of King John of England; the sixteenth century Reformation
enlarged individual freedoms in religious matters; the Bill of Rights

was adopted in England in the seventeenth century and the French Declaration of the Rights of Man in 1789; the US Declaration of Independence created unprecedented expectations and led to the US Bill of Rights constitutional amendments of 1791; the near abolition of slavery in the world was accelerated by the US Emancipation Proclamation and the subsequent Civil War (1861–1865); and the 1878 Treaty of Berlin obligated Turkey and the Balkan countries to refrain from discrimination against religious minorities.

These and other events, however significant, were limited for the most part to one nation, culture, or region, and they occurred mostly in the Western world. Human rights progress in other parts of the world has been less formal.

Global concern for human rights is of recent origin. The Council of the League of Nations (1918) was given the responsibility to administer certain provisions of World War I peace treaties protecting the rights of racial, religious, and linguistic refugees and minorities. Thus some few principles of humanitarian intervention were institutionalized by the League of Nations. Beyond this, however, the League had little involvement with human rights, and its covenant did not mention them.

The Atlantic Charter, proclaimed in August 1941, by President Roosevelt and Prime Minister Churchill, established guarantees of human rights as an objective of the World War II allies. It called for "assurance that all may live out their lives in freedom from fear and want" and "traverse the high seas and oceans without hindrance." It further demanded "the abandonment of the use of force."

It remained for the United Nations after World War II to make the quest for human rights a truly global one. The UN Charter provides the foundation for a global approach to human rights:

. . . to reaffirm faith in fundamental human rights, in the dignity and worth of the human person, in the equal rights of men and women of all nations, large and small. [Preamble]

. . . to achieve international cooperation in solving international problems of economic, social, cultural, or humanitarian character, and in promoting and encouraging respect for human rights and for fundamental freedoms for all without distinction as to race, sex, language, or religion. [Article 1]

The United Nations lost no time in dealing with human rights. *Global* The 3rd General Assembly (1948) adopted and proclaimed a Univer- *Standards* sal Declaration of Human Rights submitted by the UN Commission on Human Rights chaired by Eleanor Roosevelt. The several articles cover a wide range of basic human rights and fundamental freedoms, as developed in the Western world. Article 29 imposes duties and restrictions upon those enjoying rights and freedoms—a proper recognition that individual duties and responsibilities go hand in hand with personal rights and privileges. The declaration sets:

> . . . a common standard of achievement for all peoples and all nations, to the end that every individual and every organ of society, keeping this Declaration constantly in mind, shall strive by teaching and education to promote respect for these rights and freedoms and by progressive measures, national and international, to secure their universal and effective recognition and observance, both among the peoples of Member States themselves and among the peoples of territories under their jurisdiction.

As a lofty statement of human rights objectives, the Declaration of Human Rights set the stage for General Assembly adoption of a long list of covenants, protocols, and conventions. Those of primary interest are listed in table 1, along with the status of US ratification.

Table 1

SELECTED UNITED NATIONS TREATIES
CONCERNING HUMAN RIGHTS

Treaty	Year in Force	Number Ratifying[a]	US Status[b]
Convention on the Prevention and Punishment of the Crime of Genocide	1951	82	Signed but not ratified
Convention for the Suppression of the Traffic in Persons and of the Exploitation of the Prostitution of Others	1951	45	Not party
Protocol Amending the Slavery Convention	1953	44	Ratified
Convention Relating to the Status of Refugees	1954	69	Not party
Convention on the Political Rights of Women	1954	84	Not party
Slavery Convention of 25 September 1926 as Amended	1955	31	Signed but not ratified
Supplementary Convention on the Abolition of Slavery, the Slave Trade, Institutions and Practices Similar to Slavery	1957	90	Ratified
Convention on the Nationality of Married Women	1958	52	Not party

Treaty	Year in Force	Number Rati- fying[a]	US Status[b]
Convention Relating to the Status of Stateless Persons	1960	33	Not party
Convention on the International Right of Correction	1962	10	Not party
Convention on Consent on Marriage, Mini- mum Age for Marriage, and Registration of Marriages	1964	29	Signed but not ratified
Convention on the Elimination of All Forms of Racial Discrimination	1969	97	Signed but not ratified
Convention on the Non-Applicability of Statutory Limitations to War Crimes and Crimes Against Humanity	1970	21	Not party
Convention on the Reduction of Statelessness	1975	9	Not party
International Covenant on Economic, Social and Cultural Rights	1976	46	Signed but not ratified
International Covenant on Civil and Political Rights	1976	44	Signed but not ratified
Optional Protocol on Complaints from Individuals	1976	16	Not party

a. As of December 31, 1977.

b. United States signature on an international treaty or convention indicates that the Department of State agreed to it when it was before the UN General Assembly. Ratification indicates approval by the US Senate, at which time the agreement is binding.

Sources: United Nations, *Multilateral Treaties in Respect of Which the Secre- tary-General Performs Depository Functions*, New York, 1978; US Depart- ment of State, *Bulletin*, Washington, D.C., April 1978.

In addition to the initiatives taken by the UN General Assembly, several other international organizations have made important con- tributions to human rights standards. The European Convention on Human Rights and affiliated protocols have established workable procedures and precedents. The United Nations Educational, Scien- tific and Cultural Organization has instituted conventions against discrimination in education. Member states of the International Labor Organization have agreed on a number of labor practices, including the right to organize and bargain, the abolition of slavery, and the establishment of equal remuneration for equal work. Members of the Organization of American States, as far back as the early 1900s, have been parties to agreements on such matters as asylum, the rights of aliens, and the nationality of women.

Hence many human rights standards have been established and some have been observed. Unfortunately, some basic instruments, such as the recent Draft Declaration on the Right of Asylum, have been drafted but are not in force. United States reluctance to ratify many of the treaties already in force is not only frustrating but a hindrance to the advancement of human rights.

United Nations Activities

Beyond establishing standards, the United Nations has sought to expand the observance of human rights in several ways. Organizations have been established to deal with human rights matters; nation-states periodically report on the status of human rights in their countries; attention is occasionally focused upon human rights; some flagrant violations have been investigated; and, less frequently, violators have been censured.

Article 13 of the Charter lodges primary responsibility for human rights matters with the General Assembly.

The General Assembly shall initiate studies and make recommendations for the purpose of . . . assisting in the realization of human rights and fundamental freedoms for all without distinction as to race, sex, language, or religion.

Accordingly, annual agendas contain numerous items concerned in whole or in part with this subject. Some of the proposals reaching the General Assembly come through the overloaded Third Committee which handles human rights in addition to social and cultural matters inevitably interlinked with development matters. The General Assembly has created several organizational units to address specific human rights problems including:

SPECIAL COMMITTEE AGAINST APARTHEID—18 member states organized in 1962 and renamed in 1970; to review and report on South Africa's racial policies

UNITED NATIONS TRUST FUND FOR SOUTH AFRICA—authorized in 1965 with five trustees appointed by member states; to assist persons persecuted for their opposition to apartheid

SPECIAL COMMISSION TO INVESTIGATE ISRAELI PRACTICES AF-
FECTING THE HUMAN RIGHTS OF THE POPULATION OF THE OC-
CUPIED TERRITORIES—created in 1968 and composed of three
member states reporting annually to the General Assembly

COMMITTEE ON THE ELIMINATION OF RACIAL DISCRIMINA-
TION—organized in 1969 with 18 experts elected by states but
serving as individuals; to report annually and make recommendations based upon its examination of the reports provided by states

GROUP OF EXPERTS ON THE DRAFT CONVENTION OF TERRI-
TORIAL ASYLUM—established in 1974 with individuals from 26
nations; to review the text of proposed conventions

Additionally, several commissions, agencies, or working groups
have been established to deal with refugee problems principally in
the Middle East.

The Economic and Social Council (ECOSOC), too, deals with
human rights matters. Article 62 of the Charter states that ECOSOC:
. . . may make recommendations for the purpose of promoting
respect for, and observance of, human rights and fundamental
freedoms for all.

ECOSOC's power to draft conventions for submission to the General
Assembly and to call international conferences thus extends to questions of human rights.

In 1946 ECOSOC established the Human Rights Commission
(32 member states) to prepare studies, reports, and recommendations. This role was performed well in early years. The commission
ruled in 1947, however, that it lacked the power to take action on
human rights complaints. In recent years the commission has moved
away from complete noninvolvement toward limited involvement in
specific violations, in particular cases arising in South Africa, Israel,
Chile, and, more recently, Uganda and Cambodia. But political bias
tends to undermine the commission's ability to deal effectively with
many barbaric violations of rights and fundamental freedoms.

The Subcommission on Prevention of Discrimination and Protection of Minorities (26 individuals appointed by member states) was
established by the Human Rights Commission in 1946. It is
charged to study and make recommendations regarding prevention
of discrimination against racial, national, religious, or linguistic
minorities. This subcommission functions largely through a working group of 5 persons, reporting in turn to the subcommission.

ECOSOC also established the Commission on the Status of Women in 1946. This commission of 21 members is directed to prepare recommendations and reports to ECOSOC on the promotion of women's rights in political, economic, civil, social, and educational fields. A number of conventions dealing with progressive women's rights have been developed.

Most UN agencies claim some contribution to the quest for human rights through their economic and social development activities. Most of these contributions are indirect. Between 1930 and 1958, the International Labor Organization adopted several conventions in the field of labor relations. Nations which have ratified them report upon the application of these conventions within their countries. Five ILO organs involved in investigating and enforcing these agreements contribute to UN knowledge and impact on the subject and set some interesting precedents on national reporting.

UNESCO, too, makes some direct contribution to human rights. Its purpose, as defined in its constitution, is:

. . . to contribute to peace and security by promoting collaboration among the nations through education, science, and culture in order to further universal respect for justice, rule of law, human rights, and fundamental freedom for all.

The 1949 Geneva Conventions also contributed to the accumulation of human rights agreements. Four documents concerning wartime treatment of wounded, sick, and imprisoned armed forces members were adopted.

The United Nations, through the General Assembly and certain agencies, periodically focuses worldwide attention upon various facets of human rights through conferences and special programs. The 1968 Tehran International Conference on Human Rights highlighted the international year for human rights with its Proclamation of Tehran. The 1975 International Women's Year Conference in Mexico City produced the Declaration of Mexico emphasizing the need to extend human rights to all women. A Decade for Women and Development to last until 1985 was endorsed, and a World Plan of Action was projected for the ten-year period. The 1973–1983 Decade for Action Against Racism, highlighted by the 1978 World Conference to Combat Racism and Racial Discrimination, is an effort to focus attention upon another area of human rights.

On a number of occasions, the United Nations has identified and publicized alleged flagrant violations of human rights. General Assembly resolutions have censured offending nations, particularly in southern African situations where independence has not been achieved and apartheid prevails. Economic sanctions were imposed against Rhodesia in 1971. The 29th General Assembly took the drastic step of ousting South Africa. The same Assembly sought to rebuke Israel and its supporters for the festering Palestinian situation by according Yassir Arafat of the Palestinian Liberation Organization rights generally reserved for heads of state. While the frustrations provoking such official actions are understandable, they do reflect political bias.

Many observers and a number of governments, while endorsing the several UN human rights roles, are increasingly disturbed by their imbalance. Attention is given properly to discrimination in southern African countries and injustices to Palestinians. But numerous deprivations of human rights in communist states, some independent African nations, and dictatorships elsewhere are largely ignored. Hence there is a need for more balanced investigation, concern, and action regarding human rights violations (including political harassment, genocide, torture, forced labor, and terrorism) wherever they occur.

Significant human rights progress has been made in Europe. Eighteen Western European nations in 1949 formed the Council of Europe. This led to the 1950 adoption of the European Convention on Human Rights and Fundamental Freedoms (only France and Switzerland have not yet ratified) and the subsequent creation of the European Court of Human Rights and the European Human Rights Commission. These units, together with the Consultative Assembly (the council's deliberative body) constitute the infrastructure for ongoing attention to human rights. *Regional Activities*

This European system incorporates several advanced means of protecting and enhancing human rights. The convention provides the right of individual petition (now recognized by 11 of the 16 ratifying nations), an obligatory mechanism to deal with state versus state controversies, and a means to transfer to the Court of Human Rights those matters the commission is unable to resolve. Judgments of the court are binding. The commission, through its secretary-general, is charged with fact-finding, and its Committee of Ministers has adjudicatory authority.

This system has handled thousands of petitions, mostly intrastate but some transnational. Several member states have permitted the commission to investigate internal affairs. Although the European system has weaknesses, observers generally consider it to be the best yet initiated on an international basis. They note also that it has had an important impact on internal legal systems of member states.

Between 1948 and 1954 the OAS adopted several human rights conventions concerning aliens, naturalized citizens, asylum, and nationality of women. In 1959 and 1960 OAS again turned to the subject. The Inter-American Commission on Human Rights was established and, finally, in 1969 a Convention on Human Rights was adopted with but two reservations. The commission makes recommendations, requests reports from governments, and acts upon complaints on violations of the convention. The statute of the commission has been interpreted to permit examination of petitions from individuals. An Inter-American Court acts upon cases submitted by the commission or by states. Judgments are final. If noncompliance prevails, the case goes to the OAS General Assembly for political decision. The International Conference of American States (not the same as OAS) in 1948 adopted conventions regarding political and civil rights of women.

The Organization of African Unity in 1969 adopted its first human rights convention pertaining to refugees. It is not yet in force. The League of Arab States established a Commission of Human Rights in 1970. A Council of Asia and the Pacific to deal with human rights has been proposed.

The regional approach to the management of human rights matters has promise. One of its advantages is the greater ease of gaining agreement on fundamental concepts due to fewer cultural diversities and the presence of certain unifying forces. Regional organizations do not inject political issues into human rights matters as readily as the United Nations, ECOSOC, and the Commission on Human Rights. Progress toward human rights and fundamental freedoms may come more rapidly through regional units than through the United Nations.

Appraisal: Obstacles to Progress   High tribute is due the United Nations and regional organizations for their accomplishments in establishing global standards. The world community should be grateful for the many dedicated representatives of member states who have guided these international efforts. Through their persistence, after centuries of slow and scattered initiatives, important first steps have been taken. The Universal Declaration of Human Rights, regional declarations, and related conventions speak for the conscience of all people.

Despite these important beginnings, human rights and fundamental freedoms are widely disregarded in most parts of the world.
Fewer people have basic freedoms now than ten to twenty years ago.
Many countries have slipped back, including a number that achieved
independence since World War II and older, tolerably democratic,
and open societies.

According to a 1976 Freedom House survey, only 57 of 158
nations could be considered free societies in terms of political and
civil rights. The fundamentals of liberal democratic structure were
absent in some 100 countries. Since 1970 the Human Rights Commission has received over 100,000 complaints from individuals and
organizations about alleged violations of human rights throughout
the world. Amnesty International has repeatedly reported on the
treatment of political prisoners in a number of countries, Chile
being the latest. Massacres have come to world attention: Indonesia
(1965), Burundi (1972), Equatorial Guinea (1972), Bangladesh
(1971), Ethiopia (1974), Cambodia (1975), and Uganda (1976), to
mention a few. Terrorism and other forms of violence are increasingly inflicted upon bystanders and uninvolved people. Harassment
of dissidents in the Soviet Union and other countries is frequently
reported by news media. While a number of nations have been cited
for massive violations, very few others are entitled to outstanding
commendation for efforts to enhance the dignity and worth of all of
their constituents.

Only 17 of the principal UN initiated conventions (table 1) are
now in force; others languish in the pigeonholes of national governments awaiting ratification. Attempts since 1965 to strengthen the
capability of the United Nations to deal with human rights by
naming a high commissioner for human rights have been repeatedly
thwarted by opponents who consider it an invasion of national
sovereignty. Attempts by the United Nations to adopt and place in
force declarations or conventions on matters of current urgency, such
as asylum and terrorism, have failed. The Human Rights Commission's Subcommission on Prevention of Discrimination and Protection of Minorities has yet to demonstrate an effective, evenhanded
approach. Both the highly touted Decade Against Racial Discrimination and the 1978 UN Conference to Combat Racism have suf-
fered setbacks because of the votes of a bloc of nonaligned countries
in the General Assembly and at the conference equating Zionism to
racism.

Obviously, a wide gap remains between the high principles of the

Universal Declaration of Human Rights and subsequent conventions and the current practices of many nation-states. Why have so few nations ratified the conventions and even fewer observed them? Why are human rights so widely ignored?

Undoubtedly, the strong reluctance of many nation-states to accept any encroachment on national sovereignty is a major obstacle to the extension of human rights and fundamental freedoms. This is also the principal obstacle impeding most world community efforts. The normal desire to protect national sovereignty is usually reinforced by a determination to avoid the focus of public attention. The Soviet Union, though obviously mindful of the tyrannies of the Stalin regime and prevailing harsh treatment of dissidents, has opposed UN activities in this field from the beginning.

Coups and other nondemocratic changes of government in many countries have been accompanied by political imprisonment, torture, and, in some cases, massacre. But repugnant violations are not limited to precipitous government turnovers; they are all too often practiced by dictatorial governments determined to suppress dissenters and opponents. The nations involved in such practices constitute an informal, unpublicized bloc working behind the scenes to stifle enlarged UN human rights activities. Exceptions may be made when it seems politically expedient to investigate the actions of unpopular governments: apartheid in South Africa, treatment of Arabs in Israel, and treatment of political prisoners in Chile.

Other less insidious factors also impede progress, including differing concepts of the nature of human rights and fundamental freedoms, dominating impacts of international and domestic matters upon national priorities, and inertia and resistance to change.

The Universal Declaration of Human Rights and the various covenants subsequently adopted by the UN General Assembly document Western concepts of human rights and fundamental freedoms. The same is true of the declarations and covenants adopted by the European and Latin American regional organizations. This is not surprising, because recent human rights progress has occurred largely in the Western world, and the General Assembly that made modern human rights history was controlled by Western democracies. When the Universal Declaration was adopted, only two— India and the Philippines—of its 58 members were newly independent nations. Under these circumstances, both the declaration and subsequent covenants placed emphasis upon civil liberties, personal security, privacy, and other freedoms as practiced generally in the

Western world. The Soviet Union, committed to a different concept of people's relationship to the state, abstained and influenced its allies in Eastern Europe to do the same.

As UN membership more than doubled through the admission of numerous newly independent former colonies, the strong base of shared human rights concepts was severely weakened. The leaders of these new nations, influenced by diverse cultures, ideologies, and economic situations, tend to view human rights from perspectives which are different from those of Western Europe and the United States. Key words—rights, freedoms, dignity, justice, liberty, privacy, security, and quality of life—are interpreted differently; this is a basic problem of human rights agreements. Leaders of new nations are prone to view independence, self-determination, nonintervention, and economic progress as fundamental freedoms. Eradication of the last vestiges of colonialism and blatant racial discrimination in southern Africa, together with achievement of higher living standards, are viewed as prerequisites to civil and political rights. The new nations also view greater participation in international decision-making as an important human right. Many are quite willing to tolerate terrorism as a means to self-determination. Freedoms of speech, assembly, movement, political action, and privacy seem secondary. Undoubtedly, these differences in perception contribute to the world community's abysmal failure to strengthen and enhance human rights and fundamental freedoms. Despite some validity, these perceptions are overemphasized; they are somewhat reminiscent of the excuses kings and dictators have always used to deny freedoms to their people.

Another factor hindering progress is the paralyzing impact of pressures and exigencies arising from international and domestic problems. Today's emphasis upon national security encroaches upon personal freedoms. Defense preparations inevitably restrict freedoms; war itself becomes the ultimate human indignity. National leaders, struggling with serious economic and development problems, find it difficult to attend to sophisticated rights and freedoms. Some have no time to look much beyond survival. Political instability within nations is likewise distracting; governments which concentrate upon staying in power often limit human freedoms.

Inertia and resistance to change handicap the enhancement of human rights in most countries. Established governments take for granted placid endurance on the part of their constituents for the long-standing patterns and traditions. Leaders of dictatorships—

whether military or civilian, of the right or of the left—feel threatened by Western-type freedoms and civil rights. Bolstered by concern for personal safety, inertia is common even among those most deprived of fundamental rights and freedoms.

While human rights progress around the world appears bleak to most Western observers, the overall situation should be kept in perspective. Human rights is now a global concern. A challenging declaration has been adopted, experiments in international oversight have been initiated, and an ongoing dialogue has been started. Nation-states are increasingly compelled to justify their failures. These are vitally important beginnings for the enormous and difficult task lying ahead.

What Roles for the United Nations?   The burden of responsibility to extend human rights and fundamental freedoms rests primarily upon nation-states. The United Nations and regional systems may propose, adopt, and advocate, but they lack authority to compel member states to ratify or enforce covenants. However deplorable, this is a fact of current international life. Hence the propriety of the following words from the 1968 Proclamation of Tehran:

> It is imperative that the members of the international community fulfill their solemn obligation to promote and encourage respect for human rights and fundamental freedoms.

How then can the international community aid the conversion of high aspirations to workable precepts and enforceable practices reaching 4 billion people in more than 150 nations?

Both the direct and indirect avenues now open should be pursued. The indirect approach, stated simply, is better management of other critical world issues. The direct approach calls for continuing, but intensifying, established UN and regional human rights activities, strengthening mechanisms to deal with them, and implementing new programs. The United Nations can properly have impact in the following areas: (1) encouraging nations to ratify, promote, and enforce existing human rights conventions; (2) establishing additional standards for human rights and fundamental freedoms and focusing world attention upon human rights matters; and (3) monitoring human rights progress, investigating violations and complaints and recommending remedial action, and censuring nations committing or permitting gross violations of established standards of human rights.

The world community should also provide mechanisms for peti-

tion, asylum, relief, and equitable treatment for individuals al-
legedly deprived of rights, and establish peaceful procedures to deal
fairly with massive violations of human rights affecting minority or
political groups. These difficult roles will more likely be played in
the longer range.

Human rights matters need stronger emphasis and greater visibility. To accomplish this, the United Nations should rank human
rights matters as equals with peace and security and with economic
and social development.

*New
Approaches:
A Human
Rights
Council*

First, and most importantly, a Human Rights Council (HURCO)
patterned after ECOSOC could be established and assume those
human rights responsibilities now assigned to ECOSOC. Its functions and powers, paralleling Article 62 of the UN Charter, might
be stated as follows:

1. The Human Rights Council shall make or initiate studies and
   reports with respect to human rights, fundamental freedoms,
   and related matters and shall make recommendations with
   respect to such matters to the General Assembly, to the members of the United Nations, and to the specialized agencies
   concerned.
2. The Council shall make recommendations for the purpose of
   promoting respect for, and observance of, human rights and
   fundamental freedoms for all.
3. It shall prepare draft conventions for submission to the General Assembly with respect to all matters falling within its
   competence.
4. It shall call, in accordance with the rules prescribed by the
   United Nations, international conferences on matters falling
   within its competence.

Such a council, replacing the present Human Rights Commission
and perhaps of the same size, would, by its very nature, elevate the
stature and visibility of human rights matters. A by-product would
be removal of these matters from an already overburdened and unwieldy ECOSOC, where human rights now compete for attention
with economic and social development.

Creating the Human Rights Council could be achieved by trans-
forming the existing Trusteeship Council now nearing the end of its
mission. In any event, a new HURCO requires amending the UN
Charter, a move likely to be strongly opposed. But an interim step,
not requiring Charter change, would produce many of the suggested

benefits. The Human Rights Commission, instead of being phased out, could be transferred from ECOSOC to the General Assembly with a status similar to such agencies as the United Nations Industrial Development Organization or the United Nations Environment Programme.

With either HURCO or the transfer of the Human Rights Commission to the General Assembly, two other structural changes would strengthen the management of human rights matters. One would transfer social and cultural items from the Third Committee of the General Assembly to the Second Committee, thus allowing the Third Committee to concentrate upon human rights matters. All ECOSOC matters would then flow to the General Assembly through the Second Committee and human rights matters through the Third Committee.

Establishing within the Secretariat a deputy secretary-general for human rights would be a second desirable change. All functions and staff now related to human rights matters, including the staff of the Human Rights Commission, could come under this deputy's administration. This proposed structure is similar to that proposed in chapter 7 for development matters. From an organizational point of view, it is sounder than the establishment of a high commissioner for human rights.

With or without these basic organizational changes, the following near-term steps would help the United Nations fulfill its role:

1. Convening the Human Rights Commission more frequently
2. Assuring greater independence for experts on subcommissions and working groups
3. Establishing procedures to allow and encourage non-governmental organization (NGO) and individual input on alleged violations
4. Establishing a subcommission to continuously review and update conventions and standards
5. Investigating more thoroughly all alleged violations rather than only those having political overtones
6. Advising the General Assembly annually of the violations investigated and disposition made in each case
7. Periodically reviewing progress made by nation-states in remedying situations referred to them by the commission (or council)

It must be recognized, however, that such measures fall far short of what is needed. The world community's impact upon enhancement of human rights would still be minimal. Human rights and fundamental freedoms would remain a national prerogative closely guarded behind bulwarks of national sovereignty.

Looking farther ahead, effective management of human rights and fundamental freedoms calls for global and regional mechanisms and procedures permitting the world community to discharge longer range roles regarding equitable treatment of individuals and massive violations of rights.

The European Human Rights Commission and Court of Human Rights have pioneered the way. The European system provides for (1) developing a treaty establishing the principles to be applied; (2) establishing mechanisms to facilitate asylum, petition, investigation, and temporary protection; (3) establishing procedures for obtaining warranted relief through consultation with the government involved; and (4) providing tribunals for justly resolving appeals that are not satisfactorily handled by consultation. Such regional mechanisms may continue to be desirable, but global management should be attempted as well. Certainly principles should be developed on a worldwide basis.

Establishing peaceful procedures to deal fairly with gross, massive violations of human rights affecting minorities or political groups will be even more difficult. This calls for world community intervention into national affairs, a concept now unthinkable in the minds of valiant protectors of national sovereignty. Intervention or sanctions of some sort are needed, however, unless we are willing to tolerate more cases of genocide, continued torture of political prisoners, and harassment of disfavored groups.

For the world community to be effective in cases of large-scale rights violations, the following steps are necessary: (1) establishing the basic principles to be applied; (2) expanding the United Nations as a focal point for information and intelligence on violations to enable it to handle petitions from minority or disfavored groups, NGOs, or individuals; (3) adapting its procedures for prompt, unbiased investigation to take into account national sensitivities; (4) utilizing the prestige of the General Assembly and/or the Security Council through censure or negotiation to encourage the nation-state to correct the situation; and (5) developing mechanisms for physical intervention or sanctions when censure, consultation, and negotiations fail. Intervention of such nature is not unrelated to that required in the longer range for the world community to carry out its peace and security roles. It is comparable to the police function practiced in certain nations to protect citizens from harassment.

While human rights and freedoms are certainly fundamental to the ongoing quest for human dignity, the path from the present to the ideal is a thorny one. Nation-states must be persuaded to ratify, implement, and practice within their boundaries the many conventions dealing with human rights and fundamental freedoms. It is not difficult to understand why human rights often receive a low priority. Substantial improvements will be more likely when national leaders are less occupied with peace, security, development, population/resource balance, and political survival; tolerable progress in these areas will make it easier for them to give more attention to human rights. Constituents' demands for rights and freedoms intensify as progress is made in other areas. Obviously, the resolution of long-standing volatile issues, such as apartheid in southern Africa, the Palestinian problem, and conflict in the Middle East, would stimulate human rights progress.

United States
Posture
Unfortunately, the role of the United States regarding human rights has deteriorated in three decades from one of dynamic leadership to one bordering on evasive disregard. The United States was actively and aggressively involved in the formulation and adoption of the Universal Declaration of Human Rights. Without US participation, inspired by Eleanor Roosevelt's leadership, it is doubtful that the United Nations would have acted as boldly as it did.

Tragically, our official posture has undergone a major shift. Our record on ratification of the many human rights conventions adopted by the United Nations is miserable. Of the 17 principal conventions in force by 1976, we have ratified only 2. Six other conventions have been signed on behalf of the United States but are yet to be ratified by the Senate.

Arguments advanced by US senators who opposed human rights treaties in the 1950s included: (1) human rights are domestic matters; (2) international covenants could weaken existing freedoms and rights; (3) the covenants could enhance federal powers at the expense of states' rights; and (4) certain social, economic, and cultural rights of the treaties conflict with US conceptions of human rights. More recently, there is suspicion of any UN convention adopted by a General Assembly where dictatorships and totalitarian states are the majority. Fundamentally, the genesis of most opposition has been fear of encroachment on our national sovereignty.

Former Congressman Don Fraser, when chairman of the Subcommittee on International Organizations and Movements of the

House of Representatives, summarized the conclusions of extensive findings by that subcommittee in 1973:

> Our Subcommittee, looking first at our own government's role, finds that regard for human rights too often becomes invisible on the horizon of US foreign policy.

Beyond inaction on ratification, the United States' image as a human rights advocate has been badly tarnished by events. Silence during the 1950s and 1960s on independence for the former French and British colonies created the impression of US disinterest in the right of self-determination. Cold war maneuvers fostered the impression that the United States used aid to buy allies rather than advance economic and social development, which the Third World considers basic to human rights. Our toleration of the ultimate human suffering arising from our unfortunate involvement in Indochina has been labeled as callousness toward human life and human rights. Our support—for security reasons—of dictatorial governments, which often violate human rights, has been widely scorned. The composite result is that the United States has displayed but minimal world leadership on human rights during the last two decades.

Since January 1977, President Carter has spoken out repeatedly on human rights matters in the Soviet Union and elsewhere. He also encouraged US ratification of some of the long-ignored UN human rights conventions. His administration has cut back some US aid to some dictatorships that flout human rights.

These actions seem to indicate renewed US attention to fostering the fundamental freedoms—from want, poverty, ignorance, disease, and fear. We are perhaps beginning again to work to reduce hatreds and prejudices and to prevent encroachment upon the dignity and worth of individuals.

III   ACTORS
AND ACTIONS

11 THE AGENDA

Successful management of the six critical world issues cannot be taken for granted. It will not happen unless and until nation-states generate sufficient determination to overcome tradition, lethargy, and resistance to change and work to fashion better systems to deal with global problems.

Without better management systems, the probability of coping adequately with global problems is minimal. Even with better management, there is no promise of satisfactory solutions. Sound decisions are more likely, however, with workable and effective management systems, meaningful proposals, relevant and serious debate.

The action proposals advanced in the preceding chapters constitute an imposing agenda of both short-term and longer range tasks to reform existing economic and political institutions or replace them with new ones.

Overriding questions about the world community's ability and willingness to establish the needed institutions, mechanisms, and procedures remain unanswered. Will nations reconcile the conflicting demands of interdependence and independence? Where will strong leadership be found? What are the particular responsibilities of various groups of nations and what opportunities are open to them? What steps must be taken? Who are the actors most likely to influence public opinion and to encourage nation-states—and from my point of view the United States particularly—to play a leading role?

Approach

Implementation of this imposing action agenda presents the human race with unprecedented challenges. To break new ground well beyond accumulated experience will require imagination, plus a willingness to balance the potential risks of the unknown against the obvious and serious hazards of present and developing situations. Decisions on near-term proposals will prove extremely difficult, but longer range ones pose even more traumatic choices. Hence ongoing study and negotiation by the representatives of varied national interests must precede decisions by the world community as a whole.

Innovative and bold decision-making on behalf of the world community would be far more likely in a relaxed political climate. Ideally, an extended global moratorium might be placed upon current international controversies to create a calm period of examination, negotiation, compromise, and decision. While there is little probability of marshaling world opinion in support of a moratorium, the benefits would be significant enough to warrant the effort.

World leaders, however, will probably continue piecemeal management of global problems, dealing with one critical issue, or facet of it, at a time. This so-called functional approach has pragmatic appeal, but it also presents hazards. The functional approach fosters separate and partial solutions, thus increasing the difficulty of coordinating the management of interrelated issues. Even so, progress is possible with this approach if nation-states will act. Even limited progress in one area should encourage more intensive efforts in other areas.

Proposed near-term objectives can be accomplished within the context of the present nation-state international political system, within a reasonable time frame and without major revision of the UN Charter. Their implementation could assure the world community of stopgap action to arrest further political, economic, and environmental deterioration and could foster a more favorable climate for the permanent changes needed for longer range management.

The longer range proposals, on the other hand, call for greater delegation of authority to extranational or supranational, global or regional mechanisms. This requires modification of the present international political system and, if the United Nations remains the world's major institution, significant revision of its Charter. While near-term proposals are given first priority, opportunities may arise for early action on longer range proposals and should be sensed and acted upon promptly.

The Crucial Question   Reluctance of nation-states to delegate power and authority to regional or global institutions not only handicaps the existing international organizations but poses a serious obstacle to implementation.

One primary source of this reluctance is widespread, deep commitment to sovereignty. All nations, old and new, guard their political independence jealously. People have fought and died to achieve it; neither governments nor their constituents are prepared to let independence slip away. Traditional pride and reverence for the homeland and continued reliance upon nation-states for security further stimulate nationalism.

Furthermore, open and democratic societies worry about decisions that might be made by a governing body with heavy representation from dictatorships. Affluent countries fear share-the-wealth measures promoted by poorer countries. The resource-rich are concerned that the resource-poor would promote measures to confiscate or control vital resources. Such fears intensify dedication to the protection of national sovereignty.

But what is national sovereignty? Does not ultimate sovereignty rest with the people and do not governments exist to serve, not dominate? If this is so, sovereignty becomes a question of delegating to governmental units on the world level sufficient, but specific, authority to manage certain affairs affecting the well-being, peace, and security of people. To date there has been negligible delegation of sovereignty—authority to act in the common good—beyond that given to nation-states.

No matter how much states enjoy their independence and proclaim their sovereign rights, coping with global problems is not within their capability, individually or collectively. The world community must now find ways to pool sovereignty equitably and to minimize the potentials for intervention in domestic matters and encroachment upon national independence.

Hence success in managing the critical world issues depends, in the last analysis, upon a successful reconciliation of the pressing realities of global interdependence and the deeply entrenched emotional and political attachment to national sovereignty.

Two alternative scenarios emerge: one, forced by events, emphasizes catastrophe; the other emphasizes wisdom and leads to a common sense response.   *Scenarios*

The potential of catastrophe hangs over the world. Nuclear or conventional war, ecological disaster, food shortage, widespread terrorism, and breakdown of overloaded economic systems are all realistic possibilities, and some are probabilities. In the aftermath of any such global tragedy, it is doubtful that action to establish more effective management systems would be well thought out and broadly agreed upon. The probability is that the great powers would dominate the precipitous decisions taken.

A more hopeful scenario envisages early action with the participation of all nations. Decisions would then be reached deliberately through the exercise of judgment, negotiation, and compromise, thus yielding better management systems.

Unfortunately, people have an unwarranted confidence in the status quo which prevents their sensing the urgency of action; they fail to recognize the pace of recent global changes.

Nonetheless, concern about urgency is spreading. Recognition of the magnitude and scope of change is growing. International cooperation is more and more looked to as a key to preserving national independence. More people are aware of the limitations of the nation-state political system. More people understand that the common sense approach is the only way to avoid the dangers of inaction. More people recognize the need for bold, innovative, and effective leadership within nations and transnationally. Time is short; the potential consequences of procrastination and failure to act are overwhelming.

Having examined needed changes in world organizations in terms of the six critical world issues, let us turn to procedural changes that will facilitate improved management in all areas.

In spite of their inadequacies, the United Nations, its agencies, and many regional organizations serve the dual functions of policy development regarding political, economic, and social problems and the operation of programs resulting from policy decisions. These institutions facilitate joint action by nation-states; they will continue as important actors on the world stage.

The United Nations

The search for effective global and regional international institutions begins with the United Nations, still our greatest hope but increasingly a source of frustration and despair.

The United Nations is the second international organization formed by the world community to preserve peace. Its predecessor, the League of Nations, handicapped from its beginning by US failure to join or support it, collapsed when it failed to restrain aggression in China and Ethiopia. Steps which might have restrained Japan or Italy as they embarked on aggression were never taken: the member nations could not agree on the application of sanctions. The League was unable to preserve peace primarily because it lacked authority and power. With no peacekeeping power of its own, it was completely dependent upon the cooperative action of its members.

The United Nations was born in San Francisco in June 1945, two months prior to the tragic birth of the nuclear age at Hiroshima, and its Charter was drafted by the coalition of nations that won World War II. Broad outlines were developed at the Dumbarton Oaks Conference in 1944 by representatives of the United States, the United Kingdom, the Soviet Union, and China. Many of the Charter principles were agreed upon at Tehran and Yalta by Winston Churchill, Franklin D. Roosevelt, and Joseph Stalin.

These leaders faced a historic and serious dilemma. Although they recognized the utter necessity of a world organization more effective than the League of Nations to preserve peace, they were not prepared to design one with any real autonomy, authority, or power.

The United Nations Charter supposedly overcame most of the weaknesses of the League Covenant. A close comparison of the two documents does reveal some improvement in the UN Charter and even some suggestions of greater delegation of authority. However, the United Nations, like the League, is clearly an instrument to serve nation-states, not a world authority to serve the earth's peoples.

The San Francisco drafters anticipated none of the revolutionary events of the next decades: the A-bomb, the end of Western colonialism, the rapid pace of technological change, the bitter East-West split, and the frustrating North-South confrontation. Unfortunately, the Charter was patterned to fit the conditions of 1945, with too little flexibility for change.

A Center for Cooperation   The United Nations has played an important role in world affairs, albeit far short of that envisaged by its sponsors and early advocates. As the world's major international political organization, the United Nations and its affiliated agencies have served as the center for cooperative efforts by nation-states. Beyond the accomplishments and lack of accomplishments in managing each of the six critical world issues detailed in earlier chapters, the United Nations must also be given credit for the following:

1. Despite great diversity and substantial disunity among its members, it has survived for more than 30 years. The mere continuing existence of the United Nations demonstrates widespread recognition of the need for a global organization.
2. The General Assembly provides a forum where any nation, large or small, powerful or weak, can voice its aspirations, concerns, and complaints, challenging even the superpowers. This brings a desirable and healthy, but often abused, openness to international affairs.
3. Alternative approaches to world problems are repeatedly offered within the UN system: multilateral action, nonmilitary initiatives, and third-party interventions. These are important substitutes for the traditional exercise of unlimited national sovereignty, divisive power balances, and ultimate resort to armed force.

4. The United Nations system promotes and tests methods of cooperation among nation-states by revealing weaknesses as well as strengths and pointing the way to needed reforms.

5. Finally, the United Nations occasionally encourages member states to rise above narrow national interests and act in the common long-term interests of the world community.

World cooperation would be much less advanced had the United Nations not been in operation since the end of World War II. If the United Nations system suddenly vanished, a great clamor would arise for a substitute.

UN weaknesses have long been recognized; they are inherent in its structure and Charter. The United Nations is not a self-sustaining, independent institution. It has but minimal autonomy and authority. It recommends but cannot compel. Large majorities pass resolutions; but action occurs only when essentially all nations—certainly including those who furnish financial support—want it to happen. This explains the stream of nonimplemented General Assembly resolutions. *Deficiencies of the UN System*

UN procedures tend to be nonproductive and complicated; words are easily substituted for action, and controversy for cooperation. The more populous and powerful nations dislike and distrust the one-nation/one-vote pattern of the General Assembly; they doubt the ability of the limited staff of many smaller states to deal objectively with issues. Smaller nations, enjoying the power of equal vote, are frequently tempted to embarrass the Western world. Concern about the "tyranny of the majority" has emerged. On the other hand, the powerful veto accorded permanent members of the Security Council is greatly resented by most member states.

Confrontation of diverse cultures and interests is to be expected within the United Nations. The manner and style of confrontation, rather than confrontation itself, paralyzes constructive action. The alarming trend toward bitter dialogue and turbulent controversy subverts cooperation and further impairs the United Nations' already tenuous ability to manage political and economic matters. Ideological, cultural, and religious animosities are too often injected into confrontations over basic issues. Debate is poisoned by polemic appeals to fears and hatreds.

Arrogant charges deaden the will to cooperate. Repeated Arab verbal attacks upon Israel and the nations that support it marshal votes for General Assembly and Security Council resolutions but do little to bring peace to the Middle East, solve the Palestinian problem, or reduce racism. The constant accusatory din of imperialist aggression leveled against the West, particularly the United States, handicaps reasoned consideration of important issues. So, too, does the continuing harangue against communism in general, and the Soviet Union in particular. The charges of Western economic imperialism by the Group of 77 (currently consisting of 119 developing nations loosely banded together) hardly encourage serious discussion on desired capital and technology transfers from the Western world.

Examples of distrust abound: economic socialists versus economic capitalists; Moslems, Christians, and Jews; powerful nations and large blocs of the less powerful. Often more emotional than intellectual, distrust and cultural differences interfere with international negotiations.

Bloc voting—whether by industrial nations, socialist states, or Afro-Asian countries—frequently precludes objective consideration of the merits of proposals. This advance commitment of a group of states to vote together as a reflection of economic, ideologic, or geographic ties becomes objectionable when the desire for unity causes bloc members to disregard the merits of an issue. Both developed and developing nations frequently charge each other with irresponsible bloc voting.

The proceedings of agencies are politicized by matters belonging in the political arenas of the Security Council or General Assembly. Such practices, added to the constant pressures of near-term national interests, overwhelm constructive efforts to deal with longer range concerns.

Global frustration over the elusiveness of peace, the growth of terrorism, widespread hunger and poverty, troubled domestic economies, lagging development, and trampling of human rights push most governments toward defensiveness. This frame of mind encourages tension; scapegoats must be found and blamed.

All these factors combine to handicap UN efforts and to encourage nations to bypass the international organization. Despite the ongoing attention of the Security Council and General Assembly to Middle East matters—including the festering Palestinian problem—the most productive efforts toward peace have so far taken place outside the United Nations. Multilateral action on crucial resource problems precipitated by action of the Organization of

Petroleum Exporting Countries (OPEC) were dealt with by the International Energy Agency and the new ad hoc Paris forum called the Conference on International Economic Cooperation (CIEC), neither under the UN umbrella. Western nations that export nuclear technology, facilities, and materials are considering their problems outside the United Nations.

Clearly, the United Nations approaches an important fork in the road. Its future is clouded. Unless a tolerable degree of cooperation and compromise is soon restored, its effectiveness will be further impaired.

The proposed procedural changes that follow are mostly taken from the recommendations developed at ten annual Conferences on United Nations Procedures and fourteen Conferences on the United Nations of the Next Decade sponsored by The Stanley Foundation. Conference participants, coming from many nations, have offered reform suggestions achievable without Charter change or with minor changes of a relatively noncontroversial nature.

Reform of UN Decision-Making and Policy Formation

Decision-making in the General Assembly would be improved by:

1. Electing the officers of the succeeding assembly and constituting its General Committee (consisting of the president, 17 vice presidents, and chairmen of the main committees) at the close of the prior General Assembly or at a brief session early in the calendar year

2. Revising General Assembly rules to establish additional categories of questions to be decided by a two-thirds, rather than a simple, majority and/or counting abstentions as negative votes in determining the majority required to pass a resolution

3. Holding more frequent special sessions on specific matters, including a special session on UN decision-making

4. Improving preparation for assembly sessions and limiting general debate (Currently, the opening three weeks of each General Assembly are devoted to general statements by member states. Subsequently, undue General Assembly time is taken by members repeating prior committee debate and explaining their vote.)

5. Shortening and simplifying the agenda

6. Using more committee working groups on a year-round basis; reducing or eliminating committee general debate; eliminat-

ing assignment of the same subject to more than one committee; and using more informal consultations

7. Replacing committees of the whole with smaller committees of balanced representation
8. Restructuring committee assignments

In the Security Council, the current trends toward gradual limitation of the use of the veto, including passing of resolutions with abstention of one or more permanent members, should be encouraged. Decision-making would be facilitated by achieving an appropriate balance between official and informal meetings; by clearing the agenda of superseded items; and by increasing the use of special fact-finding, consultation, and negotiation commissions.

To strengthen the important role of the Secretariat in support of the General Assembly and the Security Council, the suggestions are (1) encouraging the Secretary-General to take greater initiative in pointing out trends and policy alternatives to the General Assembly in carefully defined areas; (2) providing more adequate services to the main committees of the General Assembly; (3) establishing a permanent office within the Secretariat to assist small delegations; and (4) raising the caliber of Secretariat staff by using personnel policies encouraging recruitment and advancement based more upon merit.

Among other possibilities, a form of optional associate membership in the United Nations for mini states may be worth considering. The world organization would also benefit from developing independent sources of revenue and from a special UN peacekeeping fund, allowing advance accumulation of voluntary contributions.

Longer Range Charter Revisions   Improvement of UN procedures and decision-making within the framework of the present Charter is of utmost importance. But even successful early reform will not alter what the United Nations is today—an association of nation-states lacking inherent power and authority. Something more is required: international cooperation based on near unanimity and voluntary performance is not enough.

What reforms are needed and what Charter revisions are required for the United Nations to play a central role in the future? Major reforms are not required in broad objectives and purpose, but rather in emphasis, authority, decision-making, and finance.

EMPHASIS: IN THE INTEREST OF THE GLOBE Revision of the basic emphasis of the United Nations is a delicate, but necessary, undertaking. The objectives of the United Nations cited earlier from the Charter Preamble and Article I are both proper and fundamental. The evident weaknesses of the aggregate UN organization arise not from smallness of objectives and purposes but from the approach to their achievement.

In practice, the United Nations functions to serve the often narrow and selfish interests of its member states rather than the broad human objectives enunciated in the Charter. As a vehicle of international cooperation, the United Nations often lags far behind demonstrated need. It responds to the least common denominator of varied national interests. To make the United Nations more effective, its basic emphasis, in practice as well as theory, must be shifted from serving nation-states to serving the world community. It must be more able to make things happen; it must be able to act, not react. Such a shift in emphasis and priority may appear to be a trivial matter of semantics because nation-states will still exist and contribute significantly to the global organization. Nevertheless, change in priority to place the interests of the world community first is fundamental. It is the first key to effective management of the critical world issues.

THE AUTHORITY TO IMPLEMENT An institution serving the longer range common interests of humanity must be delegated adequate autonomy and authority. As a tolerably independent entity, it must be free to agree upon and initiate those actions essential to managing global problems. Success is not likely if either decision-making or action can be blocked by a few powerful nations or a large bloc of less powerful ones. Once overall objectives and general policies are established by an equitable decision-making process, the institution needs enough authority and power to implement programs. It should also be free to initiate study and research and to submit proposals for dealing with global problems to the decision-making body.

Safeguards must accompany delegation of power and authority in order to reduce the potential of abuse. They may be provided in several ways, such as limiting delegated authority to carefully defined functions, assuring balanced representation in decision-making bodies, establishing proper checks upon funding, and adopting an appropriate bill of rights. Delegation of even carefully defined and safeguarded authority and power to a world organization raises genuine fears and emotional reactions. Nevertheless, the need here is effective management of global problems. The creation of an all-powerful super state to replace national governments and deal with domestic matters is neither desirable, realistic, nor acceptable. But the world does need an organization that assures effective management of global problems to avoid catastrophes and, at the same time, protect national political independence.

DECISION-MAKING AND VOTING A third prerequisite for a truly effective United Nations of tomorrow is a workable and fair decision-making process. No nation, however powerful, should be able to block action to deal with global problems, as is now the case with the permanent members of the Security Council. Nor should a group of like-minded nations, however numerous, representing but a small minority of the earth's population, be able to impose its will upon the great majority. This means that the United Nations must find alternatives to both the Security Council veto and the one-nation/one-vote system of the General Assembly. Until this is done, the powerful and less powerful nations will strongly resist the proposed shift in the basic emphasis of the United Nations and the delegation of adequate power and authority to it.

Numerous proposals for changing the voting system have been offered. Several of these are worthy of consideration. The widely criticized veto of the Security Council might be eliminated altogether; or the range of questions subject to the veto might be limited (for example, removing the applicability to actions that require disputing parties to negotiate). Another proposal would require two or more vetoes to stop an action. Enlargement of the Security Council, perhaps with semipermanent members, could provide better balance for decision-making.

Proposals for altering the voting system in the General Assembly fall into several broad categories. The famed Clark-Sohn proposals [1] would establish a graduated schedule of voting power ranging from one vote for the smallest member state to a maximum of 30 votes each for China, India, the Soviet Union, and the United States. The number of votes for intermediate member states would be related to population. Variations of this approach have been proposed by others.

Weighted voting is another option. Population is one obvious factor to be involved. A second element might be related to economic power, such as GNP, energy consumption, or agricultural

1. Grenville Clark and Louis B. Sohn, *World Peace through World Law*, 3rd ed. (Cambridge, Mass.: Harvard University Press, 1966).

and industrial production. Due to my background as an engineer, I look with favor upon the use of energy consumption as a factor in potential weighted voting. It is simple, understandable, and bears a direct relationship to stage of development and economic strength. Energy consumption, as a weighting factor, may be criticized as placing a premium on waste. Economic and supply factors, however, will compel conservation of energy, particularly by industrial powers, thus lowering their comparative weight. Energy consumption should provide more consistent weighting than GNP or other economic factors.

Dual voting in the General Assembly is a suggested means of maintaining one-nation/one-vote while injecting a weighted formula of some type. Votes on important matters would be counted twice, first on a one-nation/one-vote basis and then upon a weighted basis. In order to adopt a measure, both votes would have to carry by a stipulated margin. Dual voting might be applied only to resolutions on specified matters, leaving the one-nation/one-vote on all others.

Another possibility is a bicameral system wherein the General Assembly would continue to function on a one-nation/one-vote basis. A second body—some suggest an enlarged Security Council, giving greater representation to the larger and more powerful nations—would also consider the measure. Adoption would require a favorable vote by a stated majority in each body.

The ultimate alteration of the voting system in the United Nations will require compromise; and, in that process, quite new concepts may emerge. Such was the case nearly 200 years ago when the Constitutional Convention at Philadelphia created the US bicameral system with representation by population in one body and by states in the other.

In the necessary trade-offs, the veto may be eliminated or curtailed in exchange for one or another of the alternatives injecting the reality of power into the General Assembly decision-making system. Theoretically, a system weighting population and some economic factor makes sense. In any case, reaching compromise will be most difficult, if the United Nations is to have real authority.

FINANCE: TOWARD INDEPENDENCE The old adage that he who pays the piper calls the tune applies also to the United Nations system. So long as it is primarily dependent upon essentially voluntary national contributions, it will serve the interests of states rather than the world community. The precarious financial situation of the

United Nations from year to year demonstrates this fact. The Article 19 fiasco of 1965 is a good illustration. The Soviet Union and France refused to pay assessed costs of the UN peacekeeping operations in the Congo. The United States insisted that Article 19 (under which any member more than two years in default on its UN assessments loses its vote in the General Assembly) be enforced upon these two nations. Deadlock resulted in near paralysis of the United Nations for many months. The United States did back down eventually, saving face by proclaiming an unwillingness to wreck the organization. Although the sale of UN bonds covered part of the costs of the Congo operation, the financial strength of the United Nations is still impaired.

So long as UN agency activities are financed by voluntary contributions, nation-states will contribute only to those programs they favor or benefit from. Agencies will continue to compete with one another for support, and there is no assurance that optimum use is made of available funds or that maximum aggregate amounts are raised. The importance of independent funding and possible sources of revenue have been suggested in the previous discussion regarding management of economic and social development. For example, a two cent (US) surcharge per piece of mail crossing national borders would produce $310 million annually; a one dollar (US) per ton annual levy upon all commercial vessels for use of ocean space would raise $343 million annually; a one cent per kilogram surcharge on current total of fish catches in ocean space would raise $698 million annually. As stated earlier, a 1 percent global tariff upon the 1975 volume of international trade would have produced $8.78 billion.[2] Other possibilities include surcharges on commercial airline international flights; on petroleum and mineral resources extracted from the seabeds, including those in proposed national economic zones; and on radio, cable, and television communications using the air space above the oceans.

Functional Organizations

Several existing world organizations with minimal ties to the United Nations already perform specific functions for the world community. The World Bank and the International Monetary Fund are outstanding examples. Although blessed by the United Nations

2. Compiled from data found in the United Nations *Statistical Yearbook 1975*, New York, 1976.

and generally considered to be under its umbrella, they are, for all intents and purposes, autonomous organizations. The General Agreement on Tariffs and Trade, too, is beyond the authorized reach of the United Nations.

The outlook is for more organizations of this type. They will be established when the need in a given problem area becomes critical and the United Nations has been unwilling or unable to deal with it. Potential areas for such functional organizations include food, trade, commodities, environment, and perhaps others. In some cases, UN action or a UN conference may initiate proceedings leading to the creation of the functional organization. Ocean law is a case in point. Discussion in the UN General Assembly, followed by extensive explorations by the ad hoc seabed study group, culminated in the UN Law of the Seas Conference. Nevertheless, the treaty being developed by the conference will likely create a new organization to deal with the seabeds, with its own decision-making and administrative organs. The organization will thus be autonomous with but token, if any, ties to the United Nations.

A similar approach, the International Disarmament Organization (IDO), was proposed by President Kennedy in 1962 when the United States responded to a Soviet proposal regarding general and complete disarmament. The autonomous organization would have supervised the disarmament process and dealt with related problems. The concept is likely to surface again whenever serious arms reduction is undertaken.

A clear distinction exists between functional organizations and the various agencies closely affiliated with the United Nations. The constitutional relationships between the United Nations and such agencies are governed by the UN Charter for agencies in existence prior to the adoption of the Charter, or by General Assembly resolutions creating agencies after Charter adoption. The United Nations has the authority to renegotiate these relationships, a process that is desirable. Functional organizations created in the future, however, are likely to be more independent of the United Nations.

New functional organizations are attractive because they permit proper emphasis, adequate delegation of power and authority, balanced decision-making procedures, and access to new sources of funding. Negotiations to develop a treaty creating a new functional organization may be lengthy and heated (witness the UN Law of the Seas Conference). But the process accomplishes, for the management of a specific function, the very changes proposed for the longer range revision of the United Nations. The result is an organization with at least extranational, and perhaps limited supranational, authority.

When faced with a functional need, nation-states are more prepared to delegate authority. Decision-making can be balanced by such measures as dividing powers between an assembly (one-nation/one-vote) concerned with general policy only and a smaller council concerned with management, structuring council membership to fairly represent interest groups, requiring greater majorities (two-thirds or three-fourths) on important issues, and requiring concurrence of the majority of votes within each specified interest group. Safeguards are more easily established because they are limited to a specific function.

Functional organizations have certain disadvantages despite their attractiveness. Coordination of management of interrelated issues becomes difficult. The independence of a functional organization tends to insulate it from the world community as a whole and from the United Nations. Creation of functional organizations lessens the pressures upon nation-states to reform the United Nations.

Regional Organizations

Many regional organizations which foster cooperation on a limited geographic basis were mentioned earlier. While they differ in type and function, each is addressed to the management of regional aspects of one or more of the critical world issues. They are important for the same reasons that world organizations are important. Regional organizations have the advantage of more homogeneous constituencies which often can reach consensus and implement action more harmoniously than worldwide organizations.

The several Western European organizations provide an outstanding example of the favorable use of regional organization. Western Europe has the European Economic Community (EEC) and the European Free Trade Association (EFTA) in the economic area. The European Atomic Energy Community (EURATOM), the European Organization for Nuclear Research (EONR), and the European Space Agency (ESA) deal with problems of modern technology. The North Atlantic Treaty Organization (NATO) is concerned with security. The Council of Europe described in chapter 10 is a most significant omen; along with its human rights activities, the council deals with terrorism, migrants, and the environment. The recent change from appointment by member governments to direct election of members to the Parliament of Europe is another important omen.

Although perhaps less advanced, regional organizations of various types exist or flourish elsewhere. In Eastern Europe the Warsaw Pact and the Council for Mutual Economic Assistance (COMECON) are counterparts to NATO and EEC. The Americas have their Organization of American States (OAS), Africa its Organization of African Unity (OAU), and Southeast Asia its Association of Southeast Asian Nations (ASEAN).

The potentials available to regional organizations are nearly as varied and useful as those awaiting a strengthened United Nations. They can be structured to assume the management of important segments of critical world issues and to play supportive roles in others. Greater reliance upon regional organizations conforms to the political wisdom that the best management of political matters is the one closest to the local problems and the people. Homogeneity and proximity encourage greater acceptance of their programs. However, regional organizations can be most effective if their operations are consistent with global objectives and if suitable coordination is maintained with worldwide organizations. *Regional Opportunities*

Regional organizations are particularly well suited to deal with such economic matters as joint development programs regarding transportation, communications, and water resource projects. The several existing and proposed regional trade pacts have already been mentioned in connection with the global trade system. The outstanding progress of the EEC points the way. The Inter-American Development Bank has demonstrated the value of a regional approach to development banking. Agreement on guidelines and practices regarding transnational enterprises may be reached more easily among neighboring nations than on the world level. Finally, regional approaches to establishing exchange rates—recently initiated by EEC—could contribute toward the development of a common world currency.

Regional institutions could also contribute much to the management of peace and security. Latin America's Tlatelolco treaty and OPANAL, its concurrent institution, point the way to weapons-free zones (both nuclear and conventional) and perhaps to regional centers to store, process, and recycle nuclear fuel and wastes. Ventures of this type would economically benefit treaty parties while lessening chances of the use of armed force. Controversies among neighboring nations could often be more readily resolved if dealt with regionally by heads of the neighboring governments through the auspices of regional organizations.

Regional approaches to environmental protection and enhancement and to resource/population imbalances are promising means of dealing with these problems. Agreement upon standards and enforcement for environmental protection should be more easily reached by nations facing common problems. Action to protect rivers, lakes, and adjacent seas that serve several nations must be cooperative. Neighboring coastal states face common problems regarding marine protection and conservation measures within their economic zones. As the resource/population balance issue becomes more pressing, regions will tend to have similar concerns and outlooks.

Finally, regional organizations have a unique opportunity to stimulate progress toward greater reliance upon law for the resolution of international controversies. Here again, the European community is leading the way. The OAS, OAU, and ASEAN, together with future regional organizations, should be encouraged to follow the leadership of the European community.

Reform   Increased effectiveness of regional organizations requires reforming and restructuring not unlike that proposed for the United Nations. With varied structures, different governance, and diverse functions, the common need of regional organizations is greater emphasis upon serving the common interests of a region, not the interests of member nation-states. Hence nation-states can strengthen these organizations by orienting functions toward shared concerns, by delegating adequate authority and power, by improving decision-making procedures, and by providing enlarged and independent financial support.

Outlook

The members of the United Nations have been pathetically slow to alter traditional patterns. Their reluctance reminds one of the slowness of the US Congress to change its own archaic procedures. But fortunately there are stirrings. One ad hoc committee is looking into restructuring of the UN economic and social systems. Another is wrestling with UN reform in general, including Charter revision.

The probability is good that the United Nations will soon make some minor near-term reforms. Substantial strengthening of UN capability to manage adequately the six critical world issues is unlikely, however, until stronger leadership for change emerges. Even the current reform initiative could be undermined if the North-South economic confrontation or a deteriorating East-West détente were permitted to rigidly polarize the United Nations.

Further, it is not likely that nation-states will soon agree upon longer range UN reform measures affecting emphasis, authority, decision-making, and independent financing unless they are jarred into action.

Many facets of global problems, nevertheless, are too critical to await a hesitant United Nations' willingness to change. Nation-states will inevitably seek other means of dealing with serious problems. One way to do this is to set up ad hoc committees having no connection with the United Nations, such as the Conference on International Economic Cooperation (CIEC). While such committees can deal effectively with specific immediate problems, they have disadvantages as ongoing organizations. They lack a political base because they are not tied into the world organization.

A second alternative is greater use of functional organizations having but token, if any, connection to the United Nations; they can be structured with reasonably adequate authority, suitable decision-making processes, and more independent funding. Or additional responsibilities could be given to such organizations as the World Bank, IMF, UNEP, and other institutions. This functional pattern of dealing with problems has certain initial advantages. Nevertheless, in the longer range, extensive use of it will create a hydra-headed world network with inadequate ties and liaison to the desirable central policy-making body, the United Nations itself.

Regional organizations, the third alternative, should be strongly encouraged. Adequate linkage and appropriate coordination with the United Nations, however, are needed for these organizations to make an optimum contribution to the management of global problems.

Each alternative has certain merits if used in conjunction with a stronger and more effective United Nations that develops broad policy, determines priorities, and oversees the management of critical world issues.

In the last analysis, though, decisions on the pattern of world organization will be made by nation-states. Only they have the power and the responsibility. Their acts of commission or omission will determine how the world community manages, or fails to manage, critical world issues.

13   NATION-STATES

Nation-states are the prime actors in the global arena. They will retain this role until *they* create extranational or supranational mechanisms and institutions. Only nation-states, acting through treaties, have the power to create such organizations and transfer authority to them. International and national nongovernmental organizations, as well as public opinion, have important and persuasive supportive roles, but they cannot take action. Such is the reality of today's international political system.

There is little likelihood of bypassing the nation-state system with people-to-people movements. So-called constitutional conventions of unofficially selected representatives of the people from all nations have been proposed from time to time. Such proposals usually emanate from groups within democratic nations who naively assume that the people of other nations have the same democratic rights and privileges. But even if such a convention with broad participation assembled, it could not conceivably usurp the power of all nation-states, even though it could affect public opinion.

The Dilemma of Obsolescence

Today's frightening dilemma is that nation-states, while absolute in their monopoly of power, are obsolete in their ability to cooperate in making and implementing decisions about the management of critical world issues. They have clearly demonstrated their capacity to make war but have failed miserably to unify to maintain peace. They precipitate economic crises but are unable to manage the world economy. They pass resolutions but do not implement them. They castigate one another but cannot sustain cooperation. The near-term interests of nation-states are so diverse that agreements upon global action, if reached, are usually too little and too late. Most international controversies arise from self-serving appraisals of immediate concerns and from failure to recognize the commonality of longer range interests; others are the result of basic religious, ideological, or cultural differences intensified by prejudices and attitudes arising from tragic and frustrating historical experiences.

Reluctance to surmount these obstacles stems in part from fear of the unknown and in part from internal political pressures. Pressed by day-to-day domestic crises, too few leaders find time to anticipate the possiblity of failure to manage world problems and assess the impact of such failures upon their own countries. A strengthened United Nations can wait, they say; jobs for the unemployed cannot. A hard line and status quo posture are less risky at the ballot box.

Will nation-states rise above their actual and perceived conflicts of interest and overcome inherent reluctance to build adequate global and regional organizations? This depends largely upon the wisdom and leadership of individual statesmen and the attitudes of key nations and groups of nations. For convenience, therefore, let us review briefly at this point the clusters of states relevant to global issues. *Groupings of Nations*

At the end of World War II, three groups stood out: the nations united in victory, the defeated Axis powers, and the neutrals. As the cold war developed, alignments changed to the communist bloc, the so-called free world, and the neutral or uncommitted nations. Western colonialism phased out and the term Third World emerged, encompassing numerous less developed nations, mostly new but some of longer standing. The First and Second Worlds were those countries closely allied with the United States or the Soviet Union; but these terms were little used.

The political association of the remaining nations was formalized by their heads of state and governments in a series of Summit Conferences of Nonaligned Countries. The initial 1961 Bandung conference has been followed at intervals with four more summits, the most recent in Colombo (1976). A sixth summit meeting is scheduled for Havana in September 1979. The number of nonaligned members is now 86 nations and 3 liberation movements.

Economically, nations have been grouped for nearly three decades as the developed and the developing, or less developed, countries. Beginning in 1963, a group of like-minded nations (mostly developing and mostly nonaligned) began preparing a common platform concerning economic and social development. This led to the launching of the Group of 77 at the first UNCTAD conference in Geneva in 1964.[1] The Group of 77 (now grown to 119 nations) affords political solidarity to the developing nations on economic matters.

1. Leo Mates, *Nonalignment, Theory and Current Policy* (Belgrade: Institute of International Politics and Economics, 1972).

The memberships of the Nonaligned conferences and the Group of 77 generally overlap, but there are some exceptions. Brazil, for instance, participates with the Group of 77 on economic matters but not usually with the nonaligned. At the 1976 Nonaligned conference in Colombo, three countries (the Philippines, Portugal, and Romania) were admitted despite their respective connections with SEATO, NATO, and the Warsaw Pact. Within recent years, the Nonaligned conferences have tended toward greater political emphasis and the Group of 77 has become more involved in economic matters.

Economic realities have recently identified two subgroups within the Third World. Forty-nine of the poorest nations, sometimes referred to as the most seriously affected (MSA), have been called the Fourth World. The 13 oil-rich nations have, by their own action, become OPEC.

In chapter 7 four groups of nations were discussed: 49 Low Income, 39 Lower-Middle Income, 35 Upper-Middle Income, and 37 High Income. The High Income group includes most of the so-called developed nations. The Low, Lower-Middle, and Upper-Middle Income countries correspond generally to those considered as the Third World. The Low Income countries correspond closely to the Fourth World. OPEC nations are listed in each of these four groups, depending upon their per capita gross national product, which is very high in several of the underdeveloped OPEC countries.

Despite the similarities of interests and objectives among nations in each group, there are significant sociocultural differences. Although bloc voting in the United Nations and assorted conferences is common, nations frequently break with their associates and vote independently. Nevertheless, the groupings do come into play both constructively and obstructively during political and economic debates and decisions.

None of the groupings seems quite appropriate for appraising future attitudes and potential leadership for managing critical world issues. For this purpose, I divide the world's nations into four groups, based upon personal judgment of their needs and attitudes and their probable roles in strengthening regional and global organization.

Group A. The 5 "united" nations: China, France, the Soviet Union, the United Kingdom, and the United States

Group B. The have nations: some 30 developed nations and a few of the more advanced developing countries

Group C. The have-not nations: all other developing countries, less OPEC members

Group D. The 13 members of OPEC

How well the world community copes with critical world issues depends largely upon the leadership displayed within each of these four groups and the interplay among them. The opportunities and responsibilities for leading the world community away from its current impasse vary in proportion to the status and power of the groups. Those blessed with greater strength and maturity have a heavier responsibility; those with influence, talent, and experience, a greater opportunity. What may be expected of each of these groups of nations?

At the close of World War II, leadership rested with the five major nations united to defeat the Axis powers, namely, China, France, the Soviet Union, the United Kingdom, and the United States. Major responsibility for maintaining peace and security was delegated to them by the UN Charter through permanent Security Council membership, fortified by veto power. Each now possesses nuclear weapons. The power and influence of these five, if they cooperated, could promptly lead the world toward effective management of its critical issues.

Group A:
The "United"
Nations

The United States and the Soviet Union are, by conventional standards, the world's most powerful nations:[2] first and second in GNP, military power, and arsenals of nuclear weapons; fourth and third in population; both with high literacy and stable governments. Each fully merits the title of superpower bestowed upon it, sometimes hopefully but often fearfully, by other nations.

China, with a population of over 900 million, an expanding nuclear weapons capability, and a growing following among developing nations, is another powerful force. China's do-it-yourself, tightly controlled but significant, economic progress appeals to many poor nations. Despite frequent disclaimers of any desire for superpower status, China's strength ranks her in the top echelon.

The inclusion of France and Great Britain in this group results from permanent membership in the UN Security Council. Both have stable governments and developed cultures. Both have nuclear weapons. Hence they retain prominent positions, although West

2. Rankings are taken from Ruth Leger Sivard, *World Military and Social Expenditures* (Leesburg, Virginia: WMSE Publications, 1978).

Germany and Japan now surpass both in GNP and population, and West Germany's military expenditures exceed those of both France and Great Britain.

France, fourteenth in population, fifth in GNP, and fifth in military expenditures, has important influence, particularly among French-speaking countries in former colonial areas. With self-developed nuclear weapons and the force de frappe, France is an important military power, even though its grandeur is less than claimed by the late General De Gaulle.

Although plagued by hard times and reduced outreach, the United Kingdom retains important influence, particularly among the members of the once powerful and extensive British Commonwealth. Twelfth in population, seventh in GNP, and sixth in military expenditures, the United Kingdom has nuclear weapons through early technological cooperation with the United States.

Little change in the world's political and economic orders is likely without the formal approval or tacit concurrence of these powers. By influence, indifference, or the veto, they can obstruct any action proposed by the Security Council or the General Assembly. As the major nuclear weapon states, the Soviet Union and the United States can keep the arms race going or move to halt and reverse it. The sword of Damocles held over the world by US and Soviet nuclear weapons provides security to some but disturbs most nations. China follows behind, seeking appropriate credibility and some undisclosed degree of nuclear deterrence.

Cooperation among the once united five is now conspicuously absent. The three Western powers, from long association, work well together when they elect to do so, although they occasionally take exception to each other's proposals. The United States and the Soviet Union have been locked in ideological and military confrontation for three decades. China and the Soviet Union are bitterly debating ideology and carefully guarding their long common frontier. The current triangular relationships among the United States, the Soviet Union, and China are still somewhat divisive but are in flux. Behind a facade of declared cooperation in the interests of world community, these three seldom pass up an opportunity to criticize one another.

The self-sufficiency and strength of these five powers are viewed as too great to admit dependency upon the United Nations. The very idea of strong global institutions runs contrary to their ingrained philosophies of power politics. No one of the five nations considers its security dependent upon world organization; the NATO and

Warsaw Pact military alliances dominate European security. Neither is the United Nations system viewed as essential nor even important to economic development and well-being of these five nations; although, paradoxically, the United Kingdom welcomed the assistance of the International Monetary Fund in arranging credits to relieve its 1977 balance of payments disequilibrium. Hence they view the United Nations both as a necessary evil and an opportunity—a foreign policy instrument to be tolerated and used or abused as national interests dictate. The dependence of other nations upon the United Nations, however, is too strong to permit the five to disregard it. To walk out is hazardous, as the Soviets discovered at the time of the Korean invasion in 1950.

National attitudes toward world organization reflect the vastly different experiences of these countries. As UN membership has grown, the United States has shifted from ardent advocacy to half-hearted participation. The overwhelming majorities once marshaled to support US proposals have given way to divisive debate on many issues and frequent General Assembly majorities opposing US positions. Public unrest bursts into bitter condemnation whenever the General Assembly passes controversial resolutions, such as that labeling Zionism as racism. The attitudes of France and Great Britain have somewhat paralleled those of the United States.

The Soviet Union with a bloc of only ten reliable votes (Bulgaria, Byelorussia, Cuba, Czechoslovakia, East Germany, Hungary, Poland, Romania, USSR, and Ukraine) has been in the minority in the General Assembly from the beginning. Undoubtedly, this has fostered a negative, spoiler attitude. The Soviets dislike entrusting matters of national importance to an uncertain UN majority; they prefer bilateral approaches. Frequent use of the veto has protected Soviet interests and embarrassed the West. The Soviet Union has courted the developing world by supporting its proposed economic measures, particularly those critical of the United States and the West. But the Soviet Union has not offered development aid to match its verbal support of development.

The People's Republic of China (PRC) has represented the world's most populous nation in the United Nations only since 1972. During the preceding three decades when it was on the outside looking in, the PRC had every reason to be distrustful of the United Nations and its early United States–led majority. Such a background is hardly conducive to strong reliance upon the United Nations. Chinese attitudes toward the United Nations, however, are not yet fully revealed. The few years of PRC membership in the United Nations have been marked by caution and propriety except for diatribe against the superpowers, particularly the Soviet Union. China certainly does not view itself as dependent upon the United Nations and, undoubtedly, shares with the others the strong commitment to national sovereignty and respect for national military power.

It is obvious that considerable change in national attitudes must occur before these five nuclear-armed, veto-endowed nations will respond fully to the leadership responsibility that goes with power.

There is little probability that these powerful nations as a group will voluntarily alter their attitudes on world organization in the near future; dedication to national sovereignty is too fundamental; relationships are too belligerent; and commitment to power balance is too strong. Suspicions of world organization run deep, and vested military interests are politically and economically influential. These nations are thus deadlocked in what constitutes an applied veto over the efforts of the rest of the world. They default regularly on their responsibilities of leadership.

While Group A nations should be encouraged to reexamine their posture, the current impasse is more likely to be broken by means other than logic—internal pressures and crises, unpredictable external events, and world opinion.

Group B: The Have Nations   The nations classified as Group B include most of the High Income nations, excepting those falling within Group A plus a number of the more advanced Upper-Middle Income nations. Despite diversities, they share somewhat common needs and attitudes toward international organization.

Group B nations are mature with tolerably stable governments, capable political leaders, and experienced public servants. They have reached a stage of economic development requiring little direct assistance from UN agencies. In fact, most of them contribute capital and technology in varying amounts to developing nations. Unlike Group A powers, they know they lack the national power to go it alone; they recognize their interdependence in both security and economic matters. Hence they need similar approaches to maintaining peace, stimulating the world economic order, attending to environmental matters, and resolving resource and human rights issues. Accordingly, Group B countries are more aware of the urgent need for effective global and regional organizations.

These nations are generally dependent upon others for military security. Most have participated in NATO, the Warsaw Pact, or the defunct SEATO treaties, or have arranged defense treaties for coverage by the military and nuclear umbrellas of a superpower. Any third world war would find most of them hopelessly engulfed; they are helpless to escape it. These nations share a common interest in reducing tensions among the Big Three, halting the arms race, and developing alternative security arrangements.

Because few have sufficient natural resources for their needs, they are concerned with maintaining access to commodities and raw materials from both developed and developing countries. Because most have manufactured products to export, they are concerned with maintaining access to markets. They must generate foreign exchange to pay for imports and maintain acceptable balances of payment. These dependencies cause recognition of the importance of a strengthened world economic order with better management of the trade and monetary systems. These dependencies also heighten desire for accelerated economic and social development and for the proper management of the multilateral aid, bilateral aid, development banking, trade, transnational enterprise, and monetary systems of the world economic order. Hence the nations of this group tend to view stronger world organization not as a threat to their political and economic independence but as essential.

Many of these nations already exert effective leadership in world affairs, though some are restrained by external alliances or internal political or economic situations. Their relative maturity and strong economies provide qualified professionals and leaders; adequately staffed missions, embassies, and delegations to international conferences; and effective research and backup. Even a casual following of proceedings of the Security Council, the General Assembly, UN agencies, regional organizations, and conferences reveals constructive leadership by the diplomats and negotiators from nations within this group. They play key roles in developing and advocating new approaches to problem-solving and frequently facilitate compromise between the superpowers and the developing world.

The have nations as a whole enjoy valuable influence with both the developing nations and the five major powers. Developing nations court their favor both as sources of capital and technological transfers and as supporters of a new world economic order. The major powers must also lend an ear to the concerns and the advice of this group; their support is needed for the powerful to avoid becoming isolated, prime targets for the initiatives and invectives of the developing world.

For these reasons, Group B nations are a reservoir of potential leadership. Looking ahead, the emergence of a coalition for action greatly depends upon them.

Group C:
The Have-Not
Nations

The have-not group—a sizable one—consists of all developing nations except several of the more advanced (included in Group B) and the OPEC members (considered separately as Group D). All are strongly tied politically and economically to the United Nations, its agencies, and other international and regional organizations; the General Assembly provides a forum for their complaints, hopes, and criticisms; the UN agencies and certain regional organizations are sources of funding and technical assistance; their security depends upon maintenance of peace by the world organization since few of them have sufficient military power to engage in or resist a major armed challenge.

Hence it is not surprising that these nations generally believe in and support the United Nations and other international organizations. Developing countries want the United Nations and regional organizations to increase development funding. They advocate enlarged UN capability to assure security, keep international peace, and create a new world economic order.

The power of have-not nations to effect change is substantial but less than recent General Assembly occurrences might indicate. Although adopted by lopsided majorities, the resolutions promoted by this group often are not implemented because they lack the support of the industrialized world in the form of transfers of capital and technology. Nevertheless, the persistent demands of the developing world have stimulated the United States and other nations to give serious attention to reform of the world economic order and acceleration of economic and social development.

These Group C nations can be counted upon to actively support strengthened world organization, provided they are given participation in decision-making and management. While some of them can provide leadership, the human and monetary resource limitations of many of the smaller and poorer (including most of the Low Income) countries must be recognized. Ministries, embassies, and missions are often too thinly staffed to keep abreast of current affairs, let alone move into leadership roles. According to a recent UN Directory of Permanent Missions to the United Nations, 58 nations, mostly within this group, had professional staffs numbering six or less. Such pathetically small staffs cannot adequately cover the General Assembly and other UN activities. Some of these smaller countries, though, have been, and hopefully will continue to be, represented in international circles by dynamic and able diplomats who are effective leaders.

The 13 oil-rich OPEC countries share a unique near-term economic strength that separates them from fellow developing nations. The world needs their petroleum; and its sale greatly increases the revenues of OPEC nations. Petroleum-based economic power has increased their influence with both the petroleum importers and nations seeking development funding. *Group D: OPEC Nations*

With their new financial capability, OPEC members have the means to accelerate their own economic and social development and several should rise to the developed nation status within the next two or three decades. Some OPEC nations—Saudi Arabia, Kuwait, Qatar, and the United Arab Emirates—have, in the immediate future at least, more money than they can use on their own development; hence they have suddenly become sources of development funds for transfer to developing nations. While both their capacity and willingness to provide development funds have probably been overestimated, they are helping other countries, particularly in the Middle East. Saudi Arabia has not only greatly expanded its military capability, but also has given military assistance funding to other Arab nations. Prior to the recent revolution, Iran had done the same.

The ongoing unity of OPEC nations is not assured: witness their squabbles over pricing and production. Located in the Middle East, Africa, Latin America, and Southeast Asia, they share oil power as the all-pervasive unifying factor; but their politics and ideologies vary greatly. Their political postures range from liberal to conservative; their economic systems encompass varying degrees of free enterprise and state ownership. In the longer range, the interests of most of this group of nations are similar to those of Group C for they are, in fact, developing nations. They need the United Nations as a forum to express concerns, gain access to needed transfers of technology, and assure international peace and security. On the other hand, several of them already have interests more like those of Group B nations.

In the past, the individual postures of Group D nations toward world organization have paralleled those of other developing nations. They have produced a number of able and effective diplomats and leaders at the United Nations and in other multinational gatherings. Improved economic status should now facilitate larger and better qualified staffs in their ministries, embassies, and missions, allowing greater attention to global issues. These factors, together with the leverage of oil diplomacy, should increase the ability and perhaps the willingness of some OPEC nations to play a more meaningful leadership role.

Leadership: Breaking the Deadlock

To be effective, leadership must involve nations from the several groups not only to encourage others within each group but also to assure appropriate consideration of significantly different situations, needs, and interests. The more responsible leaders of the developing countries fully realize the need for the concurrence, cooperation, and support of developed countries. Most developed nations also recognize that a concerted approach is fundamental to solid progress. Even the superpowers are learning that they cannot dominate international decision-making. The question is not whether concerted action is required, but how to achieve it.

The world community has every right to expect Group A nations to provide dynamic leadership. Unfortunately, cooperative action from this group awaits major change in basic attitudes and relationships among China, the Soviet Union, and the United States.

Expanding détente between the United States and the Soviet Union, progress in understanding and cooperation between China and the United States, and partial relaxation of the strains between China and the Soviet Union are equally important. The appearance of new statesmen may or may not foster improved relations among these nations. Mao Tse-tung and Chou En-lai are dead and their successors are feeling their way in foreign affairs while consolidating their internal control. Kremlin watchers predict an early retirement of Premier Brezhnev. US presidents change at least every eight years. New leadership does not automatically alter basic needs and national policies; but, having little or no vested interest in prior postures, incoming governments are freer to consider opportunities for new initiatives.

Resolution of local controversies in the Middle East, southern Africa, and elsewhere could reduce the frictions among these three powerful nations. The relaxation of tensions alone, however, may merely be palliative and increase satisfaction with the current international political order, without resolving the underlying difficulties.

Domestic factors will undoubtedly generate mounting pressures to alter policies toward global problems. The three great powers would benefit substantially from the cutbacks in military expenditures permitted by reduced global tensions; each nation has its own package of pressing domestic economic needs. The United States is concerned with inflation, unemployment, and energy and will be increasingly concerned about access to raw materials and commodities, some potentially available from the Soviet Union and China. The Soviet agricultural system still necessitates repeated food imports. China, too, imports food occasionally. Both China and the Soviet Union need Western technology. Consumer demands are creating pressures for change within the USSR and, in time, will do so in China. The Soviet Union and China are inevitably becoming more involved in the world's trade and monetary systems.

Major war (whether or not any of these three nations are directly involved), an environmental crisis, or rapid deterioration of the world's resource/population balance could force a new look at managing those critical world issues. But global catastrophe is to be avoided at all costs; and external and internal economic pressures work very slowly. Thus the probability of early concerted leadership from the great powers is very low, barring some dramatic new approach.

The current deadlock will need to be shattered by a vigorous and substantial change of policy by one of the three nations. Suppose the United States or the Soviet Union—or perhaps China—were to radically alter its foreign policy, now focused upon near-term national interests, and embrace one truly compatible with the common near-term and longer range concerns of the world. Such advocacy, if matched by action, would rally amazing support.

Neither China nor the Soviet Union seem likely soon to break the shackles now binding them in confrontation and to step forward. Although France and the United Kingdom have considerable influence, both lack the clout to break these serious deadlocks.

What of the United States? Do the recent stirrings in human rights, bilateral arms reduction, and economic areas foretell a determination to assume leadership? Will this nation, frustrated by Watergate, CIA investigations, recession, and renewed debate over who is first or second in the arms race, overcome the tendency to turn inward? Are we ready to revalue our priorities, giving emphasis to what must be done if the world community is to survive and prosper? We should, and if we are wise, we will.

Until the five no longer united nations alter their approaches, leadership rests disproportionately and unfairly upon the shoulders of other nations.

A coalition of like-minded nations to propose and support measures to better manage global problems is needed. Such a coalition should include nations from among the several groups, perhaps initially excepting Group A. Participation must cut across the barriers usually dividing ideological blocs, economic groups, and regional alignments. Criteria for participation in the coalition should be simple and pragmatic: (1) national policies generally amenable to strengthening global and regional organizations, (2) dedication to early action toward such goals, and (3) willingness and ability to commit human and other resources to these ends. These criteria reflect a determination to stand up and be counted, to defy pressures, and to reject arguments of even potent powers satisfied with the status quo.

Communication and action should be the watchwords of such a coalition. Initially, its members would work informally behind the scenes to promote proposals for positive action at the United Nations, world conferences, regional meetings, task forces, and other appropriate forums. Serious, continuing communication must have a high priority and should involve diplomatic, political, academic, and nongovernmental organization leaders of the countries participating in the informal coalition. Working well ahead of immediate crises and current agendas of various regional and global international organizations, the coalition could structure proposals consistent with the longer range needs. Shared participation in this process would lead to common sponsorship of such proposals before decision-making bodies.

There are several potential advantages of such a coalition. First, it would facilitate leadership and action among like-minded nations. Second, ongoing pooling of information and research would expand knowledge about problems, approaches, and obstacles to be overcome. Third, coalition members would build confidence not only among themselves but in their ability to influence action. Fourth, the leadership of nations within the coalition would strengthen the determination of other nations. Fifth, a well constituted coalition of determined nations would exert strong pressure upon the superpowers and other holdouts.

Experiences with Stanley Foundation conferences, together with numerous discussions with diplomats and political leaders from the six continents, have demonstrated to me both the need and the viability of the coalition approach. The paucity of current communications among leaders, diplomats, and scholars of nations whose interests are similar is appalling, and the gap where interests are dissimilar is even wider. Personal communication that fosters understanding and stimulates new ideas is needed rather than structured and often polemic exchanges before public bodies. It is essential to build upon the remarkable consensus on the urgent need to improve management of the critical world issues, as observed among participants from diverse nations at our conferences.

Unfortunately, these participants also have shared a frustration that despite the urgency, little can be done because the superpowers will neither support nor concur with necessary change. This may be true when viewed by nations acting alone or only in association with members of their bloc. But substantial clout could be mustered by a balanced consortium; joint leadership and pooled influence could tip the scales from status quo to exciting change.

Once when I discussed this coalition concept as regards peace and security with a friend, he labeled it a "conspiracy for peace." Perhaps the proposed action-oriented coalition dealing with all the critical world issues might be called a "conspiracy for common sense" or a "conspiracy for survival." In any event, the coalition approach merits serious consideration and trial.

Members of a coalition would not be preselected in any formal sense. They would, in fact, select themselves, stimulated by dynamic leaders to cooperate with other nations on matters of common interest. Some nations might participate on certain proposals but not on others. Changing conditions, such as shifts in national policies and assignments of people to key posts, might alter a nation's desire and ability to play an important role in an informal coalition.

Suggesting possible coalition candidates is hazardous; errors of commission and omission are certain. Nevertheless, I offer the following subjective judgments, based upon such criteria as apparent national policy toward stronger global and regional organization, leadership displayed in various international bodies, perceived influence with other nations, caliber of diplomats, and strength of staff backup. In reaching these nominations, I have researched positions taken in international bodies, particularly the United Nations.

I have included a few nations more on their potential than their demonstrated commitment and leadership in strengthening global and regional organization. My suggested nominees (with due apology for inadvertent omissions) include Algeria, Argentina, Australia, Austria, Brazil, Canada, Egypt, Finland, Germany (West), Ghana, India, Indonesia, Italy, Japan, Kenya, Mexico, Netherlands, Nigeria, Pakistan, Philippines, Poland, Romania, Sri Lanka, Sweden, Tanzania, Venezuela, Yugoslavia, and Zambia.

Were a score or more of these nominees to cooperate as a coalition, I believe they would be joined soon by others; support would come from unexpected sources.

Enhancing
Leadership
Potential

Why are some nation-states better candidates for leadership than others? What combination of factors causes a nation to step out ahead of the pack in the important quest to manage global problems?

While no formula applies, several factors are pertinent. Certainly national leaders must be sensitive to the needs of the world. General information about the controversies and conflicts of the moment is not enough. A reasonable understanding of the current and potential threats posed by global problems, together with awareness of the inadequacies of present institutions and mechanisms, is needed. All too few national leaders measure up to these standards.

Increased awareness has to be accompanied by thoughtful reexamination of policies regarding involvement and commitment. National leaders must become convinced that something should be done and that their countries should be involved. They must commit adequate resources, assign capable diplomats, provide effective research and logistic backup, and cultivate public support. Not all nations have the necessary human and financial resources, plus the required determination.

While national leadership usually involves the composite efforts of many officials and agencies, the significant contributions of able and dedicated individuals cannot be overlooked. Jean Monnet, through persistent efforts over many years, fathered the European Economic Community. General Carlos P. Romulo of the Philippines, from the 1945 drafting of the UN Charter until the present, has kept alive the concept of Charter reform. Paul Hoffman, as an individual on the UN staff, brought new concepts and strengths to the multilateral aid program. Arvid Pardo, former ambassador of tiny Malta, almost single-handedly promoted the UN decision to reexamine the law of the seas. Maurice Strong's dynamic leadership was vital to the success of the Stockholm Conference on the Human Environment and the launching of the United Nations Environment Programme (UNEP). The dogged persistence of Ambassador Alfonso García Robles of Mexico is credited for the Tlatelolco treaty.

What will cause national leaders, buried under avalanches of pressing problems, to lose their reluctance to address seemingly remote global problems? Some impetus may come from external crises and from the advocacy and example of other nations. In reasonably open societies, the mounting pressures of public opinion and NGOs can be effective. But in most cases, the drive must be generated through internal research.

The emergence of stronger leadership should not be left to chance. Effective research focused upon longer range national interests and global problems would assist the formation of policies oriented toward more effective management of critical world issues. Most nations could benefit from some internal restructuring of administrative units dealing with the United Nations and other multilateral, global, and regional affairs; from assigning able and forward-looking diplomats and staff to missions at the United Nations and to responsible positions dealing with other global and regional organizations; from appointing to key government posts individuals having broad global outlook developed during tours of duty at the United Nations and other international organizations; and from seeking the services of policy-oriented private citizens and representatives of nongovernmental organizations.

Better management of critical world issues will occur only when nation-states act collectively to make it happen. Collective action by nation-states will occur only when the leaders of many nations accept responsibility to create extranational and supranational mechanisms and institutions. National leaders must be inspired, persuaded, or goaded to lead their nations into cooperative action, into joining a conspiracy for common sense survival.

14 NONGOVERNMENTAL ORGANIZATIONS

"Peace is too important to be left to the generals" is an often repeated cliche. Global issues are similarly too important to be left to governments. People make up the world community. People suffer or benefit from the procrastination or foresight of governments in the handling of economic, political, and social issues. People must be involved because all governments, even the most dictatorial, are influenced by public opinion and eventually stand or fall on how well they serve the needs and interests of their people.

The private sector, where it exists, is deeply and properly involved in world affairs. Since the operations of commercial nongovernmental organizations impinge directly upon the economy of nations and the world, their actions, for better or for worse, contribute to international relations and influence foreign policies. Numerous nonprofit NGOs also bear directly upon national and international public opinion and indirectly influence the decision-making processes of governments and international organizations.

Most governments need to be prodded into action by forward-looking people. Bureaucracies develop an inertia, almost human in nature, that resists innovative alternatives. Governments tend to support the status quo whether it be to the right, left, or somewhere in between. Heads of state hesitate to change the postures and positions that brought them to office: don't rock the boat, don't get ahead of public opinion. Normal governmental responses to technological, economic, and political change are seldom bold or comprehensive: go slowly and take small, safe steps. These characteristics generally prevail whether leaders are in power by virtue of inheritance, election, appointment, or military coup.

Since few individuals have sufficient stature or position to gain direct access to decision-makers and opinion-shapers, group advocacy is necessary. And this is where NGOs can serve as the vehicles for enlightened group action and expression. From nation to nation, their importance depends upon the openness of the society and the opportunities and traditions for public participation. NGO activity is minimal or nonexistent where citizen expression is discouraged or prohibited; NGOs are common and active where free speech prevails and public challenge of governmental policy is routine.

Nowhere are NGOs more numerous and influential than in the United States; they have played important roles in this country. And the shaping of future US foreign policy calls for vastly enlarged NGO participation. Obviously, the same is true in other countries where NGOs are permitted to function.

NGOs come in a wide variety of types, functions, and sizes. Commercial or industrial NGOs represent groups of people or organizations in related fields. Others pursue research, study, and education. Many are cause-oriented. They may be concerned solely with domestic matters, with the international scene, or with both. In examining the current and potential impacts of various categories of NGOs upon both opinion and policy, I emphasize the United States situation because of personal experience, my involvement through The Stanley Foundation, and my strong belief that NGOs can and must contribute importantly to the reshaping of US foreign policy and the managing of global problems.

Commercial NGOs

Private sector organizations in business, commercial, agricultural, and industrial areas constitute a large and powerful, but very diverse, group of NGOs having both direct and indirect impact upon the management of critical world issues.

The transnational enterprises, previously examined, are a sizable and unique subgroup. As profit-oriented entities transferring capital, technology, and management assistance across national boundaries, they not only contribute to economic development but also establish strong human ties. And the success of their human relations, social contributions, and economic benefits—as viewed by their host countries—is closely related to their influence. A number of observers rate the economic and social impacts of TNEs as the most significant future nongovernmental influence upon world order.

Business and business-related organizations operating within national boundaries, including corporations, trade associations, and unions, constitute another important subgroup of NGOs. Although foreign policy is not a primary concern for them, their operations do affect it. Moreover, the well-being of business-related NGOs is affected more by the international economic and political climate than is generally recognized.

The so-called military-industrial complex is a prime example of NGO influence. Its nongovernmental segments include manufacturers and exporters of weapons, military equipment, and supplies, together with labor unions and defense-related research and development institutions—all having vested interests in arms development and sales. These organizations work hand in hand with the Pentagon, members of Congress sympathetic to defense spending, and the executive branch of the US government. They strongly influence decisions and appropriations on military expenditures, weapons exports, and arms control and disarmament agreements. The efforts of these NGOs are abetted by think-tanks and academicians financed by Pentagon grants and by military-oriented membership organizations. The influence of this complex of NGOs must be rated as detrimental to managing the global peace and security issue as I have proposed it.

Other commercial NGOs with vested interests exert conflicting influence upon trade policies. Many corporations and trade associations with capital-intensive or high technological bases and forward-looking leadership have consistently supported free trade measures. Such organizations as the Farm Bureau and the US Chamber of Commerce also generally reflect this enlightened attitude. On the other hand, labor-intensive industries, and their trade associations, frequently maneuver to obtain tariff or quota protection against imports from cheap labor countries. Several formerly free trade-oriented labor unions have become more protectionist-minded and claim that imports and TNE operations export job opportunities. On balance, the conflicting influence of these two schools of thought is hardly conducive to adequate reform of the trade and TNE systems of the world economic order.

NGOs within the business community also exert conflicting influence upon US development aid policies. Some would enlarge assistance and make it more effective; others would curtail it or eliminate it altogether. Currently, the composite influence is probably negative. Leaders are handicapped in reaching compromises with the developing world to maintain a viable aid program. This bodes ill for the longer range management of both the resource/population balance and the development issues.

Commercial NGOs are a potent force. Well financed and staffed with able executives, researchers, and lobbyists, they owe it to themselves, to their nation, and to the world community to do more. Whether or not the future influence of commercial NGOs contributes to the effective management of critical world issues depends upon their willingness to take a more positive, longer range view; their own long-range interests are more achievable in the absence of unmanaged global problems. More business executives must be persuaded to place concern for improved world economic and political orders above immediate financial expediency. This is an important task for enlightened leaders within the business community, for trade associations, and for NGOs concerned with foreign policies.

Such efforts are crucial to balancing the propaganda of the military-industrial complex and to encouraging governments to base military decisions upon security rather than economics and to base decisions regarding TNE guidelines on a fair understanding of their beneficial contributions to the evolving economic order.

The various elements of the news media are a unique type of NGO. In the United States and in other countries where the media are not controlled or dominated by national governments, they shoulder a heavy responsibility for both information and influence as the major disseminators of world news. No one who reads, watches, or listens can escape awareness of crises and conflicts. In print and on the air, articles, commentaries, documentaries, and editorials present facts, analyses, and opinions. A stream of books dealing with every conceivable facet of world affairs flows from publishers.

The Media as NGOs

What impacts do media NGOs have upon the management of critical world issues? On the plus side, the media have narrowed the information gap among nations. Bringing distant events vividly into homes emphasizes the smallness of the earth and the proximity of other human groups; news undermines concepts of isolation and self-sufficiency. Telecasts relayed by satellite instantly intrude the horrors of war and violence into our living rooms.

But on the minus side, the emphasis on the immediate and the sensational, the simple good guy–bad guy view of controversies, often combines with editorial bias and reporter ignorance. The result, at times, is warped news reporting that makes minor incidents into crises, obscures underlying complications, and stresses conflict over cooperation.

Perhaps the greatest media disservice, however, is undue emphasis upon the present at the expense of the future. True, the events of today are today's news. The casual media consumer, however, is encouraged to consider a problem resolved when it no longer receives a headline in the daily paper or mention on the ABC, CBS, or NBC evening news. Satellite reporting, instant analysis, and capsulized news do not encourage deliberate ongoing attention to the resolution of stubborn problems.

How could the media have a more positive influence? News organizations could be encouraged to present a longer range view of world needs in the increasingly interdependent world community based upon a clearer understanding of underlying trends and issues. More time and space could be devoted to objective and educational presentation of emerging global issues and problems. News focus could aim well ahead of the conservative pace of governments.

Academic
NGOs   A vast array of educational institutions and associations strongly influence public opinion and, in turn, governmental policies. Local and state educational systems, although managed by public boards, can be considered NGOs because they are far removed from the mainstream of foreign policy decision-making.

Preparation for global citizenship challenges educators at all levels—elementary, secondary, collegiate, and graduate. How are graduates prepared for life in a crowded world? Will they have the tools and attitudes necessary to break with tradition and establish and operate the systems needed to manage not only today's problems but others that will surely emerge in the next few decades—deep awareness, broad understanding, high level of tolerance, and conviction regarding world affairs? The gross deficiencies of past educational patterns in this regard are evident in the attitudes and prejudices of the majority of leaders today.

Fortunately, students are now more aware of the world beyond national boundaries. Few, however, comprehend how much the present world differs from the world their parents and grandparents took largely for granted. Despite several encouraging experiments at elementary, secondary, and collegiate levels, pitifully little is being done to reshape curricula and to prepare and stimulate teachers to better educate our young people for responsible world citizenship and effective leadership.

Efforts to meet this challenge would be helped by encouraging educators to take an interdisciplinary view beyond their specialties and by giving greater attention to experimentation regarding the development of curricula and programs. Advantage should be taken of the pioneering work of such NGOs as the Institute for World Order, the Kettering Foundation, and Global Perspectives in Education, Inc.

While education of tomorrow's citizens and leaders is of vital importance, its impact is delayed. Fortunately, however, the academic world has some near-term impact upon opinion and policy through research. Policy-oriented papers and books based on investigations carried out at the graduate and postgraduate level in universities and university-affiliated research centers or institutes are widely circulated. Some of these studies, financed by Pentagon grants, focus upon military matters; other research, however, deals with broader global problems. Several NGOs provide forums for sharing and debating foreign policy proposals originating in the academic world. They reach opinion-shapers and decision-makers through printed reports and the presence of government officials at their meetings.

Individual scholars serve in personal capacities as advisors to governmental departments and agencies. A privileged few, from time to time, have the ear of high level legislators and administrators in the State, Defense, Treasury, and other departments of the US government or are appointed to fill important positions in the executive branch.

Through such channels, the near-term impact of academic NGOs may, at best, be balanced regarding the management of global problems. The impact could be made more positive in the future by expanding academic research related to the management of critical world issues, including the required institutions; making greater use of qualified academicians as advisors to the legislative and administrative branches of our government; and facilitating interchange between academic investigators, government officials, and nonofficial leaders.

Nonacademic Institutes

Considerable research applicable to the management of critical world issues is also carried on or sponsored by institutes, foundations, and organizations that are not connected with academic institutions. These so-called think-tanks are supported by private endowments, contributions, and contracts with various governmental agencies. They assemble staffs of academicians, former governmental officials, and others. While many of the think-tanks concentrate on research related to military and defense matters, several of them deal with political and economic topics related to managing global problems.

The final two groups, which I call national and international citizen NGOs, include dues-paying organizations, ad hoc committees, private foundations, and other entities financed from private sources and managed by individuals without official positions in government. They are free to propose, support, and work for changes consistent with their view of the long-term interests of all. Many focus upon various foreign policy objectives and upon domestic policies directly influencing international affairs, often concentrating upon a single issue. Most citizen NGOs in the United States confine their activities within our borders; and they will be discussed first.

Many of these NGOs operate solely within the area of foreign policy, often with concentration upon a single issue; in others, foreign policy matters are secondary. Citizen NGOs are financed from private sources, principally dues and contributions; a few obtain partial financing from private foundations. Foundations operating in this field are financed largely by private endowment. In the United States, the great majority of citizen NGOs operate on tax deductible contributions made to their research and educational programs; those concentrating upon political action to influence specific legislation or elections are ineligible for tax deductibility if political action is more than a minor part of their total operation.

The number of citizen NGOs is large and their activities fall into three broad categories.

First, because they have sufficient knowledge within their staffs and membership to challenge the validity and effectiveness of governmental economic, political, and military programs, some NGOs contribute valuable expertise to the development of policy. They are capable of relating specific proposals to the broader aspects of interdependent global problems. Input of these NGOs to policy-making is currently accomplished through conferences, publications, and consultations of members and staffs with legislative and administrative governmental bodies.

The second, and perhaps most common, opportunity for citizen NGOs is the shaping of public opinion in support of meaningful foreign policies consistent with adequate management of the critical world issues. This is an educational and promotional function aimed largely at adult audiences. NGOs now responding to this opportunity focus upon writers, scholars, educators, and political and community leaders who have, or should have, a more sophisticated understanding of global problems. Only limited appeal is now made to mass membership organizations (women's and men's groups, youth organizations, churches, labor unions, trade and business associations, and others) not primarily concerned with foreign policy. Nevertheless, on occasion, coalitions of NGOs focusing upon specific issues have enlisted the cooperation of other NGOs with more general objectives in order to give support and publicity to a timely issue.

The third opportunity is political action. Only a few of the national citizen NGOs are active in this area; most, because they enjoy tax deductibility, are barred by law from substantial involvement. Politically minded NGOs usually maintain lobbyists to work closely with legislators and administrators in governments. While they seek to inform regarding global problems, their major efforts concentrate upon specific legislation or administrative decisions. NGOs oriented to political action frequently enlist the support of sizable membership organizations interested in the particular matter under consideration.

Foundations might be encouraged to initiate or support more research and education related to the future management of critical world issues. Citizen input to opinion-shaping and decision-making is vital and should be expanded.[1]

In the United States, better channels are needed to the Congress; the Departments of State, Treasury, Agriculture, Commerce, and Defense; the Arms Control and Disarmament Agency; and ad hoc groups dealing with specific problems. Input from NGOs during bilateral and multilateral negotiations could encourage national delegations to negotiate more consistently with stated aspirations and principles of national leaders.

International Citizen NGOs

The activities of a number of NGOs reach international audiences. Many private organizations and foundations have programs seeking to promote goodwill and understanding among nations, including exchanges of many types—student, professional, tourist, and cultural. While such activities have little bearing upon near-term decisions regarding the management of critical world issues, they do enlarge understanding and reduce prejudices among people of various nations and cultures.

Unofficial international meetings and conferences convened by

1. Readers desiring involvement should contact citizen NGOs directly. The Stanley Foundation, 420 East Second Street, Muscatine, Iowa 52761, will, upon request, provide names and addresses.

NGOs make important contributions. Such conferences serve as vehicles to promote understanding among specialists and diplomats from many countries and provide the opportunity to explore new approaches to solving global problems. One outstanding example is the Pugwash Conference first convened in 1957 to bring together scientists from the United States, the Soviet Union, and other countries concerned with nuclear problems. This series of conferences initiated by Cyrus Eaton may be properly credited with creating the mutual understanding required for the initiation of bilateral nuclear arms limitation negotiations between the Soviet Union and the United States. Other noteworthy international conferences are those sponsored by the Center for the Study of Democratic Institutions, the Club of Rome, the Stockholm Institute of Peace Research (SIPRI), the Aspen Institute, the Rockefeller Foundation, the Carnegie Endowment, the Johnson Foundation, the Kettering Foundation, and The Stanley Foundation.

The ad hoc gatherings of NGO representatives and individuals at UN conferences give broad support and permit lobbying for forward-looking declarations of policy. The first of these was at the 1972 Stockholm Conference on the Human Environment. Subsequent gatherings included those at the 1974 Bucharest Conference on Population, the 1974 Rome Conference on Food, the 1975 International Women's Year Conference in Mexico City, the 1976 Vancouver Conference on Habitat, the 1978 UN Special Session on Disarmament, and several sessions of the Conferences on the Law of the Seas.

Many NGOs have been granted consultative status at the United Nations, which gives them access to UN meetings and contact with national delegations as well as the Secretariat. Unfortunately, consultative status has been used more to provide briefings and outreach from the United Nations than to encourage direct NGO input. New ground may have been broken, however, at the 1978 UN Special Session on Disarmament. Not only were NGOs permitted to submit written proposals for circulation to the delegations, but for the first time 25 NGOs and 6 research organizations were invited to address meetings of the Ad Hoc Working Committee of that session. I had the privilege of speaking for The Stanley Foundation as one of the six research organizations. I hope that further channels may be developed whereby NGOs on a consultative basis may present oral and written views to any UN organ, standing committee, or ad hoc body.

Expansion of NGO efforts across national boundaries would serve to increase their impact upon decision-making. This could be achieved by increasing the number of formal and informal international gatherings, encouraging United States NGOs to include participants from other countries in their activities, and urging US citizens to become active in international NGOs.

The future direction of foreign policy in every nation with NGOs *Opportune* can be greatly influenced by effective and expanded NGO activity. *Role* This is particularly true in the United States, but the United States is not alone in this regard. Public opinion generated through nongovernmental sources has great potential to influence governmental decisions in many countries.

The outcome, in no small measure, depends upon that small segment of the population that is concerned and aware of the hazards of failure to manage global problems. Individually, their voices will be lost in the hue and cry of big government. But concerted voices, expressed through NGOs, will be heard and should influence the shaping of opinions and the making of decisions.

If responsibility and opportunity truly parallel power and affluence, the United States ought to be the world's leading advocate of an ordered world without war and the most dedicated activist promoting wise management of the critical world issues. Currently we are neither. Although commendable and productive in some areas, our policies and actions fall far short of what the citizens of this country and the world have a right to expect.

The United States is singled out here for special examination because it is my country and that of most readers of this book. The United States is also a leading actor on the world stage. Competence, technology, affluence, experience, and heritage combine to equip us uniquely for leadership. Moreover, because of our open society, we, as individuals, have opportunities to influence policies and actions.

United States Leadership in the Past   Prior to World War II, the United States, comfortably isolated by the Atlantic and Pacific Oceans, was minimally involved in world affairs. Having "saved the world for democracy" in 1918, we stood aloof from the League of Nations, even though it was the brainchild of our President Woodrow Wilson. The 1922 Washington Armament Conference produced a five-power treaty placing a 10-year moratorium on naval shipbuilding. The 1928 Briand-Kellogg Pact seemed to assure peace and security by renouncing war as an instrument of national policy and calling for pacific settlement of international disputes. Thus assured, we reduced our military forces and turned to domestic problems. Our private sector involvement in world trade, aided by occasional bilateral government negotiations, was neither large nor economically important.

World War II shattered this comfortable, self-centered existence. Long before Pearl Harbor, moral, political, and security factors were combining to compel our entrance into the conflict. The United

States emerged as the world's strongest power; Germany and Japan were crushed, France and the United Kingdom were greatly weakened, and the Soviet Union had been ravaged and partly destroyed.

Recognizing the winds of change, our politicians and diplomats led the way in creating international organizations believed essential to peace, security, and progress in the postwar era. At Dumbarton Oaks, San Francisco, and Bretton Woods, we played a leading role.

Having provided crucial military might to crush the Axis powers, we hurriedly brought the boys home and greatly reduced our armed forces. We claimed no territory except some Pacific islands, many placed under trusteeship. We took early steps to enhance global well-being: the Marshall Plan, assistance to Japan and Germany, independence for the Philippines, the Baruch Plan to place atomic energy under international control, and Part IV Technical Assistance. We shouldered the heaviest burden of the United Nations' first and only collective security action, repelling the North Korean attack upon South Korea (1950–1953). That these measures also served our own legitimate self-interests did not detract from their worth to the world community. Our self-interests appeared to be consistent with assuring peace and security for all nations and enhancing worldwide freedom, justice, and progress. We seemed to be guided by the fine principles of our Declaration of Independence. For a few postwar years, under bipartisan leadership, we were united in support of a forward-looking foreign policy. Our reservoir of goodwill was never greater.

In a few short years, the scene changed. The Soviet Union's seizure of power in Eastern Europe shattered the supposed unity of the allied nations and revealed the East-West split. President Truman, with the support of the US Congress, formalized the cold war by extending aid to Greece and Turkey. The arms race accelerated as nuclear deterrence became the pattern for mutual security. Western colonialism ended and numerous newly independent nations, with exploding populations and rising expectations, crowded the world stage. Global dynamics became increasingly complex and unsettled.

Now, three decades later, the United States has not yet adjusted fully to the vastly changed world or fashioned a foreign policy responsive to it; we are not playing the leadership role we did in the immediate postwar period. Not only has the United States failed to respond adequately, but our public attitudes toward stronger leader- *Disillusionment* ship have deteriorated noticeably. Frustration and disillusionment are the hallmarks of US public opinion about our foreign policy and the reasons are not difficult to discern.

Our government leaders and citizenry alike are resentful and discouraged that the world community has not performed the way we proposed and expected. The Soviet Union did not play dead after World War II; instead, it has rebuilt and rearmed with a strong determination to gain stature as a world power and to export its communist doctrine. The United Nations no longer responds to our every desire and seems out of control. We see the General Assembly dominated by a "tyranny of the majority" and the Security Council impotent to assure peace and security. Our huge bilateral and multilateral aid commitments, economic as well as military, appear to have done little to foster development or win friends for the United States.

Our sacred concepts of democratic government are not working well when applied to new nations. Many democracies have yielded to military governments, often through bloody coups. Even the Philippines, our favorite developing nation, turned to martial law in 1972. Nor are our concepts of free enterprise enjoying wide acceptance. Some countries have adopted completely socialistic structures. The United States is often berated as an economic imperialist and potential aggressor.

Neither democracy nor free enterprise has received a fair test in many of them. The concept of democracy, though, should not be faulted. Democracies patterned after those of the United States and Western Europe were, undoubtedly, prematurely established in some countries; there was no other logical choice. But many new countries lack both the educated and independent citizenry and the mature leadership essential to a successful democracy. Partial governmental participation in economic affairs is inevitable in many of the former colonies. The experience and capital needed for indigenous free enterprise are lacking; distrust of foreign business, often associated with colonial masters, is common.

Humiliating withdrawal from an unsuccessful and unpopular war in Indochina capped growing disenchantment with our bilateral and multilateral activities in the world community. Revelations surrounding Watergate, CIA dirty tricks in Chile and elsewhere, misconduct of public officials, and bribery of foreign officials by Lockheed and others have undermined confidence in our government and our transnational corporations. Uncontrolled inflation, high unemployment, the energy crisis, and unsolved domestic problems raise doubts about the ability of government and the private sector to manage our economy. The result has been a loss of public confidence in government and the "establishment." The so-called taxpayers' revolt is destined to criticize and trouble government.

Thus a variety of factors combine to stimulate a harder line in foreign policy and isolationist thinking, which lead to an increasing tendency to draw back from international affairs, look at international organizations with a jaundiced eye, and rely upon ourselves. The result is stress upon military might, lessened concern for developing nations, and continued overemphasis on national sovereignty. It is no surprise that our willingness and ability to exert leadership is undermined.

The time is favorable for the emergence of dynamic and innovative US leadership. Both the need and the opportunity increase with the constant escalation of global problems; time is of the essence. *Looking Ahead*

A more positive, innovative, and active foreign policy, geared to achieving better management of critical world issues, would, at the same time, benefit the United States. The very process of developing, explaining, and implementing such a foreign policy would challenge current divisive attitudes and thwart the drift toward a more self-centered posture. Checking and reversing the global arms race—undoubtedly a high priority of a revamped foreign policy—could improve national security. It could also reduce Pentagon budgets, a highly desirable objective, in view of growing public demands for tax reduction.

But would US leadership comparable to that of the early post–World War II days be welcomed by the world community? Our allies and friends around the world are concerned that US political trends seem detrimental to a more active role in the international arena. They are highly critical of US-Soviet failure to halt and reverse the nuclear arms race and to support more positively the UN Special Session on Disarmament. Our failure to deal adequately with energy problems seems incomprehensible. Our persistent, unfavorable balances of payment, the continuing decline of the dollar, and our reduction of development assistance are alarming. Although the ratification of the Panama Canal treaties, our participation in advancing peace in the Middle East, and our normalization of relations with China have been well received and the expressed determination of President Carter to take a fresh look at a number of global problems was more than welcomed, reluctance to implement fully his aspirations has been discouraging.

Nevertheless, I believe resurgence of US leadership would be welcomed by most of the world community, provided it dealt forthrightly with the problems that are common to all. Despite their many differences, most leaders of the world's 150 plus nations recognize the urgent need to cope more effectively with global problems. Mounting economic pressures and security concerns contribute to this recognition. There is awareness, too, of the reluctance of the major powers to approach global issues on the basis of the common good.

Hence I believe that US leadership, exercised skillfully and diplomatically and aimed at improving the management of the critical world issues, would be welcomed. Some of the high regard accorded the United States a quarter of a century ago could be restored. When our leadership serves the interests of the world community as a whole, it in no way detracts from potential benefits to the United States.

Principles   Successful recasting of US foreign policy calls for this country to address proposals such as those outlined in Part II and to develop present and future policies and strategies to achieve them. This must be done in the context of the primary purpose of foreign policy—enhancing national security and well-being—with the major difference that longer range issues, needs, and hazards deserve far greater emphasis than in the past. We must translate our vague aspirations into sufficiently concrete goals and objectives to guide policy and action. Bipartisan consensus is required on the following principles:

USE OF FORCE The use and threat of military force is no longer an acceptable ultimate tool of national policy for major powers or an effective means of security for lesser powers.

POWER BALANCE Power balance as the backbone of security policy is becoming obsolete with the changing nature of national power and the declining effectiveness of military power.

ARMS RACE The future maintenance of peace and security calls for halting and reversing the arms race and developing alternate systems for peacefully settling controversies and preventing aggression.

ECONOMIC INTERDEPENDENCE Economic self-sufficiency is a luxury no longer enjoyed by any nation, the United States included.

TRADE Economic and social development and the well-being of all nations depend, in part, upon freer exchange of raw materials, manufactured products, capital, and technology.

MANAGEMENT MECHANISMS Improved multilateral and third party procedures, mechanisms, and institutions—largely non-military in nature—are essential to managing global problems related both to peace and security and to economic and social matters.

URGENCY OF ACTION Establishment of the improved procedures, mechanisms, and institutions cannot be left to chance; the hazards of procrastination are too great.

SOVEREIGNTY Effective long-range management of world problems depends upon the willingness of nations to delegate some degree of extranational or supranational authority to regional and global institutions.

THE COMMON INTEREST Successful foreign policy for any nation, including the United States, must be generally aligned with the common longer range interests of the peoples of the world. No other policy can gain broad and sustained support.

HERITAGE Successful foreign policy for the United States must be morally compatible with our heritage and capable of enjoying continued respect and bipartisan support.

Action

Were key decision-makers and opinion-shapers in this country to tacitly or formally accept these concepts, our nation would be poised for a great advance and a broad range of actions. Our president and our Congress would, in fact, have a mandate to revamp and strengthen our foreign policy and to lead efforts to manage critical world issues. Imagine the impact of presidential outreach—addresses, messages to Congress, news conferences, and appearances at the United Nations—embracing proposals for priority action.

If ultimate objectives of a world without war with adequate global institutions having extranational or supranational authority were accepted, the United States could boldly propose top priority be given to activities aimed at checking and reversing the arms race.

Bilateral discussions and negotiations with the Soviet Union might be intensified. US participation in multilateral disarmament matters—both the Committee on Disarmament and the UN Disarmament Commission—could be more forward-looking, including determined efforts not only to limit the transfer of conventional armaments but establish programs to reduce national dependence upon them.

To stimulate curtailment of nuclear weapons, the United States might declare a voluntary moratorium upon further nuclear test explosions conditioned upon (1) a reciprocal voluntary moratorium by the Soviet Union within six months, (2) UN General Assembly adoption of a Comprehensive Nuclear Test Ban treaty (CTB) within 18 months, and (3) ratification of the CTB treaty by all nuclear powers within five years.

The United States could promote disarmament by publicly reducing appropriations (in constant dollars) to its military establishment by 10 percent (3⅓ percent per year for three years), conditioned upon (1) similar action by the Soviet Union within two years, (2) development within three years of an acceptable, joint USSR-US method to monitor reductions, and (3) initiation within one year of further bilateral and multilateral arms reduction negotiations.

If the United States announced its intent to use the International Court of Justice to resolve international controversies in which it is involved and rescinded the Connally Reservation, a powerful thrust would be given to third-party peaceful settlement.

To stimulate economic and social development of the developing nations, the United States might commit additional contributions to multilateral institutions of a third or a half of that year's reduction in military budgets. To encourage necessary modifications of the systems comprising the world economic order, the United States could enlarge its dialogue with the leaders of the Group of 77, as well as with the developed nations.

To stimulate the expansion of human rights, the Senate of the United States could ratify all pending UN human rights conventions and press for the establishment of improved UN human rights mechanisms.

To encourage more extensive research on the management of the six critical world issues, the United States might offer to advance $50 million a year over the next five years to facilitate the establishment of a Disarmament Research Center (chapter 4), a Center for Economic and Development Research (chapter 5), and a World Environmental Research Institute (chapter 9). Such an offer could be conditioned upon developing matching funds from other sources within three years.

These actions are the kind we could take within the framework of a foreign policy responsive to the world of today and tomorrow. Our aspirations would then be translated into tangible proposals whose impact on the world community would be significant. At the same time that concentrated effort to solve global problems would be stimulated, some of the goodwill that has drained from the American reservoir would be replenished.

But bipartisan agreement upon revitalized foreign policy concepts   *Blocks* and actions is contingent on our nation overcoming certain barriers.

Our leadership efforts have been and continue to be severely handicapped by a number of factors—some shared with other nations, some peculiar to us. While these factors have been touched upon in earlier discussions, it is desirable to summarize them here; they constitute a ready agenda.

Nationalism unduly influences our policies and those of nearly all nations. But in the United States, excessive nationalism takes on a larger dimension. It combines with our great economic and military power, long-standing self-sufficiency, self-righteous conviction that we are chosen people, and an unbridled national pride sometimes resembling arrogance. We have little confidence in world organizations and are extremely hesitant to admit the need for more effective global and regional solutions. Many US citizens believe serious proposals to delegate any degree of authority to a strengthened United Nations border on treason.

We share with all nations a grossly inadequate understanding of the multiple impact upon our institutions of rapid, vast technological and political change. We do not comprehend the nature of the global responses necessary to cope with them. We share with most industrialized nations a stubborn reluctance to admit the inadequacies of the world economic system. Along with most older nations, we deal awkwardly and ineffectively with the problems of the developing nations.

Two typically American attitudes also handicap our leadership. One is our frustrating tendency to export our political, economic, and social systems without suitable adaptation to local conditions of other nations. The second is our insistence upon instant solutions; we overlook the vital importance of pursuing objectives patiently.

These factors contributed to our despair when our high hopes for a peaceful, orderly world at the close of World War II were subverted by the intransigence of the Communist bloc and the extravagant demands of the developing world. Undoubtedly, our expectations were too high; at least they exceeded the willingness and capacity of the world community to realize them through the United Nations.

But none of these factors is adequate to explain US failure to provide more positive leadership. Our major handicap has been nearly three decades of bitter philosophical and political confrontation with the Soviet Union and a different, but paralyzing, confrontation with China. Our response to these challenges has led us to unwarranted dependence upon military security. Ever expanding Pentagon budgets and new weapons systems invite reciprocal commitments by the Soviets and thus continue to fuel the arms race. Yesterday we were unprepared; today we are incredibly overarmed.

The domestic consequences of these face-offs include suspicion among peoples and organizations, undermining of bipartisan foreign policy, strengthening of pro-national philosophy, and enlarged influence for the military-industrial complex. Globally, we have been led to support repressive regimes and engage in covert intervention.

Our intense commitment to military power diverts US attention from the world's fundamental political and economic problems and downgrades our support of international organization. It severely handicaps the minority of our leaders who would encourage nonmilitary problem-solving. It undermines our national credibility as a champion of independence and freedom. Both the desire and the ability of the United States to offer constructive world leadership have been weakened severely.

Reappraisal   A thoughtful reappraisal of US attitudes and policies toward the communist world is long overdue. Such a reappraisal is basic to advancing beyond fragile détente with the Soviets and normalized relations with the Chinese. (Obviously, reappraisal of policies and attitudes by the Soviets and the Chinese is equally desirable.)

Despite the important beginnings resulting from Henry Kissinger's and former President Nixon's diplomacy, our fundamental relations vis-a-vis the two major communist countries have not been significantly altered. China, the Soviet Union, and the United States continue to criticize each other and maneuver to score points at home and with nonaligned nations. Fear and distrust guide military policies and cloud appraisals of each other's intent.

In retrospect, both sides have overreacted and misjudged threats and polemics. Quite naturally, US citizens find communist ideology abhorrent, ruthless tyranny as sometimes practiced by the Soviet Union and China repulsive, and some political and military moves of the communists alarming. On the other hand, the Soviet Union and China find capitalism equally abhorrent, are repulsed by some US political activities, and rightfully fear the strategic weapons focused upon them.

Undoubtedly, the United States erred by precipitously dismantling its armed forces and withdrawing troops from Europe before the dust of World War II settled. We did not know how to evaluate the actions of the Soviet Union, a sovereign state ravaged by German invasion, to protect itself. Stalin acted ruthlessly at home and aggressively in Europe. Were Stalin's moves security measures or a prelude to an invasion of Western Europe? Historians will undoubtedly debate this question for years.

US reaction certainly reflected fear that the Soviets were preparing to move westward. We embarked upon a program of rearmament and containment of communism that continues to dominate our foreign policy. In response, the Soviets stepped up their own rearmament, the cold war had begun, the arms race was under way, and the strategy of mutual deterrence—the peace of terror—emerged.

A few years later, Mao Tse-tung defeated Chiang Kai-shek and the People's Republic of China installed its brand of communism. Convinced that only the United States stood between monolithic communism and the free world, we intensified our efforts to contain the communists behind both the Iron Curtain and the Bamboo Curtain. The cold war became more intense as the communists reciprocated.

The domestic impacts of the fear of monolithic communism have been severe. Fear and panic became the order of the day; communist moves triggered near paranoiac response in this country. Demagogues like the late Senator Joseph McCarthy fanned these fears. The House Committee on Un-American Activities pried into the affairs of individuals and organizations. Those who dared speak out for international understanding and cooperation were immediately branded as suspect. The detrimental impacts of this period continue to the present. Opinion polls reveal that a significant segment of the US public anticipates war with the Soviet Union. Near hysterical anticommunism complicates efforts of our government to deal rationally with the Soviet Union and China. And, meanwhile, politicians beat the drums for greater armed might.

But time passes and conditions change. The concept of aggressive, monolithic communism has been undermined by events. The Soviet Union and China, split over ideology, have been antagonists for more than a decade. Yugoslavia has remained beyond Soviet domination. Other Eastern European countries are looking westward, edging away from Moscow. Even Hanoi tries to maintain a respectful distance from China now that Vietnam is reunited.

The influence of communist nations in the developing world has been spotty. Many developing nations have accepted economic and military aid from them. In some cases the superpowers have been skillfully played against one another, but, on the whole, the communist countries have been no more successful than the United States in dominating developing nations. Even where developing countries adopt state ownership patterns, they generally maintain independence in political and economic affairs.

Despite polemics for public consumption, both the Soviet Union and China have acted externally, more as pragmatic nation-states than as ideologists. They have aided revolutionary governments and have helped antagonists in some hot spots; the United States has often aided the other side. But, on the whole, they have been more successful than the United States in avoiding involvement of their own armed forces. Neither has become as deeply involved as the United States was in Vietnam.

Against this background, how are the superpowers to move from bitter confrontation to tolerable cooperation? Perhaps the first and most fundamental step is for these nations to recognize several areas of common self-interest.

One such interest is avoiding direct involvement in war, particularly with one another. Whatever the threats and lack of trust that initiated and continues the arms race, neither the Soviet Union nor China nor the United States want war. As members of the nuclear weapons club, they have calculated the death and destruction they could rain on one another and realized that war must be avoided lest their nation be on the receiving end of a holocaust. We know that the US military establishment is maintained to deter aggression and avoid, rather than provoke, war. Were it not so, the essential public support needed in an open society would be lacking. But we are reluctant to recognize that the Soviets and the Chinese have similar intents. Nor do the communists readily accept our claim of peaceful intent when our intercontinental ballistic missiles are targeted directly upon them.

Soviet conduct during the last three decades has revealed an intent to avoid becoming directly involved in war; their military preparations can be rationalized largely as steps to strengthen security and match deterrence with US strategic postures. Although Soviet officials bargain hard on SALT treaties and other arms control measures, they have demonstrated a desire for arms limitation, if not reduction. A most important factor is the Soviet memory of World War II. Scarcely a family was untouched; one out of every ten Soviet citizens, civilians included, died. Are Soviet leaders any more ready than US leaders to invite a war that might bring nuclear destruction upon their people?

China's yet primitive strategic nuclear capability is viewed by the United States as a lesser threat. There is, moreover, no sound basis for assuming that China has aggressive aims toward the United States. During the past two decades, China has not shown a bent for expansion. Its military posture rationally responds to a fear of Soviet invasion and, for a time, of US aggression from Korea or Indochina. Neither the conflict with India over a long-contested border, nor the recent Chinese invasion and withdrawal from Vietnam, nor the nature of Chinese armed forces is compatible with aggressive outreach. Recent understandings with the United States, plus a peace treaty with Japan, indicate desire for more rational relationships.

The validity of other common self-interests of these three great powers is less subject to argument. Each has numerous unmet needs—infrastructure, social systems, consumer products, and tax reductions—that would benefit from reduction of current commitments of money and manpower to military establishments. China's level of economic development is such that it is still classified as a developing nation. The Soviet Union is suffering from inadequate agricultural production, marginal transportation systems, insufficient housing, rising demands for consumer products, and limited capital. The United States, despite its great wealth, finds it difficult to divert sufficient financial resources into solving urban, energy, and transportation problems. Each of the three countries has a large enough agenda of domestic problems to challenge the scientists, engineers, managers, and others who would transfer from military to civilian tasks.

Not one of these three nations is likely to accomplish its desired economic objectives alone. Self-sufficiency is obsolete, despite reluctance to admit it. Clearly, in the future, United States needs for various materials may have to be met in the Soviet Union and China.

In return, the Soviet Union and China are linked to the United States by their need for our grain, our credit, and our technology. Thus the three countries have a common interest in mutually maintaining access to resources and technology.

Is it not time to deal with the Soviet Union and China more as powerful nations than as feared ideological entities? Certainly we should continue to vigorously oppose communism as economically unsound and dictatorships as morally wrong. Certainly we should continue to demonstrate by word and deed the superior performance of free enterprise and democracy.

We are compelled to coexist whether or not we like or trust one another. We must seek policies and systems enabling us to live in peace and manage mutual global problems in mutual self-interest.

Ways and Means

There is no certainty that our foreign policy can be reshaped. But to shun this challenge is to default our responsibilities, forfeit our right to influence events, and give to other nations a vetolike power over sensible and orderly progress. I believe that our people would support a president and a Congress acting with boldness and imagination to achieve our aspirations.

Several initiatives are particularly relevant. Reconciliation of the foreign policy roles of the legislative and executive branches of government deserves high priority. Integrally linked with the domestic economy, today's complex global matters present a situation quite different from that of the eighteenth century when the writers of our Constitution lodged responsibility for foreign affairs with the president. Foreign affairs can no longer be neatly separated from domestic problems. Congress controls the purse strings, and the departments of Defense, Commerce, and Treasury are involved, as well as the Department of State.

While the executive branch must lead, Congress needs to cooperate in policy formation and appropriations. Excessive secrecy generates misunderstanding and confrontation among the two branches of government and the public; it impairs the Congressional responsibility to serve as a check and balance upon the executive branch and to guide public opinion.

Secondly, to foster public understanding and involvement, the president, the administration, and members of Congress need to keep the public better informed about foreign policy, including the problems facing our nation and the world community. Improved channels for input from people to government and more formal opportunities for input from NGOs have already been suggested.

A page might be taken from the books of history. Near the close of World War II, a team of four Senators—Joseph Ball and Harold Burton, both Republicans, and Carl Hatch and Lester Hill, both Democrats—toured the country urging US participation in international organizations. Democrats William Fulbright in the House and Tom Connally in the Senate sponsored resolutions "favoring the creation of appropriate international machinery with power adequate to establish and maintain a just and lasting peace." During the Truman administration, Senators Connally and Vandenberg provided strong bipartisan leadership. More of this is needed. US foreign policy is too crucial to our country's future to allow interference by narrow party politics.

Substantial expansion of research on each of the critical world issues has been emphasized. To summarize, there is a deplorable imbalance between the human and monetary resources devoted to research on military and near-term aspects of foreign policy, compared to nonmilitary and longer range matters. The Arms Control and Disarmament Agency (ACDA) is a prime example. The organization, charged with responsibilities for studying all aspects of arms control and disarmament and for negotiating disarmament agreements, currently receives a paltry $16.5 million in contrast to more than twice that amount appropriated for Pentagon public relations and in further contrast to the billions now expended on weapons development. Obviously, serious efforts to deal with global problems require a far greater commitment for federal research.

A dynamic foreign policy undoubtedly requires independent initiatives on the part of the United States. Because this involves balancing uncertain future risks against known present risks, longer range trends and forces deserve attention. The thinking of Congress and the administration must be focused on more than immediate crises and issues. A Joint Congressional Committee on the Future could be an important vehicle for adequate dialogue. The staff work of such a committee could be supplemented by substantial input from scholars and NGOs engaged in the study of foreign policy and future trends. If given appropriate encouragement, our many NGOs can make significant contributions.

Should the United States restructure foreign policy? Should our country actively work to persuade the world community to establish the procedures, mechanisms, and institutions needed to manage critical world issues? Yes. *Why?*

Only a restructured, future-oriented foreign policy will

adequately serve our national interests. Moreover, as a nation that has been fortunate in achieving high levels of affluence, freedom, and human dignity, we owe a debt not only to the forefathers of this country but to prior civilizations. We have a responsibility to succeeding generations to preserve and enhance the concepts of democracy, enterprise, and human worth.

The time for a more balanced, innovative, and dynamic US foreign policy has come.

16 CHALLENGE

Today's efforts to manage the critical world issues appear to follow a pattern of brinkmanship. As a problem becomes threatening enough, the world community somehow attempts to deal with it; hurried and expedient reaction is substituted for careful and reasoned response. But restless political, economic, environmental, and social forces demonstrate clearly the need for and the benefit of management more adequate than the brinkmanship approach. Surely there is enough intelligence in the world to recognize the inadequacies of present global and regional procedures and institutions. Surely there is enough common sense to do something about it. Managing global problems will be difficult, but in the long run there is no other acceptable path to follow.

One certainty is that the present structure is shaky and fragmented; world community efforts are being made in an international system wherein nation-states reign supreme. Nonbinding concurrence approaching unanimity among the nation-states is the only currently available mechanism to handle crises, prevent harmful situations from becoming irreversible, and foster a more cooperative climate for building a new world order.

I find the immediate outlook far from reassuring, particularly in view of the conduct of nation-states since World War II. The world community has responded very slowly and timidly to emerging issues. The vast majority of nations has not demonstrated sufficient awareness of global problems to stimulate the implementation of even modest near-term proposals. There certainly has not been widespread recognition of the need for pooled sovereignty to implement longer range proposals. What then does the immediate future hold in store? Will nation-states rise to the occasion in common self-interest?

Fortunately, current attitudes need not dictate future conduct; they can be changed by the force of events and the power of reason.

Wars, nuclear catastrophes, environmental disasters, economic system breakdowns, famines, resource shortages, population increases, and massive encroachments upon human rights are the kinds of urgent events and trends that would, by force, convince nations of how compelling the issues are and how serious is the need for management. Resolution of current conflicts and confrontations—the Middle East, southern Africa, Korea, Indochina, the horn of Africa—could vastly improve the climate for international cooperation.

While events can positively affect the will of nations, far more is required. The urgency is great. Moreover, the nature and sequence of future events could create feelings of hopelessness and futility rather than determination to act. Rather, a grand effort is called for to persuade national leaders of the hazards of delay and the benefits of early action. This approach of reason and common sense requires statesmanship of the highest order within individual nations and among the global family of nations.

Dynamic leadership is needed at three levels: first, within each nation to conceive national policies in concert with the vanguard of forward-looking nations in quest of a sane and sound world order—joining in a conspiracy for survival; second, within regions to encourage groups of neighboring nations with similar interests to create mechanisms to handle issues and problems suitable for regional management; and, third, globally to stimulate nations to bring order out of chaos and move the world community toward effective management of its problems.

National leaders and their constituencies must look beyond narrow, near-term concerns to broader, long-term common interests. Without skillful, bold, and innovative statesmanship, the voices of reason and logic will be drowned out by the clamor of shortsighted special interests. The future of the world community, and indeed of nation-states, depends upon the response to this challenge. Stronger leaders are needed in both the public and private sectors and among opinion-shapers as well as decision-makers. More individual, group, and governmental leaders must emerge soon if the world is to avert disaster.

I believe leadership can inspire results. The skills of better management practices are known and may be applied to global problem-solving. The roles, authorities, decision-making, and financing of the United Nations can be improved without Charter change. Procedures are available for Charter revision. New institutions can be structured to supplement or even to replace the United Nations. Much technology to confront critical world issues is available; more can be developed. World problems, like national and local ones, are largely man-made. The solutions must also be man-made. With patience and determination the long and complex tasks of managing critical world issues can progress.

Statesmanship is also required to encourage a number of nations having common interests to pool their efforts to build procedures, mechanisms, and institutions for the entire world community. Statesmanship is needed to persuade still other nations to follow the lead of a coalition of future-oriented nations. Statesmanship is required to stimulate the more powerful nations, particularly the United States, the Soviet Union, and China, to accept the responsibilities and opportunities inherent in their status.

Throughout this book I have attempted to outline why improved global management of critical world issues is both urgent and beneficial for all nations and peoples, but my closing words are directed to the opinion-shapers and decision-makers of my own country. The United States belongs in the forefront of world community efforts to cope with mounting global problems. We should be a leading advocate of effective management and a persistent force in establishing the required means. Our leadership in this quest would not guarantee early success, but without US leadership progress is highly doubtful. I believe there is no excuse for our inability or unwillingness to provide this leadership.

Repeatedly, I have noted the difficulties that arise from strict adherence to the principle of national sovereignty. Of all peoples, the United States should be aware of this and be able to contribute to the resolution of the problem.

Our heritage features positive management of interdependence as well as independence. After the Revolutionary War, the 13 newly independent American states soon found that they were interdependent as well as sovereign; their political and economic fortunes were intertwined. As 13 separate and independent sovereign states, they still lacked the capacity to manage their economic and trade problems and to maintain peace and security. This situation was similar to that of the ex-colonies in Africa, Asia, and Latin America which have struggled to throw off external rule and gain political independence.

Fortunately, eleven years after the adoption of the Declaration of Independence, a significant event changed the course of US history.

A convention, cautiously endorsed by the Continental Congress, met in Philadelphia to deal with all matters "necessary to render the Constitution of the Federal Government adequate to the exigencies of the Union." The resulting Constitution, approved by the delegates of the politically independent states, acknowledged interdependence and established institutions to manage it.

Numerous parallels between the contemporary world situation and colonial America are obvious. There are differences today, of course, but they do not overshadow the urgency of managing global interdependence. This is not to propose that the formula devised in Philadelphia in 1787 is the appropriate one for today's world, but there is a lesson to be learned from the period of US history between 1776 and 1787. The lesson is a simple one. Achievement of national independence, albeit an essential step, is not enough. Interdependence, too, must be recognized and managed.

For the United States to be true to this heritage, must it not lead world community efforts to find ways to pool people's sovereignty to deal with shared and inescapable global problems? Vision and wisdom are called for. No greater challenge has ever faced the human race; no nation has a heritage contributing more to an understanding of this challenge.

The time has come for the United States to search its soul; recast its foreign policy; and dedicate its untiring efforts to advancing peace, security, progress, and human decency for the whole world. Once again we are challenged to a crusade—one whose methods will not be death and destruction as in 1917 and 1941, but peaceful and cooperative action by nation-states in response to our vastly changed world. This crusade is important; it justifies the utmost in commitment and dedication. The stakes are so high that it should be viewed as a moral equivalent of war. Have we the wisdom and courage of our nation's founders? Can we rekindle, in our time, their commitment to managing interdependence while protecting political independence? We can if we will.

APPENDIX
ACRONYMS

ABM	Antiballistic missile
ACABQ	Committee on Administrative and Budgetary Questions of the UN General Assembly
ACC	Administrative Committee on Coordination of the UN General Assembly
ACDA	Arms Control and Disarmament Agency
AID	Agency for International Development
ASEAN	Association of Southeast Asian Nations
CACM	Central American Common Market
CCD	Conference of the Committee on Disarmament
CD	Committee on Disarmament
CIA	Central Intelligence Agency of US
CIEC	Conference on International Economic Cooperation
COMECON	Council for Mutual Economic Assistance (of Warsaw Pact Nations)
COW	Committee of the Whole
CTB	Comprehensive Nuclear Test Ban Treaty
DAC	Development Assistance Countries
EAC	East African Community
ECA	Economic Commission for Africa
ECE	Economic Commission for Europe
ECLA	Economic Commission for Latin America
ECOSOC	Economic and Social Council
ECWA	Economic Commission for Western Asia
EEC	European Economic Community
EFTA	European Free Trade Association
EMS	European Monetary System
EONR	European Organization for Nuclear Research
ESA	European Space Agency

ESCAP	Economic and Social Commission for Asia and the Pacific
EURATOM	European Atomic Energy Community
FAO	Food and Agriculture Organization
GATT	General Agreement on Tariffs and Trade
GCD	General and complete disarmament
GNP	Gross national product
HURCO	Human Rights Council (proposed by author)
IAEA	International Atomic Energy Agency
ICBM	Intercontinental ballistic missile
ICJ	International Court of Justice
IDA	International Development Association
IDO	International Disarmament Organization (proposed but not established)
IDS	International Development Strategy
IFAD	International Fund for Agricultural Development
IFC	International Finance Corporation
ILO	International Labor Organization
IMCO	Intergovernmental Maritime Consultative Organization
IMF	International Monetary Fund
INFCE	International Nuclear Fuel Cycle Evaluation
IOC	International Ocean Commission of UNESCO
ITC	International Trade Center established by GATT
ITO	International Trade Organization (proposed but not established)
IWC	International Whaling Commission
LAFTA	Latin American Free Trade Association
LDC	Less developed country
MFR	Mutual force reduction
MIRV	Multiple independent reentry vehicle
MSA	Nations most seriously affected by world economic conditions
NATO	North Atlantic Treaty Organization
NGO	Nongovernmental organization
NPT	Nuclear Non-Proliferation Treaty
OAS	Organization of American States

OAU	Organization of African Unity
ODA	Official development assistance
ODC	Overseas Development Council
OECD	Organization for Economic Cooperation and Development
OIEC	Organization for International Economic Cooperation
OMA	Ocean Management Authority (proposed by author)
ONUC	United Nations Operations in the Congo
OPANAL	Organization for the Prohibition of Nuclear Weapons in Latin America
OPEC	Organization of Petroleum Exporting Countries
PLO	Palestinian Liberation Organization
PNE	Peaceful nuclear explosion
PQLI	Physical Quality of Life Index
PRC	People's Republic of China
SALT	Strategic Arms Limitation Talks
SDR	Special Drawing Rights on the International Monetary Fund
SEATO	South East Asia Treaty Organization
SIPRI	Stockholm Institute of Peace Research
SSOD	Special Session on Disarmament
TNE	Transnational enterprise
UN	United Nations
UNCTAD	United Nations Conference on Trade and Development
UNDOF	United Nations Disengagement Observer Force
UNDP	United Nations Development Programme
UNEF	United Nations Emergency Force
UNEP	United Nations Environment Programme
UNESCO	United Nations Educational, Scientific and Cultural Organization
UNFICYP	United Nations Force in Cyprus
UNFPA	United Nations Fund for Population Activities
UNIDO	United Nations Industrial Development Organization
UNIFIL	United Nations Interim Force in Lebanon
UNITAR	United Nations Institute for Training and Research
WDC	World Disarmament Conference
WERI	World Environmental Research Institute (proposed by author)

WFC	World Food Council
WHO	World Health Organization
WMO	World Meteorological Organization
WTA	World Trade Association (proposed by author)
ZPG	Zero population growth

INDEX

effects of, 61, 63, 77, 87, 133–34; US attitude toward, 128

Oman, 102

On-site inspection, 50, 52

ONUC (United Nations Operations in the Congo), 31, 36, 198

Organization for Economic Cooperation and Development (OECD), 63, 94, 102

Organization for the Prohibition of Nuclear Weapons in Latin America (OPANAL), 39, 53, 201

Organization of African Unity (OAU), 26, 172, 201, 202

Organization of American States (OAS), 26, 168, 172, 201, 202

Organization of Petroleum Exporting Countries (OPEC): economic strength of, 7, 105, 213; exports by, 86; multilateral actions precipitated by, 193; oil embargo by, 61; oil surpluses of, 77, 79–80; outlook for, 207, 213–14; power of, 82, 127, 213; price policies of, 77, 87, 133; as source of development funding, 79–80, 135, 213

Outer space, 131, 146, 157

Outer space treaties, 38, 39, 50

Overseas Development Council (ODC), 103

Ozone layer, 147, 151

Pacific islands, US, 231

Pakistan, 24, 41, 42, 218

Palestine Liberation Organization (PLO), 171

Palestinian problem, 180, 192

Panama Canal treaties, 233

Pardo, Arvid, 154, 155, 218

Paris ad hoc forum, 193

Parliament of Europe, 201

Peace and security, 4–5, 19–36, 234; and human rights, 164, 175; impact of technology on, 5; and military-industrial complex, 222; and regional organizations, 201; and resource shortages, 134, 137, 148; and rule of law, 12; and Security Council,

25–26, 28–35, 192, 232. See also Disarmament

Peaceful settlement of disputes, 19, 21, 23, 24–29, 234; and Briand-Kellogg Pact, 230; in environmental matters, 157, 158, 161; and Security Council, 25–26; and US, 236

Peacekeeping: and League of Nations, 19, 189; mechanisms for, 23, 32–35, 43, 234

Peacekeeping operations, 23, 26, 31, 198

People's Republic of China: and communism, 239; and development, 88, 99, 103, 111, 241; and disarmament, 46, 47; and family planning, 139; and IMF, 81; and India, 24; and Japan, 241; leadership of, 7, 206, 207–210, 247; as nuclear power, 41, 50, 241; and Soviet Union, 42, 214, 241; and UN, 189, 209–210; and US, 214, 233, 238–42; and Vietnam, 24, 240, 241

Pertamina Oil Co., 91

Petroleum: offshore, 154, 156, 158, 160, 161; shortage of, 130, 131, 145, 213. See also Oil prices; OPEC

Philippines, 174, 206, 218, 231

Photosynthesis, 148, 151

Physical quality of life index (PQLI), 103–104, 105

Plutonium, 51, 52–53

Poland, 100, 103, 209, 218

Policy-making, 193–94, 226–29

Political action, 227

Political pressures, 5–7, 147, 192, 237

Political rights, 167, 171, 173, 179

Political stability, 107, 175

Pollution: control of, 138, 146–48, 150–51; effects of, on the biosphere, 131, 151; at sea, 138, 150, 155, 161; standards for, 153, 154, 159, 202

Population and weighted voting, 196, 197

Population growth, 6, 129–31; and economic progress, 101

Population stabilization, 139–40, 144; and development, 108, 109; and